The Land They Found

The Land They Found
Australian History for Secondary Schools

Ronald Laidlaw

Third Edition

M

First published 1979 by
THE MACMILLAN COMPANY OF AUSTRALIA PTY LTD
107 Moray Street, South Melbourne 3205
6 Clarke Street, Crows Nest 2065

Reprinted 1980 (twice), 1981, 1982, 1983
Revised 1983
Reprinted 1984, 1985, 1986, 1987, 1988
This enlarged and revised edition 1989

Associated companies and representatives
throughout the world.

National Library of Australia
cataloguing in publication data

Laidlaw, Ronald.
    The land they found: Australian history for
    secondary schools.

    3rd ed.
    ISBN 0 7329 0044 1.

    1. Australia — History. I. Title.

994

Typeset in Plantin and Souvenir by
Graphicraft Typesetters Limited, Hong Kong.
Printed in Hong Kong.

Contents

Acknowledgements

The author and publishers are grateful to the following for permission to reproduce copyright material:

Art Gallery of South Australia, page 215; Athol Shmith, page 280; Australian Labor Party, page 295; Australian War Memorial, pages 220, 227–8, 230–1, and 264; Bank of New South Wales, page 91; BBC Hulton Picture Library, pages 39 and 42; *Canberra Times*, page 293; Coo-ee Picture Library, pages 101–2 and 125; Dixson Galleries, Sydney, pages 98–9; General Motors-Holden's Ltd, page 272; Halcyon and Oswald Ziegler Publications Pty Ltd, page 13; Hamersley Iron, page 297; Herald and Weekly Times Limited, pages 237, 244–5, 254–5, 261, 263, 265, 270, 275, 277, 279, 282, 286, 289, 294, 299–300; La Trobe Library, pages 181, 186, and 216; Mansell Collection, London, pages 38 and 76; Mitchell Library, NSW, pages 18–20, 60, 73, 75, 87, 103, 124, 187, and 196; National Art Gallery, Wellington, New Zealand, page 27; National Library of Australia, pages 5, 10, 12, 14, 32, 52, 54, 56, 62, 65, 68, 83, 95, 97, 110, 142, 145, 153, 166, 201, 208, 213–14, 217, 232, 242, 252, 262, 266, 285, and 291; National Maritime Museum, Greenwich, page 27; National Portrait Gallery, page 21; Oxford University Press, page 163; Parliament House, Canberra, page 250; Queensland Government Tourist Bureau, page 154; Queensland State Archives, page 156; Rex Nan Kivell Collection, National Library of Australia, pages 1, 4, 6–7, 17, 22, 30–1, 34–6, 40–1, 46–7, 53, 57, 64, 66, 74, 81, 89, 108, 119–20, 129, 132, 134–6, 160–1, 169, 178, 190, and 194; Snowy Mountains Authority, page 259; South Australian Archives, pages 174–6; Sovereign Hill, Ballarat, page 189; Victorian Railways, page 211.

While every care has been taken to trace and acknowledge copyright, the publishers tender their apologies for any accidental infringement where copyright has proved untraceable. They would be pleased to come to a suitable arrangement with the rightful owner in each case.

Maps: Joseph Szabo.
Illustrations: Joseph Szabo and Anne Paterson.
Cover: Aquatint by James Taylor of the entrance to Port Jackson and part of the town of Sydney, New South Wales (The Rex Nan Kivell Collection, National Library of Australia).

Preface

I see no reason why history should be a dull subject. The past, after all, was anything but dull.

In this book, I have attempted to capture the student's imagination by providing some of the details that make history interesting: sketches, paintings, letters, extracts from diaries, songs, recipes, styles of architecture and fashions in dress and grooming.

Maps help to locate the action, and every state in Australia is represented. I have tried, above all, to evoke the adventurous and rumbustious nature of Australia's past.

Chapter 1

The Aborigines:
The First Australians

Arrival

The Aborigines began to arrive in Aus
tralia about 50 000 years ago, during the
Last Ice Age. The world's geography
was different then. A good deal of water
was taken from the oceans to form large
polar ice sheets. The sea level was lower.
Australia was joined to New Guinea in
the north and to Tasmania in the south.

To the north-west lay a belt of deep
water. Prehistorians call this Wallacea.
Beyond Wallacea, Indonesia, Malaysia
and the Philippines were all joined
together.

Over thousands of years, small Abori
ginal bands moved down into Greater
Australia. To cross Wallacea they must
have constructed rafts or canoes. It is

Figure 1.1. Stalking game. *A painting by Eugène von Guérard.*

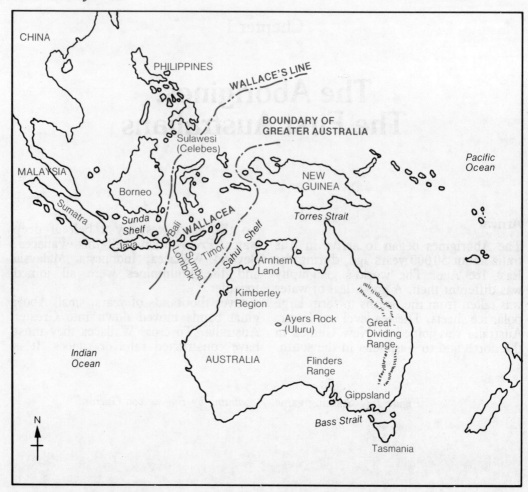

CHINA

PHILIPPINES

WALLACE'S LINE

BOUNDARY OF
GREATER AUSTRALIA

Sulawesi
(Celebes)

*Pacific
Ocean*

MALAYSIA

NEW
GUINEA

Borneo

Sumatra

Sunda
Shelf

Bali

WALLACEA

Torres Strait

Java

Lombok

Sumba

Timor

Sahul Shelf

Arnhem
Land

Kimberley
Region

*Indian
Ocean*

Ayers Rock
(Uluru)

Great
Dividing
Range

AUSTRALIA

Flinders
Range

Gippsland

N

Bass Strait

Tasmania

*Figure 1.2. 'Wallace's Line' marks a belt of deep water separating the continental shelves of the
Oriental and Australian geographical regions, with Bali belonging to the former and Lombok lying
on a long westward extension of the latter.*

not known where the Aborigines originally came from.

End of the Last Ice Age

In Greater Australia the Aborigines
witnessed important environmental
changes, including volcanic eruptions
and earth tremors. Between 18 000 and
12 000 years ago, inland water supplies
dried up, and green bushland turned
into desert. Strong westerly winds sculp-
ted longitudinal sand dunes running east
and west.

About 10 000 years ago the tempera-
ture changed. The whole earth warmed a
little, and the northern and southern ice
sheets began to melt. Meltwaters raised
the sea level again, and some depressions
and plains were slowly flooded. Torres
Strait, the Arafura Sea, and Bass Strait
came into being. Australia was separated
from New Guinea and Tasmania. Some
peaks were spared, to become islands
such as Aru in Torres Strait and King
Island and the Furneaux group in Bass
Strait. Everywhere the coastline changed.
New beaches, bays, inlets and estuaries

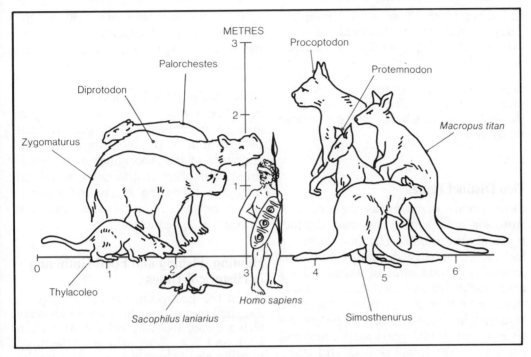

Figure 1.3. Scale diagram of some of Australia's megafauna.

were created. River mouths became silted up, creating swamps.

Hunting Megafauna

The word 'megafauna' means 'large animals' (*mega*, large; *fauna*, animals). When the Aborigines arrived in Australia, they found a number of large, unique animals. Prehistorians have found some of the bones of these animals. By analysing the bones, and fitting them together, they have been able to work out what the animals looked like.

There were several species of kangaroo and wallaby. One kangaroo, Procoptodon, stood about 3 metres in height. There was a number of lumbering, ox-like beasts called Diprotodontids. Some of these were almost 2 metres in height and more than 3 metres long. Besides these, there were large flightless birds, sloths, and large, land-prowling lizards.

Many prehistorians now believe that the Aborigines helped to wipe out the megafauna by hunting and firestick farming. Aborigines used firesticks to set fire to stands of plant food. By burning off plant foods, they encouraged and increased regeneration and regrowth. In historical times, burns by Aborigines often developed into bushfires. Many prehistorians believe the careless use of the firestick destroyed vegetation the megafauna fed on, and altered the ecology of areas. Hunting and burning, combined with climatic and ecological changes, led to the extinction of the megafauna by the end of the Last Ice Age.

The Aborigines helped to change the Australian environment in other ways too. They brought the dingo to Australia, as a pet and as a hunting aid. The Aborigines may have helped to exterminate the Tasmanian tiger (Thylacine), which at that time lived on the mainland. They dammed rivers and creeks, to catch fish and waterfowl; this stopped and diverted the flow of watercourses. They scarred tens of thousands of trees, carving out bark for shelters and canoes. They defaced hillsides, mining for flint and ochre. They pecked thousands of designs on rock surfaces, and painted many cave walls. They left mounds of shellfish on beaches, which became sandy hillocks.

Two Distinct Races

Most prehistorians today believe that Australia was settled by two distinct types of Aborigines. The first to arrive had *robust*, or rugged, skulls, and their technology was not advanced. They could make fire and manufacture simple stone tools such as 'choppers' and flake blades. The second group of people arrived about 35 000 years ago. They had *gracile*, or modern, skulls, and their technology was more advanced. They spread fairly quicky through the conti-nent, occupying land not held by the first group, and displacing or absorbing members of that group when they refused to move out of the way. Both groups of Aborigines belonged to the same species, *Homo sapiens* ('Wise man', or modern man). They were therefore able to interbreed. Most prehistorians believe that their offspring were the ancestors of the Aborigines of historical times. Offspring in the north interbred further with visting Malay and Indonesian fishermen. This resulted in more changes in appearance.

Hunting, Fishing and Food Gathering in Historical Times

When the Europeans arrived in Australia, they found that the Aborigines were well adapted to living off the Australian land and sea. The men manufactured hunting and fishing weapons and implements, and provided the band with fresh meat and fish. In dry areas, they also

Figure 1.4. Spearfishing.

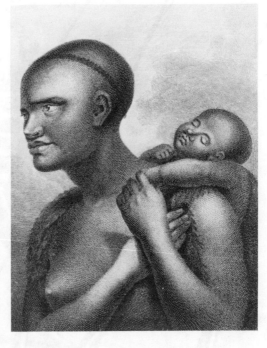

Figures 1.5 and 1.6. A man, woman, and child of Van Diemen's Land, drawn by John Webber, artist on Cook's third voyage.

found water. Women and girls hunted much smaller game (such as goannas) with clubs, and collected a rich variety of plant foods, often with a **digging-stick**. Both sexes contributed equally to the supply of food for the band.

Hunting weapons were manufactured mainly from wood. The Aborigines scraped their **spears** smooth with stone blades, straightened them by bending the shafts between their teeth, and hardened the points in their fires. Many spears were given simple sharpened points. Some were barbed, by carving notches into the point or by attaching more sophisticated points fashioned from bone. Fishing spears were fitted with a number of prongs. Fitted points and prongs were held in place with the sinews of kangaroo, reinforced with gum. Many spears were quite long, and heavy. Spears were greatly boosted in flight by the use of **spear-throwers** (*woomeras*). Some spear-throwers were narrow and elongated, some broad and leaf-shaped. At one end was a projection that fitted into a notch on the end of the spear. When the Aborigines used a spear-thrower, it became an extension of the arm, and they were able to throw their spears with much greater force. **Boomerangs** were chipped and smoothed from solid pieces of wood. Not all Aborigines made or used boomerangs, and not all boomerangs were used in hunting. Some returning boomerangs were used as playthings; some were used to stun or kill game, and to chase birds and wildfowl into traps. **Clubs** (*nulla-nullas, waddies*, etc.) varied in size.

Hunting and fishing were hard work. Men walked, jogged, and paddled for hours on end, and covered many kilometres. Kangaroos, wallabies, and emus were tracked and speared. Wom-

Figure 1.7. An Aboriginal raiding party.

bats and echidnas were dug out of burrows and clubbed. Goannas and snakes were speared or clubbed. Birds and waterfowl were speared, or driven into nets, where they were clubbed or had their necks wrung. Fish were trapped in stone weirs, and either speared or caught ('tickled') by hand. In the nineteenth century, Aborigines outside Port Fairy, Victoria, regularly harvested freshwater eels in traps constructed in weirs and ditches. On the coast and in estuaries, men speared sharks, stingrays, turtles, dugong ('sea cow') and smaller fish. In the south, seals were clubbed while ashore. Occasionally, Aborigines fed on beached whales.

Aboriginal women used their bare hands, digging-sticks, small clubs and curved wooden dishes (*coolamons*) to collect food. They killed small game such as goannas, bandicoots, and possums, and also honey-ants. They caught small fish, and collected shellfish. Sometimes they joined their men at sealing. They smoked bees out of beehives, collected eggs, and gouged witchetty grubs out of the roots of infected shrubs and the decaying branches of trees. (It has been estimated that 10 witchetty grubs are enough to satisfy the daily food requirements of one adult.) Some plant foods were regularly harvested throughout the year; some were harvested on a seasonal basis. The Aborigines ate underground roots, tubers, bulbs and rhizomes, stems, shoots, piths, leaves, flowers, fruit, and seeds. Plants or parts of plants that were unsuitable were carefully avoided.

Food preparation and cooking were done by both men and women. Food was shared out among members of a band according to age, sex, kin relations, and taboos (special bans). There were strict laws that dictated who could eat what, and in what proportions.

Social Organization

The Aborigines lived in loosely organized tribes. Members of a tribe all spoke the same language or dialect, shared the same Dreaming (religion), and displayed the same marks of initiation (e.g. missing teeth, body scars). A tribe was divided into a number of small bands of approximately 10 to 15 members. Each band had its own *range*, where it alone hunted, fished and gathered food. Tribal territories and ranges varied in size. Bands occasionally came together to trade, arrange mar-

riages or perform sacred rites. Bands were made up of families. Most men in each band were closely related. When they married, they brought in girls from other bands.

Dreaming

The Aborigines were an extremely religious people. They believed that the world had been created long ago, by powerful, superhuman, ancestral beings. The names given to these beings varied from region to region. So did the descriptions of the act of creation. The Aborigines believed that the ancestral beings created the Aboriginal people, gave them gifts such as fire, and taught them how to live. They also gave them laws to live by. Later, the ancestral beings faded from sight. Some went back to where they had come from, while some slowly turned into stars, mountains and rivers. By the end of the Dreamtime, the ancestral beings could no longer be seen. The Aborigines were

Figure 1.8. Ritual and ceremony were important in the life of the tribe and its members.

7

left alone. The act of creation was complete.

The Aborigines had no writing as we know it. They were therefore unable to compile any sacred texts. Their religion was passed on by word of mouth. It was also enshrined in dance and song. Many things an Aboriginal did reminded him of his religion — he was never able, or allowed, to forget it. The Aborigines believed that the ancestral beings were still powerful and could influence their lives. For instance, a particular dance had to be performed correctly. If it were not, the following day's hunt might not go well.

Aboriginal Art

The Aborigines developed a unique style of art. Their art is distinctive, colourful and striking. It is also very symbolic. Many of its designs and patterns are almost meaningless to people of a non-Aboriginal background. Three important art forms are rock engraving, cave painting, and bark painting.

Mining, Manufacture, and Trade

Aborigines mined such things as ochre and stone. At Wilgie Mia in Western Australia, Aborigines removed thousands of tonnes of rock, with stone hammers and wooden wedges, to get at deposits of ochre. Yarar rock shelter, in the Northern Territory, was mined for thousands of years for ochre. Aborigines used ochre to colour the hair, as a cosmetic, and for ritual purposes.

Aborigines bartered (exchanged) both raw materials and artefacts. The latter included such items as boomerangs and stone axes. Prehistorians have traced a number of long trade routes, which once crisscrossed the country.

Questions

(1) How did ancient Greater Australia differ from modern Australia?
(2) What happened at the end of the Last Ice Age?
(3) What was megafauna?
(4) How did the Aborigines alter their environment?
(5) Did all early Aborigines look the same?
(6) How did men contribute to the band's supply of food?
(7) How did women contribute to the supply of food?
(8) What was a 'range'?
(9) How did the Aborigines explain the beginning of the world?
(10) Why did the Aborigines mine ochre?

Research

Find out more about the following.
(1) Australia during the Last Ice Age
(2) Aboriginal technology
(3) Aboriginal social organization
(4) Dreamtime stories
(5) Aboriginal art and music.

Chapter 2

Traders to the North-West

Early Traders

To the north-west of Australia lie the islands of South-east Asia. These islands were colonized by a number of different nationalities after the birth of Christ. First came the Hindu and Buddhist traders and missionaries from southern India. Then came Chinese, Arabs, and Portuguese.

All of these people wanted what the islands had to offer: mace and nutmeg from the Banda Isles, cloves from the Moluccas, pepper and slaves from Java,

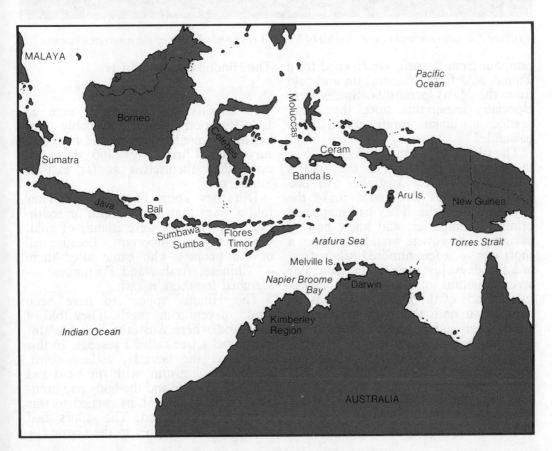

Figure 2.1. The islands of South-east Asia.

Figure 2.2. Chinese junks were capable of long sea voyages. (A junk of the nineteenth century.)

camphor from Borneo, sandalwood from Timor, gold from Sumatra, tin and gold from the Malay peninsula. Spices were especially important, since they were needed to make unrefrigerated meat palatable.

The islands of South-east Asia lie close to Australia. Did any of the traders know of, or visit, Australia? All had good solid ships that could make the voyage to Australia. They had maps and primitive compasses, and knew how to navigate. The voyage would have been a short one — a few hundred kilometres, or a few days, just over the horizon. For several months of the year, moisture-laden winds of the north-west monsoon blow down onto the coast of Arnhem Land. Even today, lost or disabled Indonesian fishing boats, pieces of bamboo, and coconut husks are washed up onto northern beaches. It may be that some early traders' ships were blown onto the coast of northern Australia. Or perhaps they found Australia because they went looking for new land?

The Hindus and Buddhists

The Hindus and Buddhists were an Indo-European people. Probably they began to colonize Java in the first century after Christ. By 1400 they had established themselves as far east as Sumatra.

Did they know of Australia? They told a story that to the south or south-east of Java there were islands of gold. This story is important, because all of the peoples who came after them — Chinese, Arabs, and Portuguese — searched for these islands.

The Hindus appear to have been afraid of venturing south. They told of an island where Australia lies. On this island was a tree called Pausengi. In this tree lived the Garuda, a huge bird, shaped like a griffin, with the head and wings of an eagle and the body and hindquarters of a lion. Ships carried to this island never returned. The sailors died of hunger, or fell prey to the Garuda.

The Chinese

The Chinese travelled in high-sterned junks, representing the Ming dynasty. By 1400 they had established trading colonies in Sumatra, Java, Borneo, Celebes, the Moluccas, and Timor. They traded earthenware, porcelain, silk yarn, satin, damask, brocades, gold, iron, beads, and coins for the products of the area. Their junks continually travelled between Canton and the islands.

Between 1405 and 1433, the admiral Ch'eng Ho made seven famous voyages of discovery. Some of his junks explored the waters around Timor — an island that lies close to Australia. It is possible that one or more of his junks sailed south, through the Wei-Lu (Unknown Sea), and found Australia.

In 1879, a small, soapstone figurine, 12 cm in height, was found at Darwin. The figurine was wedged firmly between the roots of a banyan tree, 1.2 m below ground level. It shows Shou-Lao, the Chinese god of long life. It may have been made during the time of the Ming dynasty.

In 1948, a Chinese porcelain shard was found on a beach on Winchelsea Island. It was been dated to the sixteenth or seventeenth century.

The Arabs

The Arabs colonized Malaysia and Sumatra by the fourteenth century. They came as both traders and missionaries. They searched for spices, gold, precious stones, bird plumage, and converts to their religion, Islam. They extended their trade and religion as far as west New Guinea. If they had had more time, they might have crossed to Australia. They were stopped in New Guinea by the arrival of the Portuguese. The Portuguese were an old enemy who took away much of the Arabs' power.

Did the Arabs ever visit Australia, on purpose or by accident? They were skilled navigators and visited islands as close to Australia as Aru, only 480 kilometres away.

The Portuguese

The Portuguese were the first Europeans to visit the islands of South-east Asia. They represented a new race and religion in the area: they were white, and Roman Catholic. Their ships were dif-

Figure 2.3. Shou-Lao, the Chinese god of longevity.

Figure 2.4. Portuguese ships in Lisbon Harbour.

ferent, too. At first they were small caravels, then larger carracks.

Bartholomew Diaz found a way around South Africa in 1487. Vasco da Gama, another Portuguese, found a route along the east coast of Africa to India in 1497–98. The Portuguese captured Malacca, on the west coast of the Malay peninsula, in 1511. By the end of that year, they had sent D'Abreu to establish trading stations in the Moluccas. Later they visited the north coast of New Guinea, Timor, and Melville Island. Probably they took Aboriginal slaves from Melville Island. In the nineteenth century, elderly Timorese described such slave raids.

Kenneth Gordon McIntyre, in his book *The Secret Discovery of Australia*, claims that the Portuguese charted part of the west coast and all of the east coast in the 1500s. McIntyre says their charting can be seen in the famous Dieppe Maps that were drawn in France after the Portuguese discoveries.

McIntyre believes that the Portuguese commander Christovao de Mendonca led an expedition down the east coast in 1522–24. McIntyre also believes Mendonça went ashore where Geelong, Victoria, now stands. There he dropped a bunch of keys. These keys were found over 300 years after by a workman digging the foundations of a new lime kiln.

The Geelong Keys, as they came to be known, were examined by Superintendent Charles Joseph La Trobe (a good witness), but were later lost.

McIntyre also believes Mendonça sailed on, and lost one of his ships in a storm off modern Warrnambool. This ship was washed ashore and its remains were discovered by Europeans in the early 1830s. The wreck became known as the Mahogany Ship, because the wood looked like mahogany. It was finally covered by sand sometime after 1880. Recent searches have failed to find it.

McIntyre also says that Mendonça turned back, after the loss of his ship, and spent the winter in Bittangabee Bay, south of Eden, New South Wales. There McIntyre believes the Portuguese built a stone fort, the remains of which can still

be seen. However, the New South Wales National Parks and Wildlife Service believes the ruin is that of an early house.

Malay Fishermen

Malay fishermen from the island of Celebes might have visited the beaches of northern Australia before the first Europeans set foot on them. Certainly they visited northern Australia at the same time as the European explorers, and after them.

Macassan fishermen came in boats called *praus* to fish for trepang, which is also called *bêche-de-mer*. This is a small sea animal regarded as a delicacy. Soup made from this animal was in great demand in China. The fishermen unloaded small canoes called *lepa-lepa* when they reached Australia, and fished off shore. The trepang was either collected by hand, trawled, or speared.

The fishermen set up camps ashore. They collected mangrove wood for fires, then boiled the trepang in iron cauldrons. They gutted the trepang, re-cooked it in mangrove bark, dried and smoked it. Tonnes of trepang were carried back to Celebes, and taken from there to China.

Macassan fishermen often came into contact with Aborigines, and these contacts were not always friendly. The Aborigines would have been hostile, since they would have regarded the Macassans as invaders of their tribal territory. However, some Aborigines were persuaded to board *praus*, and were even taken back to Celebes. Aborigines could not help being affected by the fishermen. They imitated the *lepa-lepa*, the Macassan sail, and use of metal. Some Macassan words became part of Aboriginal dialects. For instance, *lepa-lepa* became 'lippa-lippa'.

Figure 2.5. Probasso, a Malay chief, who visited Australia several times at the turn of the eighteenth century. A pencil sketch by William Westall.

Questions
(1) Where is Aru?

Figure 2.6. The vessels used by the Malay fishermen were called praus.

(2) What races colonized the islands of South-east Asia before the seventeenth century?

(3) What trade goods were early traders looking for?

(4) What reasons are there for believing that some early traders might have visited Australian shores?

(5) What remains have been found which show possible visits by early traders?

(6) What would the Aborigines have thought of visits by early traders?

(7) Who was Ch'eng Ho?

(8) What was a *prau*?

(9) What is trepang?

(10) Who was Probasso?

Research

Find out more about the following.

(1) Early maps

(2) Early methods of navigation

(3) Traders' ships

(4) Trade centres

(5) One of the faiths followed by early traders (such as Hinduism, Islam).

Chapter 3

The Dutch Discover Australia

The Dutch Capture Trade from the Portuguese

The Dutch followed the Portuguese to the islands of South-east Asia. They intended to take trade from them in that area. This was not difficult, since the Dutch had many advantages over the Portuguese:

- They were shrewd businessmen. Their financial methods were the most up-to-date in Europe, and they had considerable capital to develop.
- They could charge lower freight rates than the Portuguese.
- The had superior ships and were highly skilled and courageous sailors.
- The Portuguese had grown lax, and their relationship with the native people had become strained.

By 1600, the Dutch were trading with Atjeh, the Moluccas, Amboina, and

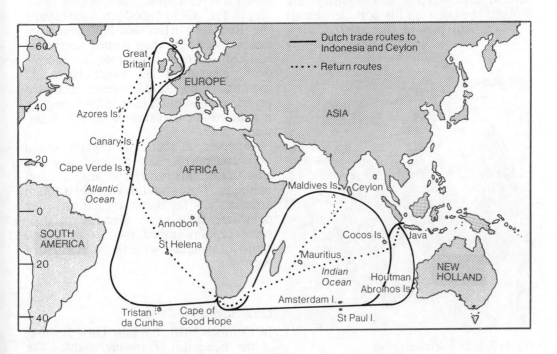

Banda. Slowly but surely they captured the trade of the area from their rivals.

Tales of Gold and Willem Jansz

In Indonesia, the Dutch, like the Portuguese, heard stories about a rich land to the south. In 1605, Willem Jansz was instructed by the Dutch authorities ' . . . to discover the great land of Nova Guinea and other East and South lands'. He was given a small boat called the *Duyfken (Dove)* and a crew of about 20.

Jansz sailed from the Indonesian island of Bantam to another Indonesian island called Banda. From there he sailed to the Kai Islands, then to the small island of Aru, then to the coast of New Guinea. Jansz followed that coast, stopping here and there to find out what he could about the country. During one landing eight of his crew were killed by cannibals.

Jansz then turned and sailed across Torres Strait, into the Gulf of Carpentaria, and down Cape York Peninsula. Strangely enough, he did not realize that he had discovered a new country. He thought the coast on his port (left-hand) side was still part of the coast of New Guinea. Perhaps he was misled by the many shallows and islands in that part of the world. Jansz ventured up one river in a small boat, to explore the hinterland (interior of the country) and meet the natives. The meeting was not friendly. The Aborigines attacked his boat and speared one of his men to death. Shortly after this, Jansz decided to turn for home. He was running short of food and fresh water, had lost about one-half of his crew, and had not discovered any gold or riches. He turned near Cape Keerweer (Cape 'Turnabout') and sailed safely back to Banda, arriving in mid-1606.

Accidental Contact with the West Coast

In 1611, a Dutch captain, Hendrik Brouwer (later Governor-General of the East Indies) pioneered a new sea route to Bantam, in Java. The old Portuguese route was to go around the Cape of Good Hope, then north along the eastern coast of Africa, before turning east. Brouwer sailed due east from the Cape of Good Hope for about 6500 km, harnessing the 'Roaring Forties' winds to gain maximum speed. He then turned north and reached Bantam in 5 months and 24 days, instead of the usual 12 to 15 months. Time saved meant increased profit, so the Dutch East India Company instructed its captains to follow Brouwer's route.

However, at that time captains could not navigate precisely because they had inaccurate instruments, maps, and methods. They could make only a rough guess at how far they travelled each day or where they were. Because of this, some captains sailed too far east, and came into contact with the west coast of Australia.

Figure 3.2. Dirk Hartog's plate.

Dirk Hartog's Island

In October 1616, Captain Dirk Hartog, of the *Eendracht (Harmony)* sighted the west coast of Australia at 26° latitude. He landed on an island lying at the entrance to a bay. He called the island 'Dirk Hartog's-reede' (Dirk Hartog's Island). Later the bay was called Shark Bay, and the land in the area became Eendracht's Land.

On the island, Hartog recorded his visit. The following was engraved on a pewter plate, and the plate nailed to a post. (The term 'supercargo' refers to a commercial agent.)

1616 on 25th October arrived here the ship *Eendracht* of Amsterdam. Supercargo Gilles Miebais of Liege, skipper Dirck Hatich of Amsterdam. On the 27th do. (ditto) she set sail again for Bantam. Deputy supercargo Jan Stins, upper steersman Pieter Doones of Bil. In the year 1616.

Too Far East

Between 1616 and 1630, a number of Dutch vessels made contact with the west coast while sailing to Bantam.

The most astonishing early contact was made by Captain Frans Thijssen in the *Gulden Zeepaart* (*Golden Seahorse*).

For some unknown reason, he sailed too far south and missed Cape Leeuwin. He reached the islands of St Peter and St Francis, which lie not far from where Adelaide now stands.

Disappointing New Holland

Dutch captains followed the west coast northwards, part of the way, towards Bantam. Sometimes they made landings, and charted parts of the coastline. They gave different names to the coast, but eventually agreed upon the name of New Holland.

The Dutch were always disappointed with the land and its inhabitants. To them, the land seemed dry and barren, its people primitive and poor. The Dutch were interested only in profit, and there seemed to be no profit in this new land.

Planned Exploration

In August 1642, the Dutch Council in Batavia (now Jakarta) proposed a Dutch

Figure 3.3. Abel Tasman, his wife and daughter.

Figure 3.4. Tasman's ship — the Heemskerck.

voyage of exploration in the seas to the south. They had a number of good reasons for wanting this:

- They needed good charts of the west coast of New Holland. This would reduce the number of shipwrecks on that coast, and save money.

- New Holland seemed to be barren and worthless, but beyond it, to the east, there might be undiscovered lands. The islands of gold, or a Great South Land, might exist. If so, the Dutch might yet open up new markets in these lands.

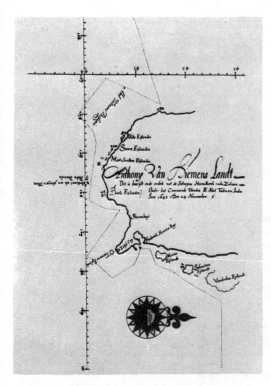

Figure 3.5. Tasman's chart of Van Diemen's Land.

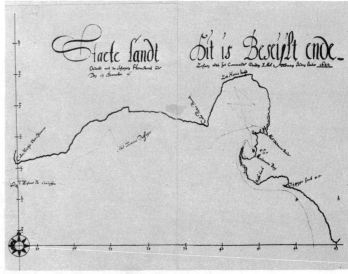

Figure 3.6. Tasman's chart of New Zealand.

• If the South Land existed, it might be a stopping-off place to Chile, on the west coast of South America. If the Dutch could sail to South America, they could seize markets from the Spanish: they could 'do great things with the Chileans, and... snatch rich booty from the Castilian'. But first they would need to find a way around New Holland.

Captain Abel Tasman

Command of the new expedition was given to Abel Janszoon Tasman.

Tasman was born in Lutjegast, Holland, in 1603, and came to Java in 1634, at the age of 31. He was given command of a Dutch East India vessel the following year. After that he transported spices, traded, and fought smugglers.

He even went, as second-in-command of a trading mission, to Japan in 1639–40.

Then, in 1642, he was appointed commander of an expedition to explore the south seas. He was given two ships: the *Heemskerck (Home Church)*, a war yacht of 60 tonnes which carried a crew of 60, and the *Zeehaen (Sea Cock)*, of 100 tonnes, which carried a crew of 50. Both ships carried enough food for an 18-month voyage, as well as goods to trade in new markets — if any were found.

Tasman's First Voyage

Tasman's voyage was a remarkable one. He sailed from Batavia to the island of Mauritius, where he stayed for just over a month, fixing gear, stopping up leaks, and taking on supplies.

From Mauritius he sailed through heavy seas, snow, and ice to the rugged south-western coast of Tasmania, which he named Van Diemen's Land (after Anthony Van Diemen, the Governor of the Dutch East Indies). We do not know whether Tasman thought this coast was part of New Holland or not.

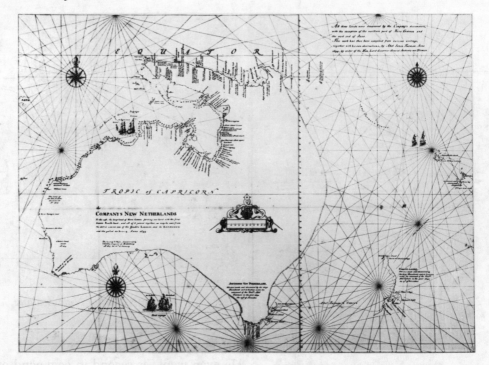

Figure 3.7. A map illustrating Tasman's voyages.

Tasman's expedition rounded the southern tip of Tasmania. He sent men ashore but they did not encounter any Aborigines. In North Bay, Tasman had a flag planted; the land was proclaimed a Dutch possession.

Tasman and his officers then decided to sail due east. If they had sailed due north, they would have discovered the east coast of Australia, somewhere near where Lieutenant James Cook was to come upon it, 128 years later. Tasman sailed for nine days across the Tasman Sea and sighted the west coast of the south island of New Zealand. He followed this coast, and crossed to the west coast of the north island. Tasman called this land Staten Land.

The expedition sailed home via the Friendly Islands and the north coast of New Guinea.

The Dutch Council was not very impressed with Tasman's voyage. Tasman himself, however, felt that he had achieved much:

- He had discovered Van Diemen's Land.
- He had mapped part of Staten Land.
- He had found a way to Chile — along the north coast of New Guinea.

Tasman's Second Voyage

Tasman was appointed to command another expedition in 1644 to explore the seas around the north of New Holland. He had three ships this time. His journal and those of his officers have not survived, but a later report and charts do exist. Tasman may have tried to get through Torres Strait from west to east, failed, and instead decided to follow and map the Gulf of Carpentaria and Arnhem Land down to North-west Cape. He added more than 3000 km to the map, but again failed to find markets.

Questions

(1) Why were the Dutch interested in South-east Asia?
(2) Who was the first Dutchman we know of to visit Australia's shores?
(3) How did Dutch vessels first come into contact with the west coast of Australia?
(4) Who visited the Islands of St Peter and St Francis?
(5) Why was Tasman sent on a voyage of exploration in 1642?
(6) What were Tasman's two ships called?
(7) What did Tasman call Tasmania?
(8) What did he call New Zealand?
(9) Did Tasman sail around Australia in a clockwise or an anticlockwise direction in 1642?
(10) Why were the Dutch disappointed in Australia?

Research

Find out more about the following.
(1) Holland in the seventeenth century
(2) Dutch Protestantism
(3) Dutch commerce in general
(4) Dutch settlement in the East Indies
(5) Dutch contact with the west coast of Australia.

Chapter 4

William Dampier: Adventurer

Figure 4.1. William Dampier.

William Dampier, the Pirate

William Dampier was one of the first Englishmen to visit Australia. He was the first Englishman to write about it.

Dampier was a lean, quiet, keen-eyed man with many interests: science, exploration, writing, adventure, fortune-seeking, and piracy. In 1688 he was one

Figure 4.2. 'Dampier and his companions in their canoe, overtaken by a dreadful storm.'

of a crew of pirates aboard a ship called the *Cygnet*, commanded by John Read. The pirates had abandoned the *Cygnet*'s proper captain, Charles Swan, in the Spanish Philippines.

Read and his men were cruising the China Seas, looking for markets and plunder, when strong winds drove the ship south. They landed on the north-west coast of Australia, somewhere near the Buccaneer Archipelago.

Read and his men established a camp on the beach, and careened the *Cygnet*. While some of the men scraped and repaired the ship's hull, others mended sails and went fishing. The Aborigines were timid, and not dangerous. Dampier, who had a natural curiosity, took notes in a journal which he carried rolled

up and stoppered inside a short length of bamboo hung round his neck.

The men stayed on the coast of Australia for two months, then set sail for Cocos Island. After another storm, Dampier slipped away from *Cygnet* at the Nicobar Islands and sailed an outrigger canoe to Sumatra, through terrible storms. He then made his way home to England.

Dampier Becomes Famous

In England, Dampier rewrote his journal and published it under the title *A New Voyage Round the World*. This book was an instant success with English readers, who enjoyed reading accounts of adven-

A
New Voyage
ROUND THE
WORLD.

Describing particularly,

The *Isthmus* of *America*, several Coasts
and Islands in the *West Indies*, the
Isles of *Cape Verd*, the Passage by *Terra
del Fuego*, the *South Sea* Coasts of *Chili,
Peru*, and *Mexico*; the Isle of *Guam* one
of the *Ladrones*, *Mindanao*, and other
Philippine and *East-India* Islands near
Cambodia, *China*, *Formosa*, *Luconia*, *Ce
lebes*, &c. *New Holland*, *Sumatra*, *Nicobar
Isles*; the *Cape* of *Good Hope*, and *Santa
Hellena*.

THEIR
Soil, Rivers, Harbours, Plants, Fruits, Ani-
mals, and Inhabitants.
THEIR
Customs, Religion, Government, Trade, &c.

By *William Dampier*.

Illustrated with Particular Maps and Draughts.

LONDON,
Printed for *James Knapton*, at the *Crown* in St *Paul*s
Church-yard. M DC XCVII.

Figure 4.3. The title page from one edition of Dampier's book.

tures in distant lands. Dampier dedicated his book to Charles Montague, President of the Royal Society. Montague was impressed by the quality of Dampier's work, and introduced him to some of the leading scientists of the day. He also introduced him to the Earl of Orford, First Lord of the Admiralty.

Dampier was able to persuade the Admiralty to give him a ship for a voyage of exploration and scientific inquiry in Australian waters. He was given the *Roebuck*, a leaking, old vessel of 290 tonnes, and a small crew of 50 men. This crew was to prove difficult to deal with.

His commission instructed him to:

Survey all islands, shores, capes, bays, creeks and harbours fit for shelters as well as defence, to take careful soundings as he went, to note tides, currents, winds, and the character of the weather . . . to observe the disposition and commodities of the natives, etc.

Australia Revisited

Dampier sailed from England to the Cape of Good Hope, and east from there across to the west coast of Australia. He sighted the coast about where Dirk Hartog had, 83 years before.

Dampier turned, and followed the coast north, sounding the depth of the water, reporting, and going ashore to sketch animals and collect plant life. He felt that New Holland might be a collection of islands instead of one large continent.

He ran low on water and provisions, and turned to the island of Timor for supplies. Refreshed there, he sailed to New Guinea, and sighted the island on New Year's Day, 1700. He sailed through Dampier Strait, and so proved that there was a strait between New Guinea and New Britain.

Shortly after, Dampier turned for home. In the Atlantic his ship broke up and sank off Ascension Island. He salvaged his all-important journal and collection of dried plants, and made his way ashore with the rest of his crew. They lived on goats, turtles, and water found high on a mountainside. The spot is still called Dampier's Spring.

Finally they were rescued by a passing East India ship, and taken home to England.

What did Dampier Achieve?

Dampier added hundreds more kilometres to maps of the coast of Australia, New Guinea, and New Britain. He described new and interesting plants, animals, and people. He helped to create an English awareness of Australia — an awareness that worried the Dutch. A number of people read and praised Dampier's work — including James Cook.

What Dampier Thought of Australia

We Saw No Trees That Bore Fruit or Berries:

New Holland is a very large tract of land. It is not yet determined whether it is an island or a main continent; but I am certain that it joins neither to Asia, Africa, nor America. This part of it that we saw is all low even land, with sandy banks against the sea, only the points are rocky, and so are some of the islands in this bay.

The land is of a dry sandy soil, destitute of water, except you make wells: yet producing divers sorts of trees: but the woods are not thick, nor the trees very big. Most of the trees that we saw are dragon-trees as we supposed; and these, too, are the largest trees of any where. They are about the bigness of our large apple trees, and about the same height: and the rind is blackish, and somewhat rough. The leaves are of a dark colour; the gum distils out of the knots or cracks that are in the bodies of the trees. We compared it with some gum dragon, or dragon's blood, that was aboard; and it was of the same colour and taste. The other sorts of trees were not known by any of us. There was pretty long grass growing under the trees, but it was very thin. We saw no trees that bore fruit or berries.

The Miserablest People in the World:

The inhabitants of this country are the miserablest people in the world. The Hodmadods [Hottentots] of Monomatapa, though a nasty people, yet for wealth are gentleme to these; who have no houses, and skin garments, sheep, poultry, and fruits of the earth . . . and setting aside their humane shape, they differ but little from brutes. They are tall, strait-bodied, and thin, with small long limbs. They have great heads, round foreheads, and great brows . . . . They have great bottle noses . . . . They are long visaged, and of a very unpleasing aspect; having no one graceful feature in their faces . . . . They have no sort of clothes; but a piece of the rind of a tree tied like a girdle about their waists, and a handful of long grass, or three or four small green boughs, full of leaves, thrust under their girdle, to cover their nakedness.

They have no houses, but lie in the open air, without any covering; the earth being their bed, and the heaven their canopy . . . Their only food is a small sort of fish . . . they have no instruments to catch great fish, should they come . . . they seek for cockles, mussels, and periwinkles . . . and what Providence has bestowed on them, they presently broil on the coals, and eat it in common.

Questions

(1) How did Dampier first come into contact with Australia?
(2) Were books on travel popular during Dampier's time?
(3) How did Dampier manage to acquire a ship for a voyage of exploration to Australia?
(4) What was the name of the ship Dampier was given?
(5) Were the English authorities interested only in scientific inquiry? What evidence is there, in Dampier's instructions, of an additional interest?
(6) What difficulties did Dampier face on his voyage of exploration?
(7) Was Dampier's voyage of exploration a success?
(8) What did Dampier think of the Australian countryside?
(9) What did he think of the Australian Aborigines?
(10) What effects did Dampier's voyages and writings have on his countrymen?

Research

Find out more about the following:
(1) The life of Dampier
(2) Science in seventeenth-century England
(3) The Royal Society
(4) Popular literature in Dampier's time
(5) Some of Dampier's famous contemporaries, e.g. Alexander Selkirk.

Chapter 5

James Cook
and the Voyage of the 'Endeavour'

Figure 5.1. Captain James Cook. A portrait by John Webber in 1776.

Figure 5.2. Model of HM Bark Endeavour.

The Ship and the Men

On 25 August 1768, Lieutenant James Cook, RN, set sail from Plymouth, England, in command of His Majesty's Bark *Endeavour*.

Cook was 40 years of age, married, a tall, businesslike man, with deep, thoughtful, brown eyes set beneath shaggy brows, his brown hair swept behind his neck in a pigtail. He had had considerable experience in ships, during both peace and war, and on both sides of the Atlantic. He was known as a capable navigator, map-maker, and astronomer.

The *Endeavour* was a slow-sailing, sturdy vessel of 374 tonnes burthen. She was an ex-collier that had been refitted with a sheathed hull. The crew numbered 92, and included officers, marines, midshipmen, able-bodied seamen, and civilians. Amongst the civilians were Charles Green, a professional astronom-

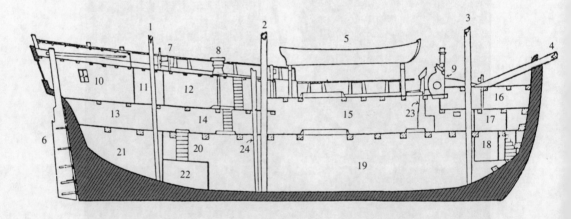

H.M. BARK ENDEAVOUR

(length of keel 27.7 metres)

1. Mizen-mast	9. Winch and belfry	17. Warrant-officer's cabins
2. Mainmast	10. Great cabin	18. Magazine
3. Foremast	11. Cook's and Banks' sleeping cabins	19. Hold
4. Bowsprit	12. Cook's and the gentlemen's messroom	20. Steward's store-rooms
5. Longboat	13. Wardroom and officers' cabins	21. Lazaret (store-room)
6. Rudder	14. Gunroom and junior officers' quarters	22. Fish room
7. Wheel	15. Lower deck (for seamen)	23. Ship's galley
8. Capstan	16. Forecastle (for the petty officers)	24. Pumps

(After the original dockyard plans in the National Maritime Museum, Greenwich, England)

Figure 5.3. HM Bark Endeavour — *a diagrammatic section of the interior.*

er, Joseph Banks, Charles Solander and Herman Sporing, botanists, and John Reynolds, Sydney Parkinson and Alexander Buchan, artists.

This was to be no ordinary voyage. It was to be a voyage of scientific observation and exploration.

Cook's Instructions

Cook carried two instructions, one from the Royal Society and one from the Admiralty:

* The Royal Society instructed him to sail to King George Island, Otaheiti (Tahiti). There he should time and record a transit of the planet Venus across the face of the sun. If he could make an accurate observation, it would be possible to calculate the distance of the earth from the sun. Observatories in Spitzbergen and Hudson's Bay would make observations at the same time. Bad weather might prevent observations at some of the observatories, but hopefully not at all of them.
* The Admiralty instructed him to make a search for the fabled Great South Land after he had observed the transit. He was to sail south from King George Island until he reached 40°S latitude, then turn westward between that latitude and 35°S, until he either found the South Land or came into contact with New Zealand. If he reached New Zealand, he should chart its coastline. He should then return home via the Cape of Good Hope or Cape Horn. He should claim all newly discovered land for Britain.

Mapping New Zealand

Cook sailed round the Horn and reached King George Island on 13 April 1769 — well ahead of the transit. The natives were friendly, and Cook and his men built an observatory and fort ashore, which they called Fort Venus. The tran-

sit occurred on 3 June, and Cook, Green, and Solander all made independent observations. (These observations eventually proved useless, because the method used was incorrect, but they did not realize this at the time.)

On 9 August, Cook set sail again to search for the South Land. As instructed, he sailed to 40°S latitude and turned west. By now he was sailing through heavy swell — a sure sign that there was no land for some distance to the south.

At the end of September he began to see birds and floating debris — signs of land ahead. The land was the east coast of the north island of New Zealand.

By sailing south and west, until he reached New Zealand, Cook had proved that no South Land existed to the east of New Zealand.

Cook charted the coast of New Zealand with great care and precision, sailing right around both islands.

New Holland

When Cook finished mapping New Zealand's coast, it was time for him to set a course for home. He decided to sail further westwards until he reached the eastern coast of New Holland. He would follow this coast northwards before returning home. In this way, he could add further detail to his map.

The *Endeavour* sailed westward, running before a southerly gale. On 19 April 1770, Cook's expedition reached the east coast of New Holland. Lieutenant Zachary Hicks saw the coast first. The point that he saw is still called Point Hicks.

Cook sailed north, noting hills and ridges, bush and the smoke from camp fires. This part of the coast of New Holland was not barren territory — indeed, it was green and fertile.

New South Wales

Cook named the newly discovered land

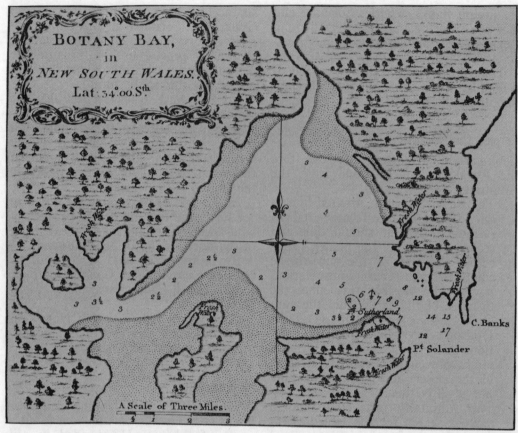

Figure 5.4. Cook's map of Botany Bay.

Figure 5.5. Joseph Banks, botanist on Cook's voyage to Australia.

New South Wales, after the land of south Wales. On Sunday, 30 April, he anchored in a bay that at first he called Stingray Harbour. He spent over a week there. During that time, Joseph Banks collected a large number of plant specimens. Because so many botanical discoveries were made, the bay was re-named Botany Bay.

The expedition left Botany Bay and continued sailing north, along the coast. Cook passed by the entrance to Port Jackson. He realized that it seemed to be a safe anchorage, but he did not turn to explore through the Heads. He did not realize that he had missed seeing one of the most beautiful harbours in the world.

He continued north until he reached another bay, which he called Morton Bay, after a former President of the

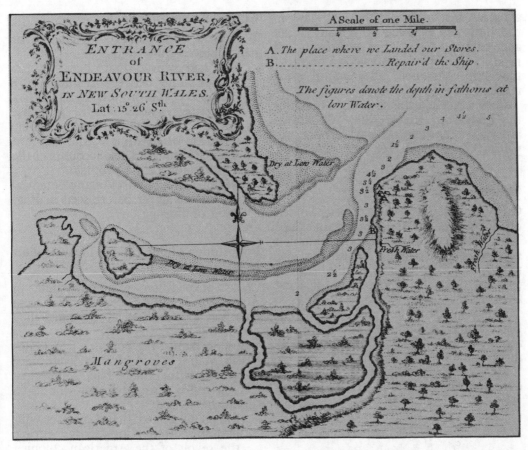

Figure 5.6. *Cook's map of the mouth of the Endeavour River.*

Royal Society. (The spelling was later changed to Moreton Bay.)

Aground on a Coral Reef

The *Endeavour* now began to thread her way through 2000 km of coral reef lying just below the waterline, running parallel to the coast.

During the evening of 11 June, while Cook was asleep in his bunk, the *Endeavour* ran aground on coral. To lighten the ship, Cook cast his cannon overboard. Then he kedged (wound) her

Figure 5.7. *The* Endeavour *careened for repairs in the Endeavour River.*

afloat on her anchor cable. The gash in the hull was plugged with canvas sail and oakum (loose fibre got from old rope). The crew was relieved to find that the ship remained afloat until they reached shore.

Cook careened the ship on a beach of the Endeavour River (where Cooktown is now), and spent 45 days ashore, repairing the damage. He then sailed on.

Heading Home

On Wednesday, 22 August, Cook landed on Possession Island, north of Cape York. He had finished his exploration northwards. He flew the British flag, and took possession of the whole eastern coast of Australia in the name of King George III.

Cook sailed home via Torres Strait, Batavia, and the Cape of Good Hope. He arrived home on 13 July 1771 — almost three years after he had left.

He had lost 38 men, 27 of them from dysentery and malaria picked up in Batavia.

Figure 5.8. A cocky apple — one of the botanical drawings make by Joseph Banks during his Australian voyage.

Cook's Achievements

What had Cook achieved? Actually, he had achieved quite a lot:

- He had proved that there was no South Land between latitudes 40°S and 35°S, east of New Zealand.
- His survey work was of immense value. He had added approximately 8000 km of coastline to the map.
- He had brought back accounts of the cultures of Pacific peoples.
- He had brought back many botanical specimens never before seen in England or Europe.

Importance of the Voyage in Australian History

Cook's expedition was important in Australian history. For the first time men saw possibilities in the land they had found.

Joseph Banks, the botanist, and James Mario Matra, a midshipman, were very impressed with Botany Bay. Later they recommended strongly that the area should be settled:

- Matra suggested that Loyalists who had supported King George during the revolt of the American colonies should be granted land in New South Wales.
- Banks suggested that the spot should be settled by free settlers; but later, in answer to the convict problem, he suggested that it should be settled as a penal colony.

Extracts from Cook's Log

(1) Botany Bay

Sunday, 6 May 1770:
The great quantity of plants which Mr Banks and Dr Solander collected in this place induced me to give it the name of Botany Bay. It is situated in the latitude of 34°S, longitude 208°37′W... We anchored near the south shore, about a mile (2 km) within the entrance, for the convenience of sailing with a southerly wind, and because I thought it the best situation

Figure 5.9. An Aboriginal house or 'humpy'.

for watering; but I afterwards found a very fine stream on the north shore, in the first sandy cove within the island, before which a ship might lie almost land-locked, and procure wood as well as water in great abundance. Wood indeed is everywhere plenty, but I saw only two kinds which may be considered as timber. These trees are as large, or larger than the English oak, and one of them has not a very different appearance: this is the same that yields the reddish gum like *sanguis draconis*, and the wood is heavy, hard, and dark-coloured, like *lignum vitae:* the other grows tall and straight, something like the pine; and the wood of this, which has some resemblance to the live oak of America, is also hard and heavy. There are a few shrubs, and several kinds of palm; mangroves also grow in great plenty near the head of the bay. The country in general is level, low, and woody, as far as we could see.

The woods, as I have before observed, abound with birds of exquisite beauty, particularly of the parrot kind; we found also crows here, exactly the same as those in England. About the head of the harbour, where there are large flats of sand and mud, there is great plenty of water-fowl, most of which were altogether unknown to us: one of the most remarkable was black and white, much larger than a swan, and in shape somewhat resembling a pelican. On these banks of sand and mud there are great quantities of oysters, cockles, and other shellfish, which seem to be the principal subsistence of the inhabitants, who go into shoal water with their little canoes, and pick them out with their hands . . .

During my stay in this harbour, I caused the English colours to be displayed on shore every day, and the ship's name, and the date of the year, to be inscribed upon one of the trees near the watering-place.

(2) The Australian Aborigines

August 1770:
The number of inhabitants in this country appears to be very small in proportion to its extent. We never saw so many as thirty of them together but once, and that was at Botany Bay, when men, women, and children assembled upon a rock to see the ship pass by: when they manifestly formed a resolution to engage us, they never could muster above fourteen or fifteen fighting men; and we never saw a number of their sheds or houses together that could accommodate a larger party. It is true, indeed, that we saw only the sea-coast on the eastern side; and that, between this and the western shore, there is an immense tract of country wholly unexplored: but there is great reason to believe that this immense tract is either wholly desolate, or at least still more thinly inhabited than the parts we visited. It is impossible that the inland country should subsist inhabitants at all seasons without cultivation; it is extremely improbable that the inhabitants of the coast should be totally ignorant of arts of cultivation,

Figure 5.10. Cook's meeting with Aborigines.

which were practised inland; and it is equally improbable that, if the knew such arts, there should be no traces of them among them. It is certain that we did not see one foot of ground in a state of cultivation in the whole country; and therefore it may well be concluded that where the sea does not contribute to feed the inhabitants, the country is not inhabited.

The only tribe with which we had any intercourse, we found where the ship was careened; it consisted of one and twenty persons; twelve men, seven women, one boy and one girl; the women we never saw but at a distance; for when the men came over the river they were always left behind. The men here, and in other places, were of a middle size, and in general well made, clean limbed, and remarkably vigorous, active, and nimble: their countenances were not altogether without expression, and their voices were remarkably soft and effeminate.

Their skins were so uniformly covered with dirt, that it was very difficult to ascertain their true colour: we made several attempts, by wetting our fingers and rubbing it, to remove the incrustations, but with very little effect. With the dirt they appear nearly as black as a Negro; and according to our best discoveries, the skin itself is of the colour of wood soot, or what is commonly called a chocolate colour. Their features are far from being disagreeable, their noses are not flat, nor are their lips thick; their teeth are white and even, and their hair naturally long and black, it is however universally cropped short; in general it is straight, but sometimes with a slight curl; we saw none that was not matted and filthy, though without oil or grease, and to our great astonishment free from lice. Their beards were of the same colour as their hair, and bushy and thick: they are not however suffered to grow long. A man whom we had seen one day with his beard somewhat longer than his companions, we saw the next, with it somewhat shorter, and upon examination found the ends of the hairs burnt: from this incident, and our having never seen any sharp instrument among them, we concluded that both the hair and the beard were kept short by singeing them.

Both sexes . . . go stark naked, and seem to have no more sense of indecency in discovering the whole body, than we have in discovering our hands and face. Their principal ornament is the bone which they thrust through the cartilage that divides the nostrils from each other: what perversion of taste could make them think this a decoration, or what could prompt them, before they had worn it or seen it worn, to suffer the pain and inconvenience that must of necessity attend it, is perhaps beyond the power of human sagacity to determine: as this bone is as thick as a man's finger, and between five and six inches long (about 16 cm), it reaches quite across the face, and so effectually stops up both the nostrils so that they are forced to keep their mouths wide open for breath, and snuffle so when they attempt to speak that they are scarcely intelligible even to each other. Our seamen, with some humour, called it their spritsailyard; and indeed it had so ludicrous an appearance, that till we were used to it, we found it difficult to refrain from laughter. Beside this nose-jewel, they had necklaces made of shells, very neatly cut and strung together; bracelets of small cord, wound two or three times about the upper part of their arm, and a string of plaited human hair about as thick as a thread of yarn, tied round the waist. Besides these, some of them had gorgets of shells hanging round the neck, so as to reach across the breast.

But though these people wear no clothes, their bodies have a covering besides the dirt, for they paint them both white and red: the red is commonly laid on in broad patches upon the shoulders and breast; and the white in stripes, some narrow, and some broad: the narrow were drawn over the limbs, and the broad over the body, not without some degree of taste. The

Figure 5.11. An Aboriginal chief from the New South Wales region, painted for a native dance.

white was also laid on in small patches upon the face, and drawn in a circle round each eye. The red seemed to be ochre, but what the white was we could not discover; it was close grained, saponaceous to the touch, and almost as heavy as white lead; possibly it might be a kind of *Steatites*, but to our great regret we could not procure a bit of it to examine. They have holes in their ears, but we never saw anything worn in them. Upon such ornaments as they had, they set so great a value, that they would never part with the least article for anything we could offer; which was the more extraordinary as our beads and ribbons were ornaments of the same kind, but of a more regular form and more showy materials. They had indeed no idea of traffic, nor could we communicate any to them: they received the things that we gave them; but never appeared to understand our signs when we required a return. The same indifference which prevented them from buying what we had, pre-

Figure 5.12. Cook setting out on his second voyage (1772–75).

vented them also from attempting to steal: if they had coveted more, they would have been less honest; for when we refused to give them a turtle, they were enraged, and attempted to take it by force, and we had nothing else upon which they seemed to set the least value; for, as I have before observed, many of the things that we had given them, we found left negligently about in the woods, like the playthings of children, which please only while they are new. Upon their bodies we saw no marks of disease or sores, but large scars in irregular lines, which appeared to be the remains of wounds which they had inflicted upon themselves with some blunt instrument, and which we understood by signs to have been memorials of grief for the dead.

The Second and Third Voyages

Cook made two more voyages of exploration.

On his second voyage (1772–75), he commanded two ships, the *Resolution* and the *Adventure*. Following Admiralty instructions, he searched for the Great South Land near the South Pole. He did not find this land, and considered that he had ended speculation about it for good.

On his third voyage (1776–79), he commanded the *Resolution* and the *Discovery*. Again following Admiralty instructions, he attempted to find a north-west sea passage between the Pacific and the Atlantic oceans. He failed in this quest, since only a modern submarine or ice-breaker can sail where he tried to sail.

During this third voyage, perhaps tired and a little careless, Cook went ashore among cannibals at Karakakoa Bay, on Hawaii Island, and was killed in petty dispute, while trying to retrieve a stolen cutter.

Questions

(1) In what year did Cook set out on his first voyage of exploration?

(2) Why did Charles Green sail with Cook?

(3) Why did the *Endeavour* carry three artists?

(4) Did Cook sail around the Cape of Good Hope or the Horn on his voyage to Australia?

(5) When did the transit of Venus

occur?

(6) Why was New South Wales so named?

(7) What was the first name given to Botany Bay?

(8) Cook was lucky to return alive from his first voyage. Why? Give two reasons.

(9) Describe some of the Aborigines that Cook encountered.

(10) Why was Cook's first voyage important in the history of Australia?

Research

Find out more about the following.

(1) Cook's contribution to science

(2) The British Admiralty during the eighteenth century

(3) Cook's second voyage of exploration

(4) Joseph Banks

(5) James Mario Matra.

Chapter 6

The British Decide to Settle Australia

An Important Decision

In the year 1786, the British government announced its intention to establish a penal colony at Botany Bay in New South Wales.

Historians have not been able to agree amongst themselves as to exactly why this decision was made. Why did the British government decide to transport convicts halfway around the world, at considerable expense, risking ships and people's lives, to establish a prison in an unknown wilderness?

What would be the benefits of such a farflung penal colony?

Surely the British were disillusioned with colonies at this time, after losing the American War of Independence?

It would seem, when the evidence is examined, that Australia was settled for more than just one reason.

A Dumping Ground for Convicts

Georgian society in the late eighteenth century was in many ways cruel and callous. Most people faced dirt, disease, poverty, lack of education, and a lack of regular police protection. The authorities found it hard to keep law and order. Cities like London, York, Glasgow, Edinburgh and Dublin swarmed with pickpockets and petty thieves. In the countryside, highwaymen

and footpads (highwaymen on foot) menaced the roads. Some people even hero-worshipped highwaymen.

Laws were extremely harsh, and many

Figure 6.1. King George III reigned from 1760 to 1820. Some have seen him as a tyrant, trying to re-establish the powers of the Crown and responsible for the American War of Independence; others have seen him as a loyal king who considered it his duty to suppress the American rebels.

Figure 6.2.

were old-fashioned. The whole legal system had been designed for an earlier society where fewer people lived in cities. More than 150 crimes could be punished by the death sentence.

The system of punishment was vicious. Convicts — men, women, and sometimes even children — were hanged from gibbets, in public, at Tyburn and elsewhere. Many were sentenced to transportation, as an alternative to hanging. Sympathetic juries sometimes undervalued articles which had been stolen so that the felon would not receive

Figure 6.3. The Discovery, *a prison hulk lying at Deptford. One of the ships that were used to house the overflow from Britain's prisons.*

Figure 6.4. The York, *a prison hulk in Portsmouth Harbour.*

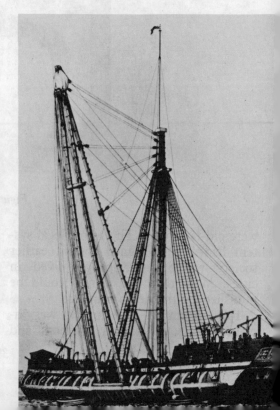

a death sentence — and King George III liked to exercise the royal pardon.

Convicts sentenced to transportation were sold to contractors, who shipped them across the Atlantic to the American colonies before the American War of Independence. There they were auctioned off to American settlers, such as the owners of tobacco and cotton plantations in the colonies of Virginia and Maryland. Convicts in America worked for the duration of their sentence, which was usually for seven years, 14 years, or life.

Most convicts in the American colonies were worked hard, and were provided with only the poorest quality food, clothing, and shelter. Some were lucky and had good masters. Many who were sentenced to seven or 14 years' transportation were able to work off their sentences eventually and make a new life for themselves in America. A few even returned to Britain. Some escaped, returned to Britain, were caught, and were either transported again or hanged.

It has been estimated that approximately 1000 convicts per year were transported to America. Convicts who were not hanged or transported were lashed, branded, or forced to stand in the pillory, or sit in the stocks in public. Some who were held in the pillory or stocks were stoned and beaten by the public. Imprisonment was not usually a form of punishment. It was used mainly for those awaiting trial or punishment.

The Hulks

In 1776, the colonists in America rebelled against British rule and refused to accept any more British convicts. This created problems for the British government. At first it was thought that the American rebels would be defeated, and transportation would resume. The contractors, after all, were still ready for business.

Convicts were held in prisons. When these became full, they were sent to old ships, or 'hulks'. Parliament passed a special *Hulks Act* to make this possible. These hulks were moored in the Thames River and in naval harbours such as Portsmouth and Plymouth. Convicts aboard them were employed during the day in chain gangs, on public works such as dredging sand and silt from harbours and rivers, and collecting and sorting ballast. Some hulks could be moved and moored near the work site.

As time passed, and the war dragged on, conditions in the prisons and hulks became intolerable. Prisoners became re-

bellious and difficult to deal with. Some escaped. Jail distemper (infectious disease) broke out, claiming the lives of guards and convicts alike. Prison reformers, such as John Howard, and the Whig opposition in Parliament protested about the situation.

A New Dumping Ground Needed — But Where?

Before the war ended, the British government was thinking seriously about finding a new destination for convicts sentenced to transportation. Some could remain in Britain, employed on public

Figure 6.5. Sir Joseph Banks when he was President of the Royal Society.

Figure 6.6. Lord Thomas Sydney, Secretary to the Home Office, after whom the city of Sydney was named.

Figure 6.7. Jean-François de Galaup, Comte de La Pérouse, the French explorer.

works, but many would have to be sent overseas. Parliament formed a committee to look into the matter. It gathered suggestions and evidence, but no decision was made.

After the war, a second committee considered a number of proposals:

- Modern, safe penitentiaries could be built at home (at Milford Haven, for instance) or in the Scottish Highlands. This idea was abandoned because of the cost of construction and fear of opposition from local people.
- Gambia, the Gold Coast, South-west Africa, the West Indies, Newfoundland, Nova Scotia and Gibraltar were all considered as new dumping grounds, but rejected. There was a large native population in Africa, and the diseases and climate there were hard on white settlers. South-west Africa was barren and lacked water, and the Dutch, at the Cape, might prove difficult. The West Indies already had a supply of black slave labour. Members of the House of Lords who owned sugar plantations on the islands would not agree

to white convicts being sent there. Disease was also common there. Newfoundland and Nova Scotia? Local settlers would object.

Joseph Banks's Solution: Botany Bay

Since his journey with James Cook in the *Endeavour*, Joseph Banks the botanist had become a gentleman of considerable influence. He was regarded as an authority on the Pacific Ocean.

For years, he had been talking about Botany Bay. Now he argued that it would be a suitable site for a penal colony. Botany Bay was far from Britain, and most convicts would never return. The natives there were not warlike (Banks called them 'cowardly', in fact). There were no dangerous wild animals. The climate was not severe, there was soil for farming and adequate water to drink.

But what of the cost of starting a penal colony? Banks argued that the colony would soon grow enough food to support itself. That would be a start.

On 18 August 1786, Lord Sydney announced that His Majesty had fixed upon Botany Bay as a place for convicts, and he later instructed the Admiralty to provide ships to transport approximately 750 convicts, staff, and provisions to that destination.

Norfolk Island

The historian Geoffrey Blainey (*The Tyranny of Distance*) has stressed the fact that Britain settled Norfolk Island at the same time as Australia.

It was decided that some ships of the fleet that would transport convicts to New South Wales should also plant a small colony on that island. The island had been discovered by Cook in 1774, approximately 1500 km north-east of Botany Bay. The Admiralty hoped that this island might be a help to British shipping. The tall, beautiful Norfolk pines could be felled and trimmed for ships' masts and spars, and high-quality native flax could be cultivated to make sail cloth and ships' cables.

Britain's commerce and defence depended on supplies of timber and flax, so Norfolk Island was too good a thing to ignore.

Rivalry between Empires

Undoubtedly, rivalry between empires played a part in the decision to settle Australia. A large continent was waiting, mostly unexplored. Nobody then knew its full potential. If the British did not occupy it, then some other nation, such as Spain or France, almost certainly would do so.

For some years, the French had been interested in the Pacific. La Pérouse, the French explorer, was given orders to explore the west coast of Australia and sail from Tasmania to New Zealand in 1785. Reports reached London that he had been instructed to establish a settlement in New Zealand. These reports were false, but they must have caused some concern at the time.

Such French measures called for British countermeasures. It would have been unthinkable to allow Australia and Norfolk Island to fall into French hands.

Trade with Asia?

Was Australia settled in order to establish trade with Asia and the Pacific? This seems unlikely. The British East India Company already had a monopoly on trade in the region of Australia, and at the time the British government did not want to infringe the Company's rights. Arthur Phillip, the first governor of the New South Wales colony, was warned in his instructions:

every sort of intercourse between the intended settlement at Botany Bay, or other places which may be hereafter established on the coast of New South Wales, and its dependencies, and the settlements of our East India Company, as well as the coast of China, and the islands situated in that part of the world . . . should be prevented by every possible means.

The new settlers were also forbidden to build ships. There was to be no trading, whaling, sealing, or any other major commercial venture in or around New South Wales.

Questions

(1) What were the major forms of punishment in eighteenth-century Britain?

(2) How did the revolt of the American colonies affect the British system of punishment?

(3) Why were modern penitentiaries not built in eighteenth-century Britain?

(4) What arguments did Banks put forward in favour of Botany Bay as a place of settlement?

(5) Why were the British authorities interested in Norfolk Island?

(6) Where is Norfolk Island?
(7) Who was La Pérouse?
(8) What did the British think of French exploration in the Pacific?
(9) What were Phillip's instructions regarding trade?
(10) Why did the British decide to settle Australia?

Research

Find out more about the following:
(1) Life in Georgian England
(2) The British Empire
(3) The American War of Independence
(4) The British East India Company
(5) The French in the Pacific.

Chapter 7

Arthur Phillip and the First Fleet

Figure 7.1. Captain Arthur Phillip.

Phillip is Appointed Captain-General and Governor

Once the British government had decided to settle Australia, it had to appoint a captain-general and governor and assemble a fleet.

The man chosen to be captain-general and governor was Arthur Phillip. He was 49 years of age, the son of a German language teacher. He had years of experience as a naval officer abroad, and as a farmer at home. He was not very tall. He was not very strong, and indeed he was a little nervous, but he was patient, efficient, and quietly courageous.

His farm was at Lyndhurst, in Hampshire, in the south of England. One of his neighbours was Sir George Rose, who was an ex-naval officer and, at that time, Secretary to the Treasury. It is possible that Rose obtained the command for Phillip. It is also possible that Phillip later named Rose Hill (now Parramatta) after his neighbour.

Phillip's Orders

- Phillip was ordered to claim the eastern part of Australia, from the extremity of Cape York Peninsula in the north (10°37'S) down to the extremity of South Cape, southern Tasmania (43°39'S), and westwards inland from the coast to 135°E. He was also to claim all adjacent Pacific islands. This was an enormous area. Phillip was to rule over more territory than any other British governor.
- He was to establish a penal colony at Botany Bay, and a smaller colony on Norfolk Island.
- He was to clear and cultivate the land.
- He was to explore the new territory.
- He was to establish friendly relations with the natives.
- He had the power to pardon convicts. Convicts who worked off their sentences, or were pardoned, were to be regarded as free people. Children of convicts were to be also free. Ex-convicts were to be granted land — 75 hectares per man, 50 hectares more if he married, and 25 hectares more for each child. Marriage was to be encouraged. Native women were to be imported from the islands to make up for the lack of females in the colony. (It can be seen that ex-convicts were to be bribed with land to stay on in Australia. They were not wanted back in Britain.)
- Philip and the settlers were not to build ships or encroach on the British East India Company's trade monopoly in the region.

Figure 7.2. Convicts embarking for Botany Bay.

The First Fleet Assembles

In March 1787, a fleet of 11 ships assembled at the Mother Bank, within the Isle of Wight, just off the great naval port of Portsmouth. The fleet consisted of a flag ship, an armed escort, and nine merchant vessels: six to transport convicts and three to transport supplies.

Special modifications were made to the convict transports. Iron bars were fitted over hatchways. Barricades were made from iron spikes to protect the upper decks. Loopholes were cut so that musket fire could be directed between decks in an emergency. The lower decks were divided into compartments separated by bulkheads one metre thick, studded with nails.

As was usual in those days, the ships were all infested with rats, cockroaches, and other vermin. The Royal Navy classified the flag ship, *Sirius*, as sixth-rate. She leaked badly. The combined tonnage of the fleet was only about 3915 tonnes. The entire cubic capacity for all 11 ships was less than for a modern Australian coastal freighter. Yet, despite this, the fleet was to carry 1472 people to Australia — Royal Navy personnel, marines, merchant crews, and 759 convicts.

It took two months to load and prepare the fleet. During that time, there was great excitement. Shopkeepers in Portsmouth feared for their property, and boarded up their windows. Wives of convict transportees came to the port,

Figure 7.3. *Wives of convicts bidding farewell to their husbands.*

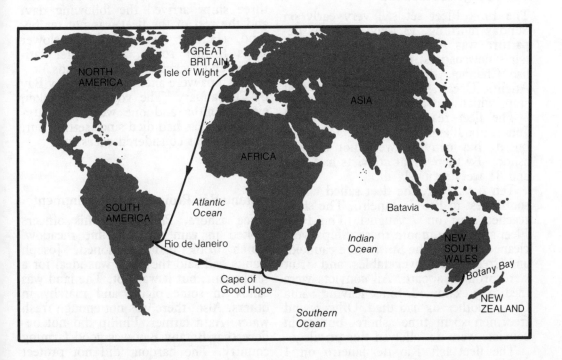

Figure 7.4. *The route taken by the First Fleet in 1787.*

begging to be taken with their husbands. The government did not wish to overspend on the venture, and the ordnance office was notorious for its inefficiency. Supplies were therefore inadequate. There was not enough food or clothing for the convicts. There were no medical supplies. There were no antiscorbutics to prevent scurvy. There was not enough grog for the marines, and no ammunition for the guns on the ships. The ships were overcrowded. The convicts lacked the skills that they would need in the new colony. There were no real farmers and few craftsmen amongst them. There were no experts in flax cultivation.

However, Phillip kept trying to improve the situation. He wrote letters pleading for further supplies, and managed to improve a little on what he had been given. He could not achieve any more than this.

The Voyage to Australia

The First Fleet set sail very early on Sunday morning, 13 May 1787. Its departure was hardly mentioned in Britain's newspapers. After it left the English Channel, the fleet sailed into the Atlantic Ocean, and headed for its first stop, which was Santa Cruz, Teneriffe.

The fleet reached Santa Cruz on 3 June. Food and water were taken on board, but convicts were not allowed ashore. By then, eight convicts had died and 81 were seriously ill.

Ten days later, the fleet sailed again, south-west to Rio de Janeiro. The ships reached port on 7 August. The First Fleet spent one month there. Ships were cleaned, leaks in the *Sirius* were caulked, and fresh meat, vegetables and fruit were brought aboard. All convicts were medically examined. Since leaving Santa Cruz, another six had died. Officers and free men spent time ashore, but again convicts were not allowed this privilege.

The fleet left Rio de Janeiro on 4 September and sailed east across to the Cape of Good Hope. Phillip was not prepared to risk rounding Cape Horn. The fleet reached Table Bay on 13 October, and spent another month in Cape Town. Here, livestock was taken aboard. The decks became crowded with cattle, sheep, pigs, goats, and poultry. The First Fleet resumed its journey on 9 November.

Arrival at Botany Bay

After leaving the Cape, Phillip transferred from the *Sirius* to the *Supply*. With the *Alexander*, *Friendship*, and *Scarborough* — the fastest ships in the fleet — he sailed on ahead, leading an advance party.

He sailed east until he reached Tasmania, then rounded the tip of that island and sailed north, up the east coast of Australia, to Botany Bay.

Phillip reached the entrance to Botany Bay first, and dropped anchor off Bare Island on 18 January 1788. The other three ships arrived the following day, and the rest of the fleet was not far behind. (Hunter had moved the slower ships further south, into higher latitudes, and picked up strong winds.)

All ships were anchored in Botany Bay by 20 January. The voyage had taken eight months and one week. Twenty-three convicts had died since setting out. This was not considered excessive.

Botany Bay Proves a Disappointment

Once ashore, Phillip and his officers looked in vain for the 'fine meadow' which Cook had mentioned. Joseph Banks had said the place was ideal for a settlement, but it was not. The land was sandy in some places and marshy in others. Also, there was not enough fresh water. As a farmer, Phillip did not believe that Botany Bay was good farming country. The harbour did not protect ships riding at anchor from winds blowing in from the ocean.

The Fleet

Sirius (c. 531 tonnes)	Flagship (20 guns)	Arthur Phillip, 1st Captain Captain Hunter, 2nd Captain	Royal naval personnel. Marines.
Supply (c. 173 tonnes)	Armed tender (8 guns)	Lt Ball, Captain	Royal naval personnel. Marines.
Alexander (461 tonnes)	Convict transport	Master: Duncan Sinclair Surgeon: William Balmain	Merchant seamen. Marines. Convicts.
Charlotte (352 tonnes)	Convict transport	Master: Thomas Gilbert Surgeon: John White	Merchant seamen. Marines. Convicts.
Friendship (284 tonnes)	Convict transport	Master: Francis Walton Surgeon: Thomas Arndell	Merchant seamen. Marines. Convicts.
Lady Penrhyn (345 tonnes)	Convict transport	Master: Wm. Cropton Sever Surgeon: (i) Jn. Turnpenny Altree (ii) Arthur Bowes	Merchant seamen Marines. Female convicts only.
Prince of Wales (340 tonnes)	Convict transport	Master: John Mason Surgeon: None	Merchant seamen. Marines. Convicts.
Scarborough (427 tonnes)	Convict transport	Master: John Marshall Surgeon: Dennis Conssiden	Merchant seamen. Marines. Male convicts only.
Borrowdale (278 tonnes)	Storeship	Master: Readthon Hobson	Merchant seamen.
Fishburn (386 tonnes)	Storeship	Master: Robert Brown	Merchant seamen.
Golden Grove (338 tonnes)	Storeship	Master: Sharp	Merchant seamen.

Those Who Sailed

(The following figures are estimates only.)

210 Royal naval personnel
211 Royal marines (4 companies)
233 Merchant seamen
568 Male convicts
191 Female convicts
 13 Convict children
 27 Marine wives
 19 Marine children

20 officials

Deaths	*Men*	*Women*
Between embarkation and sailing	16	1
Between Motherbank and Teneriffe	7	1
At Teneriffe	1	0
Between Teneriffe and Rio	5	1
Between Rio and Port Jackson	7	1
	36	4

Figure 7.5. Arrival in New South Wales, 1788.

'The Finest Harbour in the World'

On 21 January, Phillip and Captain Hunter, two other officers, and some sailors explored north in three boats — they went looking for a better spot to settle.

Cook had charted the entrance to Port Jackson and Broken Bay. Perhaps these would be more suitable. Phillip sailed into Port Jackson early in the afternoon, and was greatly impressed by what he saw. He wrote:

We got into Port Jackson early in the afternoon, and had the satisfaction of finding the finest harbour in the world, in which a thousand sail of the line may ride in the most perfect security . . .
The different coves were examined with all possible expedition. I fixed on the one that had the best spring of water and in which the ships can anchor so close to the shore that at a very small expense quays may be made at which the largest ships may unload.

The cove was named Sydney Cove, in honour of Lord Sydney, the Home Secretary.

Raising the Flag

Phillip returned to Botany Bay and made arrangements for his ships to move around into Sydney Cove. He sailed in the *Supply* on 25 January, and the other ships followed the next day.

At daylight on 26 January, officers, marines, and convicts from the *Supply* went ashore, and a small ceremony was held. The Union Jack was run up, and officers and men drank four toasts in glasses of porter — one to the health of His Majesty, King George III, one to his Queen, Charlotte of Mecklenburg-Strelitz, one to George, Prince of Wales, and the fourth to the success of the colony. The marines then fired a volley and all present gave three cheers. (Ever since then 26 January has been celebrated as Australia Day.) The First Fleet had arrived. It was now time to commence building the new colony.

Questions

(1) What experience did Arthur Phillip have which made him suitable for his new appointment?

(2) How many ships were in the First Fleet?

(3) What was the name of Phillip's flagship?

(4) What precautions were taken to ensure that convicts did not escape from convict transports?

(5) Approximately how many people travelled to Australia in the First Fleet?

(6) What problems did Phillip face in loading and preparing his fleet?

(7) The British government was not generous in supplying ships and supplies. Why do you think this was so?

(8) What three stops did the First Fleet make between England and Botany Bay?

(9) Why did Phillip reject Botany Bay as a site for settlement?

(10) Why did Phillip decide to settle at Sydney Cove?

Research

Find out more about the following.

(1) Political and social events in England in 1787

(2) Life aboard ship in the eighteenth century

(3) Teneriffe and Santa Cruz

(4) Rio de Janeiro

(5) Cape Town.

Chapter 8

Years of Struggle

Landing

Here is a description of the first days of the new settlement at Sydney Cove:

The landing of a part of the marines and convicts took place the next day, and on the following, the remainder was disembarked. Business now sat on every brow, and the scene, to an independent spectator, at leisure to contemplate it, would have been highly picturesque and amusing. In one place, a party cutting down the woods; a second, setting up a blacksmith's forge; a third, dragging along a load of stones or provisions; here an officer pitching his marquee, with a detachment of troops parading on one side of him, and a cook's fire blazing up on the other. Through the unwearied diligence of those at the head of the different departments, regularity was, however, soon introduced, and, as far as the unsettled state of matters would allow, confusion gave place to a system.

So wrote Captain Watkin Tench, a marine officer, in his journal.

Shelter

The new settlers stayed in tents at first,

Figure 8.1. Sydney Cove, as drawn by John Hunter in August 1788.

but permanent buildings had to be built. They made wattle-and-daub huts, which proved to be frail. Sometimes they collapsed in winter under heavy rain. When this happened, the settlers often found it easier to build a new hut rather than rebuild a collapsed one.

They took longer to build better quality wooden buildings, with thatched or shingled roofs, because there were only 12 carpenters amongst the convicts. The settlers found a good, local supply of clay and sandstone for moulding bricks and building. However, they could not find a supply of limestone for mortar. They burnt shells from the waterline to produce lime for mortar, but this mortar proved of inferior quality. Some of the first brick buildings collapsed soon after being built.

Farming

Phillip had a supply of food to last about two years. By the end of that time, the settlement had to be able to produce its own food. This meant that trees had to be felled, land cleared, soil turned over, crops planted, tended, and harvested.

Farming proved very difficult because few settlers had any knowledge of farming. They had no ploughs. They had poor-quality hand hoes and other implements, which broke easily. They did not have enough beasts of burden. Clearing the land was hard, blistering, backbreaking work. Everything depended on human muscle power.

Drought, intense heat, then heavy, pouring rain and mud made this sort of work very difficult. The soil around Sydney Cove was sandy and of poor quality, and the harbour area ended in shallows and swamps. The seed that the First Fleeters had brought out was eaten by weevils, rotted in the ground, and failed to germinate. They had little manure to fertilize those crops which did manage to grow. The seasons were upside down and confusing. At the outset, no one could even be sure what the seasons

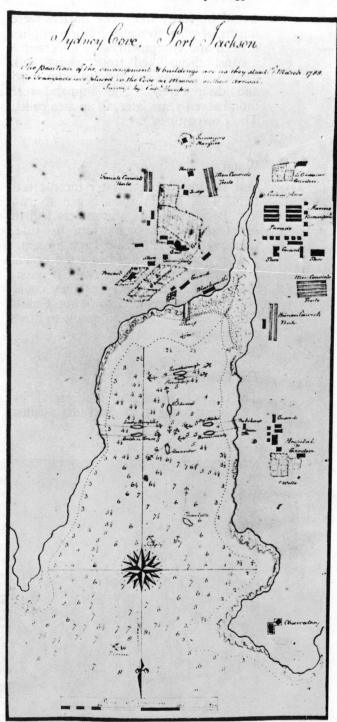

Figure 8.2. The location of the encampment and buildings as they existed in March 1789.

would be really like. The settlers were unsure of when to plant. Future supplies of seed and equipment were uncertain.

Most sheep died from eating lank grasses. Cattle wandered into the bush and disappeared. (The animals were found seven years later, in an area called The Cowpastures.)

Water

One stream supplied water for the settlers. This stream soon began to run low. Because of this, the settlers had to cut tanks or reservoirs into its side. (Hence they called it the Tank Stream.) Phillip would have liked to settle beside a larger watercourse — a river, if possible. The settlers found that they could not build a waterwheel to power a mill. They needed to build windmills to drive mill machinery.

The Convicts

The convicts made poor pioneers. They had been brought to Australia against their will, and they lacked the enthusiasm of people like the Pilgrim Fathers, who had settled North America. They did not want to obey laws or meet the challenge of beginning a new settlement. When they could get away with it, they avoided work. They lost, or deliberately broke, tools. They defied authority. They made the Rocks area, near the harbour, their retreat, and went there to indulge in drinking, gambling, and squabbling.

Most seriously, the convicts began to steal food. Phillip realized that he had to stop this at the outset. The colony could not survive without its supply of food. Therefore, Phillip sought to make an example of those convicts caught stealing. On 27 February, four convicts, Thomas Barrett, Henry Lovell, Joseph Hall, and John Ryan, were brought to trial for stealing bread, pork, peas, and other provisions. They were all found guilty. Barrett, Lovell, and Hall were sentenced to be hanged in public from a tree in the settlement. Ryan, who was considered slightly less guilty, was sentenced to 300 lashes.

Figure 8.3. A convict chain gang.

The Marines

The main duty of the marines was defence. They defended the officers and gentlemen from the convicts, and the colony as a whole from attacks by the Aborigines or from another country.

However, Phillip expected them to do more. He asked that they help supervise the convicts, that they patrol at night to prevent theft, that they sit as jurors in court, and that they co-operate with certain trusted convicts who had been given police duties.

Major Robert Ross protested that these things were all beyond the call of duty. The duties of the marines had been made clear in a letter from the Admiralty to the commanding officers of marines at Portsmouth and Plymouth, and they did not include these things. Ross was stubborn and difficult to deal with, and the marines followed him. He and his men made Phillip's task all the harder.

The Aborigines

Phillip hoped to live in peace with the Aborigines, and learn from them about the land. However, this did not happen. The Aborigines did not like to see their tribal land invaded, and they were not interested in teaching the newcomers how to survive in their new environment.

At first they were frightened by the settlers, who were a strange colour — the colour of spirit-beings. Their leader seemed kindly disposed towards them. Phillip even had a missing front tooth — an outward sign of tribal membership!

They lost their initial curiosity and awe, however, when they saw their land taken, and the game hunted and driven off. They became hostile. Settlers who had to leave the immediate area of settlement and the protection of the marines went in fear of their lives. Some settlers were killed and others were wounded by the Aborigines. Phillip himself was speared in the shoulder while trying to communicate with the warrior Bennelong, at Manly. It took him a month to recover from his wound.

The Bush

The settlement was surrounded by deep, rugged bush, and the settlers had no maps to guide them. Some became lost and died from exposure. Some disappeared without trace.

Norfolk Island

Phillip had been instructed to settle Norfolk Island as soon as possible after landing in New South Wales. In February 1788 he sent Lieutenant Philip Gidley King, in the *Supply*, to do this. King took a small party, consisting of an officer, surgeon, midshipman, six marines, two men who knew a little about flax cultivation, and 15 convicts (nine men and six women). On the way there, Lieutenant Ball, who was in command of the *Supply*, discovered and named rugged Lord Howe Island.

When the expedition reached Norfolk Island, King realized that settlement would not be easy. The island was walled in by sheer cliffs and surrounded by jagged coral reefs and crashing surf. Landing was difficult, and depended on the weather. On some days it would be impossible. (Some time before, La Pérouse had found it impossible to land.)

Once ashore, the party found that the land was very difficult to clear. The soil was good, but the Norfolk pines were very large, and they grew everywhere. Arthur's Vale, in Sydney Bay, was the first settlement.

The island had been settled for its flax and timber. Would this plan work? It did not take the settlers long to realize that the plan would fail. The flax on the island was a hardy, strong variety, and the settlers could not separate the long fibres from the stalks. They found plenty of straight timber — but it was full of

Figure 8.4. Norfolk Island.

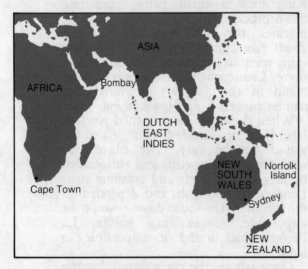

Figure 8.5. The new colony was very isolated from the rest of the world.

knots, and therefore useless for ship's timber.

Isolation

The new colony was very isolated. To many settlers, it must have appeared the end of the earth. The nearest Europeans were at Cape Town, or Batavia in the Dutch East Indies. It took months to sail there and back, and there was always the risk of storms and shipwreck. Phillip also lacked ships. Once the nine transport ships of the First Fleet had unloaded, they eventually set sail again for China and home. This left only the *Sirius* and the *Supply*. The *Sirius* was leaking badly and the *Supply* was a small ship. Then, to make matters worse, the *Sirius* was lost. While transporting more marines and convicts to Norfolk Island, it ran aground on a coral reef close inshore. Fortunately, the crew rigged up a flying fox between the ship and the shore so that everybody could escape. However, the ship could not be saved. It sat slowly breaking up on the reef for the next two years.

So the settlement had only one ship left — the *Supply*. If Phillip sent her away on a voyage, Sydney would be totally cut off from the rest of the world. Unfortunately, Phillip had to do just this. Because of a critical shortage of food, he sent Lieutenant Ball in the *Supply* to Batavia. This left the colony totally isolated.

Matters were made worse because the settlers feared that supply ships from England might have sunk. They were

Figure 8.6. The wreck of the Sirius *off Norfolk Island.*

right to fear this. A supply ship — the *Guardian* — was sent in 1789, but struck an iceberg off the Cape of Good Hope, and sailed, sinking, into Cape Town harbour.

Starvation

Lack of food became a serious problem. The land did not produce enough, and so the settlers had to rely on the supplies which had been brought out with the First Fleet. Phillip was forced to reduce the food ration for each person per week to 1.8 kg of flour, 1.1 kg of salt pork and 0.7 kg of rice. This was then further reduced to 1.1 kg of flour, 0.9 kg of pork and 0.9 kg of rice. This food was by now years old, and also lacking in vitamins — particularly vitamin C. The result was that settlers grew perpetually hungry, weak, and ill, and several died. Phillip suffered along with the rest. He ordered men to fish in the harbour, and all who were good marksmen — including convicts — to hunt kangaroos.

If a lucky man, who had knocked down a dinner with his gun, or caught a fish by angling from the rocks invited a neighbour to dine with him, the invitation always ran 'bring your own bread'. Even at the governor's table, this custom was constantly observed. Every man when he sat down pulled his bread out of his pocket, and laid it on his plate.

The Arrival of the Second Fleet

On 3 June 1790, the *Lady Juliana*, the first ship from home, entered the Heads, bringing food, supplies, and news from home. Within a month, four more ships arrived, the *Justinian*, the *Surprise*, the *Neptune*, and the *Scarborough*.

The Second Fleet brought food — but it brought more mouths to feed too. It also brought death and suffering. The fleet had sailed with over a thousand convicts. To save costs, they had been fed poorly and closely packed. As a result, a quarter of them had died on the voyage out. Two-thirds of those who landed at Sydney Cove were ill — some so ill that they could move only by crawling on their hands and knees. Several convicts died before they could be taken ashore, and crewmen dumped their bodies overboard. Some of these bodies were found washed up on the beaches.

The Second Fleet also brought out the first detachment of the New South Wales Corps, which was eventually to replace the marines. One of its officers was John Macarthur, an ambitious young man who was to prove a thorn in the side of future governors.

Rose Hill

The first settlers had more success at farming when they moved further inland, away from the sandy soil around Sydney Cove. They found much richer, alluvial soil on the banks of the Parramatta and, later, Hawkesbury Rivers.

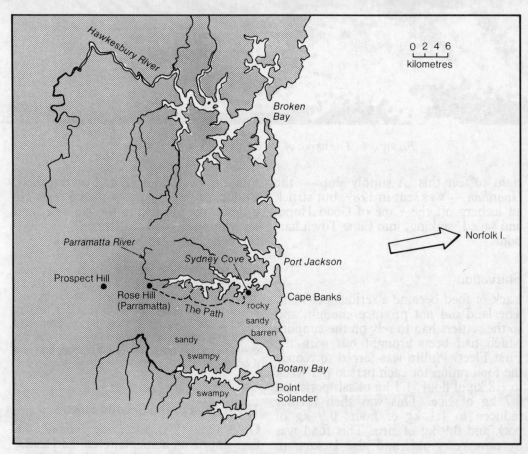

Figure 8.7. At Rose Hill on the Parramatta River, the first settlers found land more suitable for farming.

Figure 8.8. The landing place at Parramatta.

Settlers developed Rose Hill (or Parramatta, an Aboriginal name meaning 'where the eel rests') to take advantage of this better soil and the fresh water of the Parramatta River. Rose Hill lay about 24 km west of Sydney.

At first, Rose Hill was cleared and worked by convict gangs, under Henry Dodd, an experienced farmhand who had come to Australia as Phillip's personal servant. Dodd supervised the clearing and planting of some 30 ha in an area known as The Crescent on the south side of the river. He grew a good crop of corn, wheat, barley, flax, and oats. He was one of the first to become a successful farmer in the region, and he deserves to be given more credit than he has been given in the past.

The first convict to receive land was James Ruse. Ruse knew something about farming and he was a good worker. In November 1789, Phillip offered him 0.6 ha of cleared land, two pigs, and six fowls, and asked him to see if he could make himself independent of the supply store. Ruse asked for more land, and Phillip increased his offer to one hectare. Ruse accepted, and went to work. Within 15 months he was growing enough wheat, maize, and vegetables to meet his needs. He was allowed to keep his farm (called Experiment Farm), and his holding was increased to 12 ha.

Rose Hill developed quickly. More land was cleared, crops planted, houses, barns, and public buildings constructed. Phillip decided that his residence should be there, and not in Sydney. He built a small Government House near the river and spent much of his time in Rose Hill. The little satellite-settlement was reached by a small boat which sailed up the harbour and Parramatta River. The journey took about four hours. A rough road was also built along the high land on the south side of the river. At first this was called simply 'The Path'.

Figure 8.9. Whaling at Twofold Bay, New South Wales.

Whaling and Trading

The Third Fleet arrived in July and August 1791. (This time 180 convicts had died, out of 2000). After unloading, five of the ships went whaling instead of sailing for China and home. British companies, such as Samuel Enderby and Sons, had discovered that there was good whaling in Australian waters.

The ships of the Third Fleet were very successful at whaling. This gave new ideas to some of the settlers. Ships could carry convicts out to Australia, and carry whale products back to Britain. Whale products sold very well at that time. Whale oil was used in soap and for lamp fuel. The mouth bones of the whale were used in women's corsets, for hoops in petticoats and in umbrella frames. Ambergris, a grey substance from the diseased intestines of the whale, was used in perfume and cooking. Spermaceti, a solid wax taken from a cavity in the whale's head, was used for making high-quality candles. From 1791 onwards, Sydney became an important base for whaling operations.

American ships soon discovered the existence of Sydney. For some of them, it was a convenient stopover on the way to China. On 1 November 1792, the *Philadelphia*, a Yankee brigantine, dropped anchor in Sydney Harbour. It sold 569 barrels of American cured beef and 27 barrels of pitch and tar to the officers, who also bought from it rum, gin, wine, and tobacco. The *Hope*, from Rhode Island, arrived next. It arrived in time for Christmas 1792, and sold American beef, pork, flour, and alcohol to the store.

Other shipowners and masters began to look to the spice trade with India, and some to the *bêche-de-mer* trade with China. This all conflicted with the British East India Company's monopoly on trade. However, Phillip could not stop the beginnings of sea trade. Besides, the colony needed contact with more ships and supplies.

Phillip Returns Home

The struggle to build the colony and survive there made Phillip weary. He began to suffer ill health, and complained of a pain in his side. In March 1791, he wrote home, asking to be allowed to return temporarily.

On 10 December 1792, Phillip went aboard the storeship *Atlantic* to sail for home. He could not wait any longer. He took with him two Aborigines, Benne-long and Yem-mer-a-wan-nie, and two convicts. Left in power was Major Francis Grose, commandant of the New South Wales Corps and lieutenant-governor, and David Collins, the judge-advocate. As yet, no new governor had been sent to replace Phillip.

Phillip had worked hard and well, and carried out most of his instructions. The penal colony was established and now showed every sign of surviving. Farms on the Parramatta River were producing food. Ships were beginning to call at Sydney Cove. A colony had been started on Norfolk Island.

A beginning had been made, but it was only a beginning. There was still much to do.

Questions

(1) What disadvantages did Sydney Cove have as a site for settlement?

(2) Why did most convicts make poor pioneers?

(3) What did the marines think of the convicts?

(4) Why were the Aborigines hostile to the new settlers?

(5) Who was sent to colonize Norfolk Island?

(6) Why was Norfolk Island difficult to settle?

(7) What emergency measures did Phillip take to prevent the colonists from dying of starvation?

(8) Why was Rose Hill settled?

(9) Why was whaling important to Britian?

(10) Why did Phillip return to England?

Research

Find out more about the following.

(1) The geography and geology of the Sydney area

(2) The Royal Marines

(3) Farming methods in the eighteenth century

(4) Whaling

(5) American ships in the Pacific Ocean.

Chapter 9

The 'Rum Corps' and the Governors

Figure 9.1. Major Francis Grose.

Phillip sailed for England in 1792. The struggle for mere survival had nearly ended. Now there followed a struggle for political and economic power within New South Wales. For the next 17 years the colony was dominated by an exclusive ring of New South Wales Corps officers and a few wealthy free settlers, who exploited the colony for their own benefit. Three governors attempted to break the power of these men, and all failed. Eventually this conflict between governors and opportunists flared into open rebellion.

The Corps

The New South Wales Corps was raised to replace the Royal Marines. It was also raised to deal with the special problems of New South Wales. It would be a garrison regiment, not a front-line regiment. It would deal with convicts and convict problems. Officers, for instance, would perform jury service. The Corps was made up of volunteers. Three guineas was paid to each recruit when he enlisted. The only requirements were that he should be over 16 years of age, over 5 feet 4 inches (1.6 m) in height, and sound in mind and body.

Why did men volunteer for service in a penal colony on the other side of the world? Some may have joined for the three guineas; some were in debt to escape creditors; others might have wanted a free ticket to adventure, promotion, or profit. A few had no choice. They were released from prison on condition they serve with the Corps. This was a common recruiting practice at the time.

Major Francis Grose was in charge of the Corps. He received his commission in 1789, at the age of 35. He was a professional soldier who had fought against the rebels in America. He had been wounded seriously and, on returning home, had retired on half-pay. He was a rather easy-going man, ambitious, but lacking in ability. He was not a good choice for commanding officer.

Another man who enlisted was John Macarthur. He was of Scottish descent. His father had fought for Bonnie Prince Charlie against the English. Macarthur had settled in Devonshire and married Elizabeth Veale, a West Country girl. He was 22 when he enlisted, his wife younger. The couple had one child. Macarthur became one of the ringleaders of the profiteers in New South Wales.

The first detachment of the Corps sailed to Australia with the Second Fleet. Macarthur and his family sailed with them. The second detachment arrived in February 1792, with Grose. Shortly afterwards, the Corps replaced the Royal Marines. Those among the marines who did not wish to leave Australia transferred to the new Corps.

The Corps Gains Control

Grose and his officers had the colony to themselves for two years after Phillip left, and they firmly entrenched their position.

- Grose granted land to his officers and men, and certain free settlers, in lots of roughly 40 hectares. He said that this was necessary in order to develop the colony.
- Convicts were smuggled away from public works and assigned to Corps members and certain settlers. Sergeants, corporals, and even drummers received convict servants. Some men holding land were given as many as 10 to 13 convict servants each.
- Equipment, tools, clothing, food, grain etc., were all supplied, free of charge, to officers and settlers. Many men lived off the store.
- Officers purchased some of the small farms held by emancipists (freed convicts) and others. This was illegal.
- Goods were bought from visiting ships and sold for a high profit. This was against service regulations, which forbade servicemen from indulging in trade.

- Officers imported rum (any strong liquor) or distilled it, and sold it for profit. The sale of rum brought enormous profit — as high as 800–1000 per cent.
- Roads and public building were neglected.
- Officers controlled the military and civil courts.

There was little money in the colony at the time. For some reason, the British government had not included currency notes in the supplies. Therefore the Corps carried out business in promissory notes (IOUs) and government bills, as well as in wheat and rum.

Grose resigned in May 1794, because of his war wounds, and left for England in December of that year. He left Captain William Paterson in charge, with the special title of Administrator. Paterson was 39. He had served in Cape Town and India, before coming to Australia. In Australia, he had served on Norfolk Island before serving in Sydney. Unfortunately, he was a rather weak man who was easily led. The Corps had yet another poor commanding officer.

It was left to three governors to confront Paterson and the Corps. They were Captain John Hunter (1795–1800), Captain Philip Gidley King (1800–06), and Captain William Bligh (1806–08).

Governor Hunter

Many people in the colony already knew Hunter when he became governor of New South Wales. He had served as second captain aboard the *Sirius*, under Phillip, in the First Fleet. He had sailed to the Cape for supplies in the *Sirius* when there was a food shortage. He had been on board the ship when she ran aground on Norfolk Island, and he had spent 11 months marooned on that island with other seamen, marines, and convicts. He had returned to England in 1792, before Phillip. There he had published his journal and served aboard the *Queen Charlotte*. He was offered the governorship by Lord Howe, his patron. He

Figure 9.2. Governor John Hunter.

was a kindly, religious man.

Hunter's instructions included:
- Re-establish civilian control of the courts.
- Reduce the number of convicts allowed as servants to officers so that no officer could have more than two.
- Check the traffic in rum.

He failed in all these instructions. It was one thing to issue an order, and another to make sure that it was carried out. Nobody paid attention to Hunter's orders.

Hunter was shocked by the insubordination and dealings of the Corps. He said, bitterly, that its members were 'soldiers from the Savoy' (the Savoy was a military prison in England). He even tried to get replacements for the Corps. A detachment of marines was ordered to set sail for New South Wales, but it was held back at the last moment because of the war with France.

Hunter made many enemies, and they blackened his name at home. He tried to assist the free settlers, but they lacked farming skills, and were no match for the Corps. Hunter could do little. He returned to England, a disillusioned man.

Figure 9.3. Governor Philip Gidley King.

Governor King

King, like Hunter, had sailed to Australia in the First Fleet. From the beginning he had been an enthusiastic officer. Phillip had appointed him commander of the settlement on Norfolk Island in February 1788 and he served there until 1796, when he returned home on sick leave.

Sir Joseph Banks suggested him as a replacement for the ineffectual Hunter. King accepted the commission and arrived in Sydney on board the *Speedy*, on 15 April 1800. By now he suffered from gout, and looked haggard. He was given to outbursts of temper, and some people thought he acted in an eccentric manner.

King tackled the convict problem. As Hunter had done, he ordered that food and clothing should be issued to only two convict servants per officer. Later, he insisted that convicts employed on agricultural work should be supplied by the farmer entrusted with their accommodation and welfare. King tried to protect the interests of the convicts. For instance, he forbade the horse-whipping of convicts. Only justices of the peace could inflict punishment.

King encouraged settlers not to mortgage their crops. He sold goods cheaper than the officers, in competition with them.

Like Hunter, he tried hard to break the rum trade. He forbade the Corps to traffic in rum, and restricted imports. Only a fixed amount of rum was to be landed from any one vessel. Ships from India and America were ordered to carry away tens of thousands of gallons, and their governments were requested to control traffic to Australia. A trader needed written permission from the governor to land spirits, and it could not be sold ashore without a licence. At the same time, King ordered vigorous hunts for illegal stills. He also set up a government brewery, at Parramatta, in 1804, to sell beer wholesale to shops on condition it was sold at a fixed rate. Officers were tol they could not supply or sell rum from their personal allowance.

King was only partly successful:

- Officers smuggled rum into Sydney, sometimes through the new Hobart settlement, and distilled their own.
- The officers carried out business through their convict mistresses to avoid detection.
- Macarthur demanded that officers and settlers boycott the governor. When Paterson continued to dine with King at Government House , Macarthur fought a duel with him, wounding him seriously. King sent Macarthur to England to face trial (November 1801), and there Macarthur worked at damaging King's reputation.
- King had to put up with insults and slights. A number of 'pipes' (rhyming lampoons) were produced ridiculing him and those who supported him.

King was more successful than Hunter, but the most he achieved was to

Figure 9.4. *Governor William Bligh.*

counteract and undermine abuses, not stop them. As early as 1803, he asked to be recalled home.

Governor Bligh

Unlike Hunter and King, Governor Bligh had no experience in New South Wales. This may be one reason why he ruled for only 18 months before being deposed.

Bligh had had an exciting naval career. He joined the navy as a lad, and accompanied Cook on his third voyage as sailing master on the *Resolution*. He fought under Lord Howe at Gibraltar in 1782. He commanded the armed ship *Bounty* on a voyage to Tahiti to pick up a supply of breadfruit for transplanting in the West Indies. On that voyage his crew mutinied, and he and 18 others

Figure 9.5. *The mutiny on the* Bounty.

were cast adrift in an open boat. Bligh navigated, without maps, from the Society Isles to Timor, a distance of 6400 km, in 44 days — one of the most remarkable small-boat voyages in history. He commanded the warship *Director* at Camperdown in 1797, and in 1801 he was thanked personally for his loyalty and bravery by Horatio Lord Nelson.

Joseph Banks picked him as the new governor for New South Wales. He arrived in the *Porpoise* in August 1806 to begin his duties.

Bligh carried strict orders to break the power of the New South Wales Corps. Unfortunately, he had a stormy personality, which made his job more difficult. He was his own worst enemy. He used the rough language of the sea continually, and he seemed to care little for the feelings of others. 'The law, Sir?' he declared once. 'My will is the law, and woe unto the man who dares to disobey it.'

Bligh and Macarthur

Unfortunately for Bligh, he soon clashed with Macarthur. The two men had little in common:

- Bligh's life was in the navy. Macarthur's service had been in the army.
- Bligh believed that the future of the colony depended on farming. Macarthur's over-riding interest was sheep.
- Bligh was determined to destroy the rum trade. As a sea captain, he was well aware of the evil effects of rum on men, and how it undermined discipline. Macarthur saw rum as an important source of income, and objected to Bligh attempting to destroy his interest in it.
- Bligh believed in obedience to regulations. Macarthur cared only for his own advancement.
- Bligh was English. Macarthur was the son of a Scottish rebel.

What the two men did have in common

was an equal determination by each to have his own way. When they confronted one another, there was bound to be trouble.

The first round between Bligh and Macarthur was fought over two copper boilers that could be used as stills. They had been imported aboard the *Dart*. Bligh considered that they had been imported illegally and ordered them to be seized.

Unfortunately, the official who seized the boilers had no authority to do so. Macarthur saw his opportunity. He sued for wrongful seizure and trespass, and won the case.

The second round between Macarthur and Bligh proved decisive. Macarthur was part-owner of a schooner called the *Parramatta*. A convict escaped on this vessel to Tahiti. (Tahiti was the same place the *Bounty* mutineers had returned to.) When Bligh heard about the escape, he ordered the owners to pay an £800 bond and two sureties of £50 in compensation. Macarthur refused to pay. When the ship returned to Sydney, constables went aboard to prevent the cargo being unloaded. Macarthur then declared he had abandoned the vessel. This drove the master and crew ashore, and when they stayed ashore this broke port regulations.

Macarthur was ordered to appear before Atkins, the judge-advocate. Macarthur refused, stating that Atkins was his debtor, and would be against him. Macarthur was then arrested and brought before the court on 25 January 1808. Macarthur again objected to being tried before Atkins, and the officers on the jury were sympathetic to this claim. Macarthur was released on bail, pending settlement of the question of a suitable judge.

However, Bligh refused to replace Atkins. Next day, Macarthur was re-arrested, and imprisoned.

The 'Rum Rebellion'

The same afternoon, 26 January 1808,

Figure 9.6. Bligh's arrest.

Major George Johnston, commanding the military in Sydney, arrived at the military barracks at five o'clock, having come from Annandale, his residence. His superior, Colonel Paterson, was then in Tasmania. Officers and others met him excitedly, and asked him to march on Government House to depose Bligh.

Johnston sent an order to Macarthur's jailer, asking him to release Macarthur. This order was obeyed, and Macarthur walked across the road to the barracks. The following petition to Johnston was then drawn up:

Sir,
The present alarming state of this colony, in which every man's property, liberty and life is endangered, induces us most earnestly to implore you instantly to place Governor Bligh under an arrest, and to assume the command of the colony. We pledge ourselves, at a moment of less agitation, to come forward to support the measure with our fortunes and our lives.

we are, with great respect, Sir,
Your most obedient servants.

It was signed by Macarthur, the Blaxland Brothers and two others; 146 extra signatures were added later.

Johnston sent a letter to Bligh, calling on him to resign. At nine o'clock in the evening, he led 300 troops up to Government House, with bayonets fixed, colours flying, and a band playing. Bligh was arrested in an upstairs bedroom. According to the propaganda of the day, he was caught hiding under a bed. The next day, Johnston issued a proclamation stating that the rebellion was over and peace had been achieved.

Bligh Stripped of Power

Bligh remained a prisoner at Government House for twelve months. He was then allowed to take command of the *Porpoise*, on condition that he return to England.

Bligh tried to persuade the ship's company to attempt to restore him to power. They refused. He waited a month, hoping that the free settlers on the Hawkesbury River would rise to support him, but they did not. He sailed to Hobart, hoping for assistance from David Collins and the people of the town. They were not prepared to help him. Bligh quarrelled with Collins, and remained just off the southern Tasmanian coast until Macquarie, the new governor, arrived in Sydney in December 1809.

When Macquarie arrived, Bligh sailed back to Sydney. By this time, Macarthur and Johnston had gone back to England. There would be a hearing, and they wanted to make sure that their case was received well.

Macquarie welcomed Bligh in Sydney, and informed him that it was His Majesty's pleasure that he should return to England, too. Macquarie had been instructed to reinstate Bligh as governor for one day, for form's sake, so that Bligh could hand over power to him. Bligh, however, was in Tasmania when he arrived, and Macquarie assumed power on his own.

Bligh was quite prepared to go back to England, but first he wanted to search for private papers and arrange for witnesses to give evidence on his behalf at the forthcoming hearing. This took time, and it irritated Macquarie.

Bligh Goes Home

Finally, in May 1810, Bligh, the ex-governor, and Paterson, the ex-lieutenant-governor, together with the New South Wales Corps and the members' wives and children, sailed for home aboard the *Porpoise*, *Hindustan* and *Dromedary*. Paterson never saw Britain again, however. He died on 21 June,

Governor	Lieutenant-Governor	Garrison
Captain Arthur Phillip, R.N. 1788–92	Major Robert Ross	Royal Marines
First interregnum. (No official governor) 1792–95	Major Francis Grose 1792–94	New South Wales Corps
	Captain William Paterson 1794–	
Captain John Hunter, R.N. 1795–1800	Captain William Paterson	New South Wales Corps
Captain Philip Gidley King, R.N. 1800–06	Captain William Paterson	New South Wales Corps
Captain William Bligh, R.N. 1806–08	Captain William Paterson	New South Wales Corps
Second Interregnum. 1808–09	Captain William Paterson	New South Wales Corps

while the *Dromedary* was rounding Cape Horn, and was buried at sea.

During the hearing that followed in England, Bligh was cleared of all blame for the mutiny. Johnston was cashiered, and returned to Australia as a free settler. Macarthur, who could not be tried before a military court, was told he could not return to New South Wales for some time. Macquarie was ordered to arrest him if he did. It was years before Macarthur was allowed to return.

Why the Governors Failed

Hunter, King, and Bligh all failed to curb the power of the Corps because:

- The officers of the Corps had controlled all military power in the colony, and had been able to use force (or threats of force) to support their policies and demands. The governors had been surrounded, outnumbered, and intimidated.
- Members of the ring had also written letters of complaint to the authorities in England, making them doubt the abilities of the governors. The officers had developed the art of character assassination. In particular, John Macarthur used this method. He used his time in England to talk to important people.
- The British government was slow to act, because it was fully occupied with the war against Napoleon, and the threat of a French invasion.

The End of the Corps

The Rum Rebellion meant the end of the New South Wales Corps and its activities. It had gone too far. Macquarie, the new governor, brought his own troops with him, and they replaced the Corps. The Corps was recalled to England in disgrace. It ceased to be the New South Wales Corps and became simply the 101st Regiment. Its members were also split up.

Lampoon Attacking King

My powers to make great,
O'er the laws and the State,
Commander-in-Chief I'll assume;
Local rank, I persist,
Is in my own fist;
To doubt it, who dare shall presume?
For infamous acts from my birth I'd an itch,
My fate I foretold but too sure;
Tho' a rope I deserved which is justly my due,
I shall actually die in a ditch —

And be damned!

Excerpts from Johnston's Court Martial

The court martial of Johnston was held in the Chelsea Hospital, London, beginning on Tuesday, 7 May 1811.

Prosecuting Counsel Questions Bligh:

'In what state did you find the colony upon your arrival?'

'In a very miserable state.'

'Did you discover any abuses existing with respect to spirits?'

'There was a barter of spirits for articles of every description, by those persons who had spirits to purchase them with.'

'Were the officers or soldiers at all interested in that barter of spirits, and if so, how?'

'The officers were very much interested in the barter of spirits; so much so, as to be enabled to get whatever they wanted at a very cheap rate.'

'What with respect to the soldiers?'

'The observation applies exactly the same to the soldiers, provided they could get it.'

'Did you take any measures to prevent this barter of spirits?'

'Yes sir.'

'What?'

'By prohibiting the barter of spirits altogether; and it stands so in my public orders.'

'Did these measures of reform create any discontent in the colony; and, if so, mention who were discontented, and on what account; and how they showed their discontent?'

'They did create discontent among a few.'

'Mention who were discontented.'

'Those persons in particular who were connected with the mutiny, who were connected with my arrest; Macarthur and a few others whose names are mentioned in my dispatches.'

'In what state was the settlement in general in the month of January 1808?'

'In a very improved state, and the whole people happy and contented in a high degree, except as I mentioned in answer to a former question.'

'Was there the least danger of tumult or insurrection, or of any disturbance in the settlement, provided the military had remained true to you as the governor?'

'Not the least danger.'

Johnston, In Defence, Questions Bligh:

'How often has it happened to you in the course of your service in the navy that you have found it necessary to bring officers or others to a court martial for mutiny or other similar offences?'

'I think about twice I have brought persons to a court martial; twice or thrice I suppose, in the course of forty years' constant and active service.'

'How many courts martial have you obtained against individuals for other officers?'

'Really, gentlemen, it is hard for me to answer such a question... The world knows perfectly well that in 1787 there was a mutiny on board the ship *Bounty*; I presume that is what they allude to. I don't know any other mutiny that I have had anything to do with, except that dreadful mutiny at the Nore in which, of course, I was not particularly concerned...'

'Have you ever been brought to a court martial, and for what?'

'I was brought to a court martial for the loss of the *Bounty*; and my lieutenant, who I understand is now turned out of the service, brought me to trial when I commanded His Majesty's ship the *Warrior*, a 74. I cannot say how the charge was worded, but the amount of it I recollect was that I had sent for him to do his duty when he had a lame foot... and he said that it was an act of tyranny on my part to send for him, or the word might be, oppression.'

'What was the result of that last court martial to which you have spoken?'

'I think to the best of my recollection that the affair terminated with the court saying they recommended Captain Bligh to be more cautious in his expressions: I think that was just to the amount of it, word for word.'

'You have spoken of an individual of the name of Macarthur: was not Mr Macarthur one of the principal settlers of the colony?'

'Yes.'

'Had not Mr Macarthur the authority of His Majesty's Government for a grant of five thousand acres of land, together with the power of employing a certain number of labourers for the forwarding of a project of great public importance; namely, that of raising very fine wool which should supersede or supply the want of Spanish wool?'

'There were no orders of that kind came to me.'

'But do you know whether such orders did in fact come?'

'I knew he was possessed of great property in the country, and I know there was great conversation and long talk about his producing a great quantity of wool, which I believe the government of England was led to think would be brought over.'

'Did you ever forward or endeavour to forward, or did you oppose and thwart the execution of thse declared intentions of His Majesty's Government?'

'I did everything in my power to forward the views of His Majesty's Government.'

'Did you not damn the Privy Council and Secretary of State, and say that Macarthur should not keep the grant of land which he held by order of the Secretary of State?'

'No. I declare to God I never did.'

'Did you not, in the hearing of Major Abbot, use these words, or others to the like effect: "Damn the Secretary of State; what do I care for him, he commands in England and I command here."?'

'I know nothing about it.'

'Did you not say in the presence of Lieutenant Minchin, "I don't give a damn for the Secretary of State; he is but a clerk in office, in today and out tomorrow."?'

'I did not.'

'Will you venture to restate upon your oath that you never did utter any of those expressions, or any words to the like effect?'

'To the best of my recollection I know nothing of this kind of conversation taking place.'

Macarthur Gives Evidence:

'I endeavoured to appease him by stating that I had understood the government at home had particularly recommended me to his notice. He replied: "I have heard of your concern, sir; you have got five thousand acres of land in the

The Land They Found

finest situation in the country; but, by God, you shan't keep it.''

'I told him that as I had received this land at the recommendation of the Privy Council and by order of the Secretary of State, I presumed that my right to it was indisputable.

'"Damn the Privy Council! and damn the Secretary of State too!" he says. "What have they to do with me? You have made a number of false representations respecting your wool, by which you have obtained this land."'

Questions

(1) Who commanded the New South Wales Corps in 1792?
(2) Why were public works neglected after 1792?
(3) Why did the sale of rum bring such high profits?
(4) Why was the British government unable to devote a lot of time to problems in New South Wales?
(5) Who suffered most at the hands of the Corps?
(6) Why did Bligh and Macarthur argue?
(7) Why did Macarthur object to being tried before Atkins?
(8) Who led the troops to Government House to depose Bligh?
(9) Why was Bligh deposed?
(10) Why did the deposing of Bligh lead to the withdrawal of the New South Wales Corps?

Research

Find out more about the following.
(1) Francis Grose
(2) William Paterson
(3) John Hunter
(4) Philip Gidley King
(5) William Bligh.

Chapter 10

Macarthur and the Wool Industry

The Need for a Staple

New South Wales proved costly to run. The main cost involved in running the colony was the transportation of convicts. The colony received convicts and it managed to stop most of them returning to Britain — but it gave little else in return. Sir Joseph Banks echoed the feelings of many people in Britain when he argued that what Australia needed was 'some native raw material of importance to a manufacturing country such as England is'. This 'native raw material' had to fit in with the convict system. It also had to fit in with powerful trade interests, at home and abroad. It had to

Figure 10.1. John Macarthur.

supply some need in the British empire and it had to attract capital.

Various investments were tried:

- **Flax and timber:** The British government had hoped that Norfolk Island might supply flax and timber, but, as we saw in an earlier chapter, this came to nothing. The flax was too hardy. It could be cultivated, but not economically. Supplies were low, and fluctuated. The Norfolk pines were too full of knots to be of use for masts and spars. Australian timber was a possibility, and some Australian cedar was exported. Timber in general, though, proved to be too bulky and expensive a cargo, and the competition was too great.
- **Whaling** was a good investment for some time, but it did not seem enough.
- **Sealing** was tried, but declined rapidly after 1800, because too many seals had been slaughtered. This reduced their numbers and depressed the market.
- The trade in **sandalwood and bêche-de-mer** with China was ruined because the British East India Company reclaimed its right to this trade as far as British vessels were concerned. Crews also treated the natives badly, and they were not keen to trade.
- No **gold** or other precious metals or minerals were found in Australia at the time, despite wild rumours.
- **Coal** was discovered, and exported from Newcastle on the Hunter River, north of Sydney, to India and Cape Town. It was not profitable, however, to carry it all the way to Britain, which had its own local supply. There was a market in Java, but this could not be exploited because the British East India Company controlled the market there.

The Emergence of Wool

Wool was slow to emerge as a staple. The fact that it did become the main Australian export owes much to the enthusiasm and hard work of John Macarthur. Ironically enough he was at the same time one of the colony's most troublesome young settlers. Other settlers bred sheep, but mainly for mutton. Macarthur alone took the time to experiment with wool breeding and find markets for his produce.

The Work of Macarthur

Macarthur came to New South Wales as an officer and gentleman in a garrison regiment. Soon he became interested in farming. The colony had plenty of land,

Figure 10.2. Whaling provided New South Wales with a profitable industry in the early years.

Figure 10.3. Elizabeth Farm, Macarthur's first property on the banks of the Parramatta River.

and there was a supply of cheap labour. The New South Wales Corps soon controlled the colony, and Major Francis Grose could be generous. He was persuaded that a gentleman needed land, and besides, the colony needed developing.

At first Macarthur's main interest was in mixed farming. This was needed to feed the colony. He received land at Rose Hill, next to James Ruse's Experiment Farm on the Parramatta River. He called his farm Elizabeth Farm after his wife. Elizabeth Farm lay near Macarthur's barracks, and he was able to combine farming with his military duties. The farm also lay near a government store, from which he obtained supplies.

Macarthur worked hard. He was the first man in the colony to use a plough. Like other farmers in Europe, he adopted a new scientific approach to farming. For instance, he divided his land into paddocks, enclosed by fences. This kept animals separated, and protected crops. By 1795, he had enlarged his farm to approximately 160 hectares. He had wheat, corn, and maize under cultivation, a good vegetable garden and orchard, and a large number of healthy cattle, sheep, and horses.

Macarthur's interest soon turned to sheep. The sheep that were in the colony at the time were 'unsightly and diminutive . . . resembling the goat in appearance'. They were good only for mutton and lamb. Would it be possible to breed sheep for wool?

Figure 10.4. An eighteenth-century Spanish merino ram.

In 1794, Macarthur crossed an Irish ram with Bengal ewes, and produced a stock that had a mingled fleece of hair and wool. This new stock could thus be slaughtered for meat, or shorn for its wool. However, the wool was not of high quality. Could better wool be bred?

To produce better wool, Macarthur had to obtain better stock. He had travelled in Spain, and he knew the best sheep in the world came from there. This was the merino, a sheep that had rich, thick wool. However, it was hard to obtain merinos. The Spanish authorities wanted to keep their monopoly on the sheep, and stopped their sale.

Macarthur was lucky, though. A number of merinos were handed over under treaties during the Napoleonic Wars, and some of these came into the hands of Commandant Gordon at Cape Town. He had trouble selling them to the Dutch farmers at the Cape, who were not interested in them. Captains Waterhouse and Kent visited Cape Town to purchase provisions for Sydney. There they bought some of the merino sheep. Kent's died on the voyage back to Australia; Waterhouse was luckier. Macarthur, as well as Reverend Marsden, Cox and Rowley, were eventually able to buy merino lambs. These were a start.

In 1800, Macarthur was temporarily disillusioned with the colony and planned to leave. By now he had approximately 600 sheep, and he offered to sell these to Governor King. King was interested in the possibilities of wool, and he sent some wool samples home to Britain, hoping to persuade the authorities to allow him the funds to purchase the sheep.

Meanwhile, Macarthur overreached himself. Major Foveaux was ordered to Norfolk Island, and he offered his 1400 sheep for sale, too. Macarthur bought them, and tried to sell them to King, with his other sheep, at an increase of 66 per cent. He even included the flock's lambs over the next two years. King decided against the deal, leaving Macarthur with the largest flock in the colony. Macarthur then quarrelled with King and Paterson, fought a duel with Paterson, and was ordered home to face court martial.

2000 Hectares at Camden

Macarthur left Sydney on 15 November

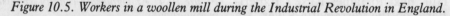

Figure 10.5. Workers in a woollen mill during the Industrial Revolution in England.

1801, for London via the East Indies and India. He reached London one year later, in November 1802. Always shrewd, he avoided court martial by resigning his commission. He also made friends with ex-Governor Hunter, and in general was rude about King's abilities as governor. He also talked about wool to government representatives and factory owners.

Macarthur did not have to go looking for manufacturers who were interested in wool: they came to see him. At this time, Britain was undergoing an industrial revolution. Factories that used new machinery powered by steam were being built. The textile industry was an important part of this revolution. Raw cotton, silk, and wool had to be imported to make cloth for clothing and bedding, etc. Markets throughout the British Empire seemed almost limitless, and many people were making new fortunes.

However, there was a problem concerning supplies of wool. At that time, it came from Spain and Silesia, and these sources of supply were being threatened by Napoleon's armies. The manufacturers wanted to know if Macarthur and his associates could provide wool.

There were problems in sending wool from Australia to Britain. Distance was one problem. It took a long time to sail to Australia and back, risking storms and shipwreck. An investor would have to wait years for a profitable return. But then, wool would not decompose during the journey.

New South Wales could not produce much wool at this time, but in the near future it might be possible. In 1804, Sir Joseph Banks suggested that Macarthur should be allowed to experiment with wool production. He should be given land, labour, and every encouragement. Macarthur had the audacity to ask for 225 000 hectares. A committee of the Privy Council, set up to examine this proposal, thought that this was too

Figure 10.6. Camden, the estate John Macarthur selected on his return from England in 1805.

much. Instead, the committee offered Macarthur 2025 hectares, with another 2025 ha held in reserve to be granted later, and up to 30 convicts for labour. Macarthur accepted. He also purchased seven merino rams and three merino ewes from King George's private stud at Kew. These merinos were a gift to the British monarchy from the King of Spain, and really should not have been taken out of England.

Macarthur returned to Australia in June 1805, and selected his land in the fertile Cowpastures area. He named his estate Camden, after John Jeffreys Pratt, the Second Earl of Camden, the Colonial Secretary, who officially granted him the land.

At Camden, Macarthur went to work, breeding merinos for wool to feed the hungry mills of industrial Britain. However, he did not live on the new property. Elizabeth Farm House, in Parramatta, remained his home.

Two and a half years later, Macarthur took part in the Rum Rebellion. This time he went back to England on his own initiative, to help Johnston prepare for his court martial.

He found that this time the authorities were not as trusting as they had been. It was eight years before he was allowed to return to Australia. For Macarthur, these eight years were a time of trial. His wife Elizabeth managed Elizabeth Farm and Camden in his absence. He did not know if he would ever be allowed to return to Australia. Should he bring his wife and children to England? If he did, he would be abandoning a profitable investment. Finally he was granted permission to return, and arrived back in Sydney Cove in February 1817.

68 000 Kilograms of Fine Wool

Macarthur spent the rest of his life in New South Wales, dedicated to improving his flocks and increasing his exports to England.

Most other farmers were slow to follow his example. They continued for the time being, to breed for mutton, and then mutton and wool.

The weight of Macarthur's fleece increased. In 1820, the average weight of his fleece was 1.1 kilograms against an average weight of 0.8 kilograms for the rest of the colony. (The weight of this wool was about one-quarter that of the modern average.) In 1822, he received two medals from the London Society of Arts for producing 68 000 kilograms of fine wool, and for successfully rivalling the wool of Saxony. Macarthur eventually went insane, died in 1834, and was buried at Camden, in a private family cemetery.

Increased Development

The coastal district around Sydney was not ideal for sheep, but in 1813 a way was found across the Blue Mountains by the explorers Blaxland, Wentworth, and Lawson. Settlers could now move into the Bathurst Plains, on the other side of the ranges. Large areas of good pasture became available. Here the 'squatters' began to develop sheep properties, and the result was a slow but steady increase in the number of sheep and the amount of wool produced and exported. A staple had been found for the colony.

Questions

(1) When did Macarthur arrive in New South Wales? (See Chapter 8.)
(2) How was he assisted to start farming?
(3) What was the name of his first farm?
(4) Where was this farm situated?
(5) Why did Macarthur wish to acquire merino sheep?
(6) Why were merinos hard to obtain?
(7) Why was wool needed in Britain?
(8) How many hectares did the British authorities grant to Macarthur?
(9) What did Macarthur call his new estate?

(**10**) Name two other farmers who bred sheep at that time.

Research

Find out more about the following.
(**1**) Sheep and wool
(**2**) Early methods of sheep farming
(**3**) The textile industry in Britain at the beginning of the eighteenth century
(**4**) The life of John Macarthur
(**5**) The early Australian wool trade.

Chapter 11

Coastal Survey

Australia Still a Mystery

When George Bass and Matthew Flinders arrived in Australia, much of the northern and southern coastline of the continent still needed accurate charting. The Dutch had slowly charted the west coast, part of the north coast, and the tip of Tasmania. Cook had charted most of the east coast.

But what of the north and south? Were the Dutch maps of the north accurate?

Was the continent split by an inland sea? Were in fact New Holland, in the west, and New South Wales, in the east, really two large islands?

Was Van Diemen's Land, in the south, joined to the mainland, or was it an islands?

Were there large inland lakes which emptied into the sea? Did the flora and fauna, and the natives, change as one moved around the continent?

The survey work of Bass and Flinders answered most of these questions. Between them, the two men showed the world the complete outline of Australia and described the nature of the coastal land. Flinders also gave the continent its name — Australia.

Two Friends

George Bass and Matthew Flinders came to Australia with Governor Hunter aboard the *Reliance*. The two men were firm friends.

Bass was 24 years old, 1.8 metres tall, and quite robust. He was a naval surgeon, but was keenly interested in exploration. So that he could go exploring, he brought with him a small dinghy, 2.5 m long, with a single mast, nicknamed *Tom Thumb*.

Matthew Flinders was 21 years of age, only 1.6 metres tall, and quite slim.

Figure 11.1. George Bass.

(Others on the *Reliance* noticed and laughed at the difference in height between the two men.) He was the son of a doctor and, like Bass, keen on the idea of going exploring. He had joined the Navy when he was 14, after reading Daniel Defoe's *Robinson Crusoe*, and had sailed with Bligh aboard the *Providence*. He had volunteered to come to Australia because of the chance to go exploring.

Out of the Heads

Not long after landing at Sydney Cove, Bass and Flinders took *Tom Thumb* to explore the entire shoreline of Port Jackson. Hunter was pleased with their work. He was a naval officer as well as a governor, and he knew how much the colony needed maps. He suggested that they explore Botany Bay fully.

Bass and Flinders were willing to make the journey. They set off through the Heads, taking William Martin, Bass's servant, with them. *Tom Thumb* must have been very cramped. Few sailors today would venture through the Heads in such a small boat.

The explorers sailed south, past deserted beaches that would later be named Bondi and Coogee, as far south as Botany Bay and Georges River. They explored the mouth of Georges River, then returned to Sydney.

Tom Thumb II

Next year, in 1796, Governor Hunter ordered a larger boat built for the two explorers. The result was *Tom Thumb II*, a craft 4.5 m long, partly decked, with lockers and centreboard. In this boat Bass and Flinders explored Port Hacking and sailed as far south as Lake Illawarra. On this trip, they nearly lost their lives in a gale.

South to Westernport Bay

In 1797, Flinders had to sail to Cape Town. In December of that year, Bass

Figure 11.2. Captain Matthew Flinders.

set out in an 8.6 m whaleboat, with six strong oarsmen, and instructions from Hunter to explore as far south as he could 'with safety and convenience go'. He sailed south, discovering coat at Bulli and charting the Shoalhaven River.

When he reached Cape Howe, Bass turned westwards, and discovered Wilsons Promontory and Western Port Bay. He tried to get through Bass Strait, but could not.

He became convinced that Van Diemen's Land was an island, and he put this to Governor Hunter when he returned to Sydney.

Discovery of Bass Strait

The following summer, Hunter placed Flinders in command of an expedition to explore west of Western Port Bay. He was to look for a strait. If it were found, he should 'pass through it, and return by the south end of Van Diemen's Land'. Bass was to accompany him. For a vessel, Flinders received the *Norfolk*, a 25-tonne sloop. (It had been built in the colony, despite the British government's ban on shipbuilding.) To sail her, Flinder was given a crew of eight.

The two explorers left Sydney on 7 October 1798, and followed the coast south. They turned west and sailed through Bass Strait, from Wilsons Promontory in the east to Cape Otway in the west, a distance of 224 km, thus proving that Tasmania was an island.

They went on, as instructed, and sailed right round Tasmania, arriving back in Sydney on 12 January 1799.

The discovery by Bass and Flinders was important because it meant that they had found a new seaway between the Indian Ocean and Sydney. Ships could save time by sailing through Bass Strait rather than sailing around Tasmania. By

sailing through Bass Strait, they would cut about 1100 km off their voyage, and also avoid a good deal of stormy weather. The expedition had been very successful.

The Mystery about Bass

Unfortunately, Bass and Flinders made no further trips together. Bass left the navy and went into business, hoping to make money by importing goods and selling them at a profit. On 5 February 1803, he left Sydney aboard the *Venus*, bound for Chile, to pick up supplies. Neither he nor the *Venus* was ever seen again. There was a rumour, afterwards, that the Spanish in Chile had seized the ship and had forced the crew to work in

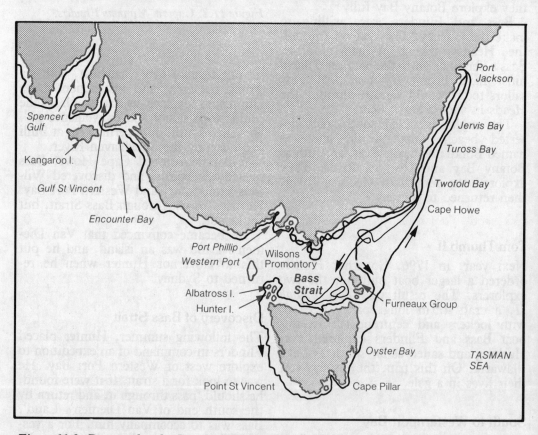

Figure 11.3. Routes taken by Bass and Flinders to survey the coast of southern Australia and Tasmania.

their silver mines. This may have been only a rumour. The fate of the ship and its crew remains a mystery still.

Flinders's Voyage around Australia

In March 1800, Flinders returned to England. There he published a book on his explorations, called: *Observations on the Coasts of Van Diemen's Land, on Bass Strait and Its Islands, and on Parts of the Coasts of New South Wales, intended to accompany the Charts of the Late Discoveries in those Countries.* He dedicated his book to Sir Joseph Banks, who was most impressed with his work. Flinders asked Banks to use his influence on his behalf. He wanted to return to Australia to chart the rest of the continent's coastline. To do this, he needed a ship and a crew. Banks used his influence, and Flinders was promoted to captain, and given a ship and a crew.

The ship was a 330-tonne warship (a sloop) called the *Xenophon*. Now she was refitted and renamed the *Investigator*. Unfortunately for Flinders, the ship was in very poor condition. Her timbers were rotten, and she leaked badly. Their lordships at the Admiralty were not very generous.

Among the crew were William Westall, a landscape artist, and Ferdinand Lukas Bauer, a botanical draughtsman, who were to draw the landscapes, flora, and fauna found during the journey.

At this time, France and England were at war, and there was a danger that the *Investigator* might be attacked at sea. However, because Flinders's voyage was to 'enhance human knowledge', the French authorities issued him with a special passport.

On 17 April 1801, Flinders married. He asked the Admiralty if he could take his wife, Ann, on the voyage, but this was not allowed. Flinders set sail from England on 17 July 1801.

Flinders sighted the coast of Australia on 6 December 1801, and began slowly to circumnavigate the whole continent.

Figure 11.4. William Westall.

First, he surveyed the south coast. He explored and charted Spencer Gulf and Gulf St Vincent (near Adelaide). From there, Flinders sailed around to Sydney, where he arrived on 9 May 1802.

In Sydney, the *Investigator* was refitted. Flinders left Sydney on 22 July to continue the journey. Cook had charted the east coast, but there were small gaps in his maps. Flinders filled them.

However, by the time the expedition passed into Torres Strait, the *Investigator* was leaking so badly that it was shipping a metre of water an hour. Flinders hugged the coast, charting as he went, and anchoring the ship each night. In March 1803, he turned to Timor for fresh water and supplies, and to rest his crew. Some of them were suffering from scurvy.

From Timor, Flinders continued south down the west coast of Australia, then back around the south coast again. The *Investigator* limped into Sydney on 9 June 1803.

Flinders was the first captain to make a close circumnavigation of Australia. His ship was examined and declared no longer seaworthy (although, incredibly, it was later sailed to England without sinking).

Shipwreck, Imprisonment and Death

Flinders now fell upon hard times. He knew only hardship and suffering for the rest of his life.

On 10 August 1803, Flinders sailed for England with charts and reports for the Admiralty. He sailed aboard the *Porpoise*, with two other ships, the *Cato* and the *Bridgewater*. As they entered the Barrier Reef, the *Porpoise* and the *Cato* ran aground on coral and sank, while the *Bridgewater*, for some unknown reason, sailed on. Flinders and more than 90 men were marooned on a sandbar. Fortunately, Flinders and 13 others were able to launch a cutter from one of the

wrecks and sail back to Sydney to break the news. Help was then sent, and the men were rescued.

Flinders set out for England again in command of the schooner *Cumberland*. The *Cumberland* was a Sydney-built vessel of poor quality, and she began to leak badly. Also, the pumps were worn. Flinders was forced to put into French Mauritius (then called the Ile de France) to make repairs. The French governor, Charles Decaen, thought Flinders was a spy. The passport he carried had been made out for a vessel called the *Investigator*, not the *Cumberland*. Flinders was held on the island under arrest for seven years. In July 1807, orders from France arrived for his release, but Decaen refused to obey them. He thought that Flinders knew too much about the island's defences. During the time of his captivity, Flinders's health broke down. He was released in June 1810, a gaunt white-haired man, old before his time.

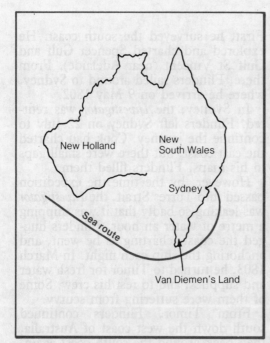

Figure 11.5. Map of Australia before the survey of Bass and Flinders.

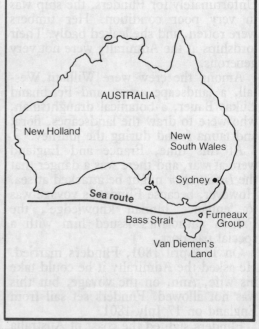

Figure 11.6. Map of Australia after the work of Bass and Flinders.

Figure 11.7. Flinders and his crew were marooned on Wreck Reef after the loss of the Porpoise *and the* Cato.

Flinders arrived in England on 23 October 1810. An ageing Sir Joseph Banks welcomed him with a dinner, and he was appointed to the rank of post-captain. However, he was given no honours, and no back pay. His book, *A Voyage to Terra Australis*, was published on 18 July 1814. On that day, Flinders lay dying. His wife, Ann, pressed a copy of the book between his fingers, but he was already unconscious. He died the next day, aged only 40, and was buried in St James's Graveyard, Hampstead Road, London.

Questions

(1) What contributions did Bass and Flinders make to Australian geography?

(2) How did their survey work assist shipping near the Australian coast?

(3) Name three natural features, such as bays, gulfs, or rivers, surveyed by the explorers.

(4) Did Bass and Flinders circumnavigate Tasmania in a clockwise or an anticlockwise direction?

(5) Did Flinders circumnavigate Australia in a clockwise or anticlockwise direction?

(6) How many books did Flinders publish?

(7) Name two men in authority who assisted the explorers in their work.

(8) What dangers did both explorers face?

(9) Was the *Investigator* a good ship?

(10) Where was Flinders shipwrecked?

Research

Find out more about the following.

(1) George Bass

(2) Matthew Flinders

(3) Early methods of survey

(4) The art work of William Westall

(5) The botanical drawings of Ferdinand Lukas Bauer

Chapter 12

Macquarie the Builder

Figure 12.1 Lachlan Macquarie.

The New Governor

Lachlan Macquarie landed in Sydney Cove on Sunday, 31 December 1809, from the storeship *Dromedary*. The next day, at a public ceremony, he was sworn in as governor — the fifth governor of New South Wales.

Macquarie was a 48-year-old professional soldier of noble Scottish descent. He had served loyally in North America, India, Egypt, and Europe, and had been presented to the King. He was keen enough to serve as governor, to show what he could do and perhaps gain further promotion or even honours (such as a knighthood). He was a very ambitious man.

Macquarie's own regiment, the 73rd Highlanders, an offshoot of the Black Watch, now took over duties from the New South Wales Corps, which went back to England. Fortunately for Macquarie, he did not have to engage in a trial of strength with that Corps, as previous governors had had to do. Lieutenant-Colonel Maurice O'Connell, the commanding officer of the 73rd, and the men of the regiment were loyal to him. This was a great advantage.

Within a few months of landing, Macquarie found himself free of many difficult men and troublemakers. Bligh had gone. Paterson had gone. The Corps had gone. Macarthur and Johnston were still in England. Therefore Macquarie could settle down to the demanding task of restoring law and order, and improving the colony. There was certainly a lot to do.

Figure 12.2. St Matthew's Church, Windsor, designed by Francis Greenway. Macquarie laid the foundation stone in 1817.

Figure 12.3. A group of convicts outside a jail. Macquarie formed street-cleaning gangs to remove rubbish.

Public Morals

Macquarie was appalled at the low moral tone of the colony. All the rumours he had heard about the colony appeared to be true. Everywhere people, in particular the lower class, seemed to be set firmly on the road to damnation. What should be done?

- Macquarie reduced the number of public houses, and placed an import duty on spirits. He hoped that the import duty would raise the price of grog, and thus help reduce the amount of drunkenness.
- He encouraged convicts and others to marry by abolishing the marriage licence fee of 5 guineas and giving freedom to women convicts who married.
- He built a number of schools, and found school masters and school mistresses to cater for the needs of the youth of the colony. (Many young people were born illegitimate, and lived in a state of poverty and ignorance.)
- Above all, he promoted church attendance. He ordered that all convicts should attend church services regularly each Sunday, and that public houses should close during the times of service. Any proprietor who sold spirits during the time of services would lose his licence. Also, anyone drinking or creating a disturbance on the Sabath would be arrested and clapped into jail.

Public Works

Macquarie had an eye for neatness. He disliked untidiness and dirt. He did not like much of what he saw in Sydney and other settlements. Houses, shops, barns, and public buildings had been built according to fancy, here, there and everywhere. As a result, streets were narrow and crooked. Many streets did not have names, and were full of holes and tree stumps. People allowed their properties and buildings to encroach onto the street. They dumped their rubbish onto the streets, and pigs and other animals were allowed to wander at will. Many buildings were little more than shanties — low, poorly designed (if designed at all), and constructed from the poorest quality materials. Obviously, there had been a deplorable lack of planning and care in the past. Macquarie determined to remedy this situation:

- He formed street-cleaning gangs to remove rubbish.
- He had tree stumps removed and holes in streets filled in.
- Many streets were widened and straightened. If a building was in the way, and of poor quality, it was demolished.
- Macquarie instructed that the streets of the colony should be straight. The blocks should have corners as near as possible to right angles. This was hard to achieve in some areas, where a great deal of solid building had taken place (for instance, Sydney Cove). Elsewhere, Macquarie could achieve a more rectangular plan. Most blocks in the old, inner areas

Figure 12.4. The first Government House in Sydney, built for Governor Phillip in 1790.

Figure 12.5. Macquarie Light, South Head, designed by Francis Greenway.

Figure 12.6. Government House, Parramatta Park. Macquarie had the house, which had been started by Phillip, remodelled. Greenway designed the portico and fanlight. (It is now called Old Government House.)

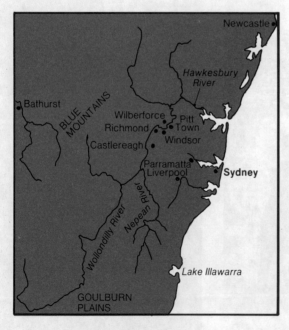

Figure 12.7. Growth of settlement around Sydney during Macquarie's governorship.

of Sydney, Hobart, and Launceston are at least roughly rectangular because of his instructions. Streets were also given new, dignified names, such as George Street, Prince Street, York Street, Pitt Street, Castlereagh Street, Phillip Street, Hunter Street, etc.

- He drew up new regulations for building. Shanties were prohibited.
- Macquarie built widely: a general hospital, a military hospital, a lighthouse on South Head, a new Government House at Parramatta, a fort, extra military barracks, a number of convict barracks for males, females, and juveniles, a jail, a new stone wharf and dockyard, a market, churches, schools and offices.

Macquarie was fortunate in acquiring the services of a convict architect, Francis Howard Greenway, who had been sentenced in 1813 to 14 years' transportation for forgery. Greenway arrived in Sydney in February 1814, with a letter of recommendation from Arthur Phillip. Macquarie appointed him civil architect and assistant engineer, on a salary of three shillings a day. On 16 December 1817, Macquarie gave Greenway his freedom. Together the two men planned a new colony. Only lack of funds, and displeasure in Britain, stopped them achieving this.

Extension of Settlement

While Macquarie was governor, the colony was extended. Macquarie toured the Hawkesbury region in 1810, and planned a number of settlements to stimulate farming. The townships of Windsor, Wilberforce, Richmond, Pitt Town, Liverpool, Castlereagh, and Campbelltown all grew during this time. Some were named after political figures, and some were names. All lay reasonably close to Sydney, within 48–65 km.

Macquarie improved the road to Parramatta. When the Blue Mountains were crossed in 1813, he saw his chance to extend roads and settlement inland. He ordered William Cox to build a road, using convict labour. By 1814–15, a permanent road had been built as far as the new township of Bathurst.

After the war with France ended (in 1815, at the Battle of Waterloo), transportation was stepped up. More free settlers arrived in New South Wales to increase the population of these settlements. More roads and bridges were built to improve communications and transport within the colony.

In 1818, a small stone obelisk was set up in Macquarie Place, Sydney. All roads in New South Wales were measured from this point.

A New Currency

Many problems in New South Wales had been caused by the lack of a proper currency. Macquarie determined to solve this problem. If he could not get stocks

Figure 12.8. The 'holey dollar' and the 'dump' — the first currency made in Australia.

Figure 12.9. The first Bank of New South Wales, founded in 1817. The building, situated in Sydney, was formerly a private residence owned by Mrs Mary Reiby.

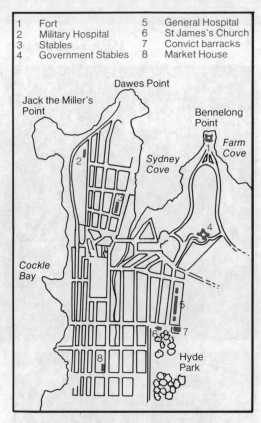

1	Fort	5	General Hospital
2	Military Hospital	6	St James's Church
3	Stables	7	Convict barracks
4	Government Stables	8	Market House

Figure 12.10 Street plan of Sydney in Macquarie's time.

of British currency, he would have to improvise and issue a token currency. He imported 40 000 Spanish silver dollars via India and Mexico. Thomas Henshall, who had been transported for forging coins, was employed to punch the centre out of these dollars.

Macquarie gave a value of five shillings to the outer ring, or 'holey dollar', and a value of one shilling and threepence to the middle, or 'dump'. Shopkeepers were allowed to issue tokens, valued from one halfpenny to sixpence. These tokens were stamped with the proprietor's name and value.

In 1817, Macquarie arranged for the first bank in Australia to open. Appropriately, this bank was called the Bank of New South Wales. The colonial secretary was not keen for this to happen, but he allowed the bank to continue. Macquarie's currency and bank had no real standing in law, but they served a useful function. If nothing else, Macquarie's system was an improvement on the traffic in barrels of rum.

Macquarie and the Emancipists

Macquarie looked upon New South Wales as primarily a penal colony. His main concern was convicts, and ex-convicts (emancipists) and their families. His ideas about emancipists were, for the day, regarded as radical. He believed that past mistakes should be forgotten and that emancipists should help build the colony for the future. Their pasts should not be held against them. Various reasons have been put forward to explain why Macquarie followed this policy:

- He was a devout, practising Christian, concerned with ideas of redemption and atonement. He believed that all people are equal in God's eyes.
- He soon discovered that many emancipists, such as D'Arcy Wentworth, Simeon Lord, Andrew Thompson, and Francis Greenway, were dependable men. It helped the colony

Figure 12.11. Simeon Lord.

Figure 12.12. St James's Church and the Supreme Court.

if he encouraged and assisted them.
- He was influenced by such people as Governor Duncan, with whom he had served in Bombay, and who advocated a humanitarian approach to convicts. Macquarie's wife, Elizabeth, was in favour of assisting emancipists. So was Lieutenant-Colonel Joseph Foveaux.
- Macquarie had commanded troops who had been convicts, and these men had performed their duty.
- There was a movement in Britain to abolish the slave trade, and this may

have influenced Macquarie. In 1796, he had given freedom to his own slaves. White convicts in New South Wales had a similar position in society to that of black slaves in America.

Macquarie encouraged emancipists to make a new life for themselves in the colony. Many convicts were emancipated, and given positions important to the welfare and development of Australia. Some were employed in the law courts. Macquarie even invited certain emancipists to dine with him at Government House.

Many free settlers did not share Macquarie's ideas about convicts. They believed that the governor should not concern himself so much with convicts, emancipists, and small-time farming. Instead, he should give more emphasis to large land grants, wool, and commerce in general. They were hostile towards convicts and emancipists. They regarded themselves as morally superior to them. They would not accept emancipists socially, and thought it was scandalous that Macquarie should take their side.

Those who did not favour emancipists came to be known as 'Exclusives' or 'Pure Merinos'. They made Macquarie's task even harder.

Not all free settlers were rich or educated. Many arrived in the colony knowing little or nothing about farming, and with little capital. This meant they had to rely on the Government for supplies and assistance. This cost money. Money spent on these free settlers meant less spent on building and the penal programme, and this annoyed Macquarie. No wonder that Macquarie and the free settlers did not see eye to eye.

The Bigge Reports

In 1819, Lord Bathurst, the colonial secretary, sent a special commissioner, John Thomas Bigge, to examine the affairs of the colony of New South Wales. Lord Bathurst did this because:

- He had received a number of petitions and letters of complaint about Macquarie, asking that he be withdrawn. These were written by free settlers.
- He was concerned at the amount of money that Macquarie was spending on building.
- The government, in Parliament, was being asked to justify the effectiveness of transportation to Australia, and answer questions about what was going on there. Since the end of the war with France, Britain had suffered widespread unemployment, unrest, and crime. Many were concerned that transportation was not a sufficient deterrent.

Bigge's Terms of Reference were wide. Bigge, who had served as chief justice of Trinidad (another colony), was to investigate 'all the laws, regulations and usages of the settlements' in Australia.

- He should examine the treatment of convicts. Were they being punished harshly enough? In fact, were they subjected to sufficient 'salutary terror' (enough to deter others from breaking the law)?
- If the convicts were being treated too leniently, Bigge was instructed to suggest possible sites for new, harsher penal colonies.
- He should look at the matter of emancipists, and how they could fit into a free, colonial society.
- He should examine the conduct of officials, including Macquarie himself. He was to examine the courts, and their decisions.
- He should assess the potential of the colony. Should it continue as predominantly a penal colony? Could it become a worthwhile, free, commercial colony? A colony based on wool?

A Bias Against Macquarie?: Bigge sailed to Australia on a convict transport, the *John Barry*, accompanied by Thomas Hobbes Scott, a private secretary. He arrived on 26 September 1819, was received politely by Macquarie, sworn in as a justice of the peace, and went to work. He spent about a year and a half in Australia. During this time, he travelled widely on the mainland and in Van Diemen's Land, and interviewed many people.

He tended, because he was a gentleman, to take the side of the exclusives. He failed to notice a lot of the good work that Macquarie had done. He had not seen the colony in 1810, and therefore could not draw comparisons.

Figure 12.13. Sydney from the Domain.

He tended to be a little thoughtless in his approach. He took down a good deal of evidence casually, and without interviewing people under oath.

Bigge was guided by Macarthur, who was now back in the colony. Macarthur told Bigge that the future of Australia should depend on wool-growers. Men of capital should be allowed to develop large sheep properties, not less than 4000 hectares in size, worked by assigned convict labour, and the free, hired labour of emancipists. Convicts and emancipists would, according to Macarthur, benefit from working in the country. They would be removed from the vices and temptations of the settlements, and would have time to reflect on past follies. Macarthur also told Bigge that the production of wool would be to Britain's advantage as well. British factories needed all the wool they could get. The governor favoured emancipists on small farms, but how could they develop the country? Land should not be granted to emancipists, and duties on colonial wool should also be dropped.

What Macarthur wanted (and had wanted for a long time) was a system similar to that in Europe. Aristocratic (or, in New South Wales, rich and respectable) families would hold large estates, and their labour would be supplied by loyal workers of lower class who lived locally or on the landowner's property. Macarthur was not very interested in real democracy.

Three reports were prepared by Bigge when he returned to England. They were:

- *On the State of the Colony of New South Wales*
- *On the Judicial Establishments in New South Wales and Van Diemen's Land*
- *On the State of Agriculture and Trade in the Colony of New South Wales.*

In these reports:

- Bigge criticized Macquarie's extensive building programme, including the cost involved in some of Greenway's designs.
- He criticized Macquarie's personal ambitions. He suggested that, in the

future, the governor should be given an advisory body to help him manage the colony.

- He recommended that convict punishment should be made harsher. Secondary penal stations should be established to isolate and punish the worst offenders.
- He followed Macarthur's opinion entirely and advocated that men of capital should be granted land and labour. He said the growth and export of Australian wool should be encouraged.

Macarthur and his Exclusive friends must have been very pleased with Bigge's reports.

population in general depressed by poverty; no public credit nor private confidence; the morals of the great mass of the population in the lowest state of debasement and religious worship almost totally neglected . . .

. . . That the colony has, under my orders and regulations, greatly improved in agriculture, trade, increase of flocks and herds, and wealth of very kind; that the people build better dwelling-houses, and live more comfortably; that they are in a very considerable degree reformed in their moral and religious habits; that they are now less prone to drunkenness, and more industrious; and that crimes have decreased, making due allowance for the late great increase of convict population; every candid, liberal-minded man, at all acquainted with the history of the colony for the last twelve years, will readily attest.

Macquarie Goes Home

Macquarie asked to be relieved of his command, and returned to England in 1822 with his family, aboard the *Surry*. The first of the Bigge reports appeared before he landed.

Of course, Macquarie was offended by what Bigge had to say. He did his best to defend his reputation and achievements with the King, the lords of the realm, and others. However, he did not receive a knighthood, and was awarded only a small pension of £1000 a year. He died on 1 July 1824, a disillusioned and embittered man.

Macquarie's Achievements

Macquarie had achieved much. His achievements can be summed up in his own words:

I found the colony barely emerging from infantile imbecility, and suffering from various privations and disabilities; the country impenetrable beyond forty miles (65 km) from Sydney; agriculture in a yet languishing state; commerce in its early dawn; revenue unknown; threatened with famine; distracted by faction; the public buildings in a state of dilapidation and mouldering to decay; the few roads and bridges formerly constructed rendered almost impassable; the

Questions

(1) Name two buildings designed by Francis Greenway.
(2) Name three new settlements built during Macquarie's period as governor.
(3) In what year were the Blue Mountains crossed for the first time?
(4) Why did Macquarie issue a token currency?
(5) Where was the first Bank of New South Wales situated?
(6) What was Macquarie's policy regarding emancipists?
(7) Why did many free settlers, such as Macarthur, object to Macquarie's policies?
(8) Why was Commissioner Bigge sent to Australia?
(9) Were Bigge's reports fair?
(10) Why was Macquarie hurt by Bigge's reports?

Research

Find out more about the following.
(1) Lachlan Macquarie
(2) Francis Howard Greenway
(3) Australian colonial arhitecture
(4) The Hawkesbury River district
(5) John Thomas Bigge, and his reports.

Chapter 13

Life in Macquarie's New South Wales

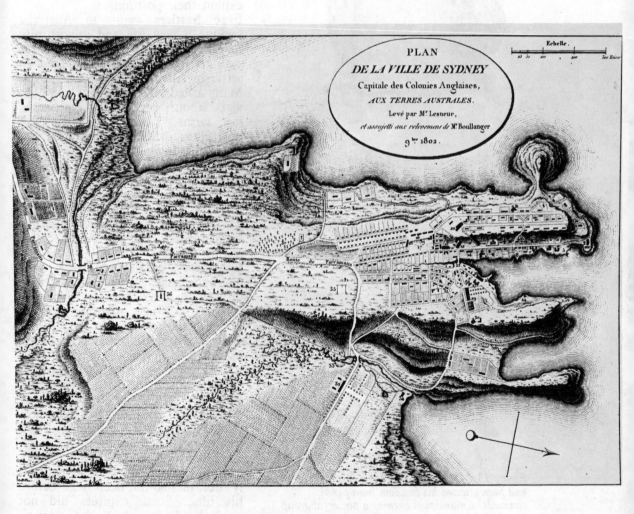

Figure 13.1. An early plan of Sydney.

Social Groups

Much depended on the social group to which you belonged. The different social groups included:

- **Officials:** These included the governor, lieutenant-governors, judges, and other, high-ranking officials, together with the lesser officials. These officials were always men, and usually represented the public service and the army. Some educated emancipists were appointed officials by Macquarie. Officials enjoyed considerable prestige and power in the colony. Unfortunately, some tried to exploit their position.

- **Free Settlers** came to Australia seeking a new life and opportunity for advancement. Some, such as younger sons, were encouraged to settle in Australia by their families. Many asked for land grants and convict labour, and tried to develop farms. Others opened small businesses, or looked for general employment. Some were reduced to relying on the government for support.

- **Currency Lads and Lasses** were those people born in the colony. They were the first white Australians. Usually they were raw and unsophisticated. Many were children of convicts.

- **Exclusives, or Pure Merinos** were mainly officials and free settlers who refused to mix socially with ex-convicts and their offspring. Not all exclusives were wealthy, educated, or even law-abiding themselves.

- **Emancipists:** An emancipist was, strictly speaking, a convict who had been granted his freedom from penal servitude. The term came to refer to all ex-convicts and their offspring, whether they had been emancipated or not.

- **Expirees:** An expiree was a convict whose sentence had expired naturally, i.e., he had not been freed before his time. Some expirees did not work hard enough to be emanci-

Figure 13.2. An emancipist — a convict who had been granted his freedom from penal servitude. Emancipists became a powerful group in colonial society.

pated; some were just unlucky.

- **Convicts** existed on the lowest level of society in Australia. They formed a hard core of cheap labour, which was harnessed to build and develop the colony. Men with few skills were employed in road gangs, as builders and as agricultural labourers. Women were employed as gardeners, washerwomen, cleaners, etc. Many women were also employed at the Female Factory, in Parramatta.
- **Ticket-of-Leave Men:** A ticket-of-leave man was a convict who was trusted to work for wages and find his own accommodation. However, he was not allowed to leave the police district in which he was placed. He had no legal rights in a court of law.
- **Assignees:** An assignee was a convict who was 'assigned' to an official free settler, or emancipist, to work for him for a fixed period of time, often the remaining part of his sentence. In return for his labour, he received shelter, food, and clothing. He was trusted, in that he was allowed a measure of freedom, and worked unguarded. Some assignees were treated very harshly by their masters, and given only the barest essentials to subsist on. Others were treated quite well. Much depended upon the personalities involved, and the nature of their work.

Figure 13.3. An English officer and his lady.

Fashions in Dress and Grooming

Dress and grooming were important in the nineteenth century because they were used to advertise social position and occupation. Most styles and fashions were imported directly from England, without considering the differences in climate and land.

Gentlemen in New South Wales often wore military uniforms. These uniforms varied in design according to rank and regiment. At the time, the British had not adopted the idea of camouflaged warfare, so uniforms were designed to stand out on the battlefield. Many uniforms were brightly coloured and elaborate in design. Officers wore epaulets on their shoulders and carried swords. The uniforms were made from woollen cloth;

fastenings were brass buttons and buckles, which had to be polished continually.

Gentlemen not in uniform wore clothing of various styles. These included a wide jacket, breeches, and waistcoat. Shirts were made from cotton or silk, and were often white. Cravats were tied around the throat and leather boots pulled up to the knees.

Most gentlemen rode horses, so their clothing was tailored to fit comfortably in the saddle.

Beards and moustaches were not fashionable. Gentlemen shaved their chin and upper lip, and grew medium to long sideburns or mutton chop sidewhiskers. They grew their hair down onto the back of the collar. Short hair was unknown. Gentlemen shaved with an open razor, stropped on a leather belt, and warm soap suds, mixed in a bowl and applied with a small shaving brush. After shaving, they applied shaving powder or toilet water. Gentlemen smoked pipes and inhaled snuff, which was carried in small, ornate, metal snuff boxes. Also they wore small watches of silver, gold, or plain metal on chains inside their waistcoat pockets. There were no wristwatches.

Ladies always wore long dresses over a number of petticoats. These dresses were of wool, satin, silk, or lace, and varied in design and colour. Petticoats were usually of white cotton. Ladies pulled in their waists with corsets manufactured from cloth and whalebone. The zipper had not yet been invented, and ladies were laced or buttoned into their dresses.

Ladies wore jewellery around their necks and wrists, small, leather boots on their feet, and grew their hair down onto, or below, their shoulders. In public, they sometimes tied their hair up in a bun. A hat or bonnet was worn, and a parasol carried as a protection against the sun and rain.

During the time of Macquarie, the 'romantic' look came into fashion, with its soft, simple lines.

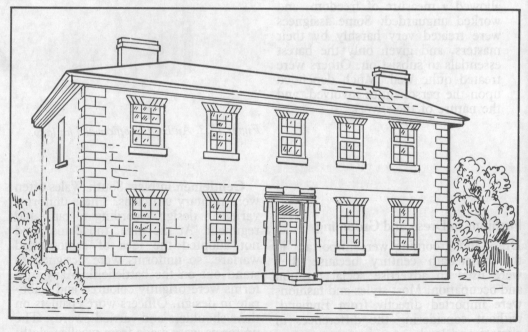

Figure 13.4. Georgian architecture.

Among the **lower classes**, clothing was less expensive and fashionable, and more practical.

Privates and non-commissioned officers in the army wore uniforms with fewer tassles and insignia.

Tradesmen wore open-neck shirts and aprons. Working girls wore plain woollen dresses and aprons.

Farmers and agricultural labourers wore breeches, open shirts, boots, and hats during the day in summer. At night, or during winter, they added a jacket.

Convicts wore the cheapest and poorest of clothing. Many, in fact, wore rags called 'slops'. At that time, there were no convict uniforms as such.

Housing

The Upper Classes lived in large brick or sandstone houses, with whitewashed walls and terracotta-tiled roofs. Some were two storeys high, but many had only one storey. These houses were modelled on the houses of Georgian England.

A visitor to one of these houses passed through a central front door into a wide, straight hallway, from which opened small, square rooms with high ceilings, to the left and right. The bedrooms, together with a sitting room and a dining room, were at the front of the house, and upstairs if the house was two-storeyed. Most rooms had an open fireplace for heating in winter, and whale oil lamps or candelabra and chandeliers for lighting in the evening.

Floors were made of plain, polished boards, covered with rugs and carpets. Oil paintings and water colours decorated the walls. Much of the furniture was imported. It was heavy, sturdy, oaken — and uncomfortable. Everybody had to sit bolt upright in chairs and on stools. Beds were covered with soft, thick, feather mattresses, which sagged and lacked resilience. Bedrooms were

Figure 13.5. A Georgian staircase.

Figure 13.6. The bedroom of an upper-class home.

provided with china basins and jugs for washing.

At the back of the house were the serving quarters. There was a kitchen, pantry, and laundry. Here the domestic staff worked. They cooked over a large, open fire in the kitchen, using iron or copper pots suspended from pot hooks, and frying pans. Butter was churned in the kitchen, and bread was baked in the kitchen as well.

Outside, many people attempted to cultivate a typically 'English' garden around the house. Many people kept dogs to deter convict intruders.

Middle Class Settlers lived in smaller, less pretentious houses. The roofs had shingles instead of tiles, and the furnishings were not so expensive.

The Poorest Class of settlers, assignees, and others lived in small wattle-and-daub or timber cottages of only one, or sometimes two rooms, with thatched roofs and earthen floors. Windows were small and covered with wooden shutters. Poorer settlers often made their own furniture or bought furniture made in the colony.

In these houses, the one central fireplace tended to be the focus of much activity. Meals were cooked there, and families sat and ate and talked in the glow of the flames.

Working Conditions

Hours of work were very long. Most people worked six days a week, Monday to Saturday, from early in the morning until early in the evening. Sunday was a day of rest, and work on this day — the Sabbath — was frowned upon. On Sunday, one attended church in the morning (either willingly or reluctantly) and

Figure 13.7. The bathroom of an upper-class home.

Figure 13.8. The poorer settlers lived in timber cottages.

THE
SYDNEY GAZETTE,
And New South Wales Advertiser.

PUBLISHED BY AUTHORITY.

Vol. I.	SATURDAY, MARCH 5, 1803.	Number 1.

It is hereby ordered, that all Advertisements, Orders, &c. which appear under the Official Signature of the Secretary of this Colony, or of any other Officer of Government, properly authorised to publish them in the SYDNEY GAZETTE, AND NEW SOUTH WALES ADVERTISER, are meant, and must be deemed to convey official and sufficient Notifications, in the same Manner as if they were particularly specified to any ONE Individual, or Others, to whom such may have a Reference.

By Command of His Excellency the Governor and Commander in Chief, WILLIAM NEATE CHAPMAN, Secretary.

Sydney, March 5th, 1803.

General Orders.

REPEATED Complaints having been made of the great losses sustained by the Settlers at Hawkesbury, from the vexatious conduct of the Boatmen by whom they send their Grain to Sydney, the following Regulations are to be observed.

Every person sending grain from the Hawkesbury to Sydney in an open boat, or a boat that is not trust-worthy, the Magistrates are directed to take no notice thereof.

If on proof it appears that the Master of a Boat receives more grain than the vessel ought to take with safety, the Master shall make good any quantity he may throw overboard, or otherwise damage, lose the freight of that part, and, on conviction before two Magistrates, forfeit 5l. to the Orphan Fund.

If it shall appear to the Magistrates that grain coming round to Sydney has been wetted, that it might weigh heavier or measure more than the quantity put on board, the Master will, on conviction, forfeit 5l. to the Orphan Fund.

The Commanding Officer of the New South Wales Corps will direct the Corporal of the Guard on board the Castle of Good Hope to read the General Orders that are marked off in the Extracts he is furnished with, to the Corporal, and the Party that relieves him; the said Orders are also to be read to the Guard on board the Supply Hulk.

By Command of His
Excellency   W. N. CHAPMAN, Sec.
Government House, Feb. 21, 1803.

THE Receiving Granaries at Parramatta and Hawkesbury, being filled with Wheat which is spoiling, no more can be taken in at those places until further Orders, except in payment for Government Debts, and the Whalers Investments lodged in the Public Stores.

Wheat will continue to be received into the Stores at Sydney, until further Orders.

Wheat will be issued to the Civil, Military, &c. until further Orders; except to the detachments and labouring people at Castle-Hill, Seven-Hills, and other Out Posts, who will receive Flour, as they have not the convenience of Mills.

By Command, &c.   W. N. CHAPMAN, Sec
Government House,
Feb. 24, 1803.

THE GOVERNOR having permitted Mr. Robert Campbell to land 4000 Gallons of Spirits for the domestic use of the Inhabitants, from the Castle of Good Hope, it will be divided in the following proportion, viz.

For the Officers on the Civil Establishment, (including Superintendants and Store-keepers), 1000 Gallons;

For Naval and Military Commissioned Officers, 1000 Gallons;

For the Licensed People, 1000 Gallons;

To be distributed to such Persons as the GOVERNOR may think proper to grant Permits to, 1000 Gallons.

The above to include the Civil and Military Officers at Norfolk Island.

By Command, &c.   W. N. CHAPMAN, Sec.
Government House, March 4, 1803.

ADDRESS.

Innumerable as the Obstacles were which threatened to oppose our Undertaking, yet we are happy to affirm that they were not insurmountable, however difficult the task before us.

The utility of a PAPER in the COLONY, as it must open a source of solid information, will, we hope, be universally felt and acknowledged. We have courted the assistance of the INGENIOUS and INTELLIGENT:— We open no channel to Political Discussion, or Personal Animadversion :—Information is our only Purpose; that accomplished, we shall consider that we have done our duty in an exertion to merit the Approbation of the PUBLIC, and to secure a liberal Patronage to the SYDNEY GAZETTE.

Figure 13.9. The Sydney Gazette *was the main newspaper in the colony and published mainly local news.*

TABLES OF WEIGHTS AND MEASURES

AVOIRDUPOIS WEIGHT
For General Merchandise

16 drams	make 1 ounce	(oz.)
16 ounces	,, 1 pound	(lb.)
28 pounds	,, 1 quarter	(qr.)
4 quarters (112 pounds)	1 hundredweight ,, (cwt.)	
20 hundredweight (2240 pounds)	,, 1 ton.	

Also,

14 pounds ..... make 1 stone
8 stone ...... ,, 1 hundredweight
Used for Flour and Meat sold wholesale
100 pounds ..... make 1 central or 1 short hundredweight
20 centals (2000 pounds) .... ,, 1 short ton.

TROY WEIGHT
Gold and Silver

24 grains	make 1 pennyweight (dwt.)	
20 pennyweights	,, 1 ounce (troy)	
480 grains	,, 1 ounce (troy)	
12 ounces	,, 1 lb. (troy)	
5760 grains	,, 1 lb. (troy)	
437½ grains	,, 1 ounce (avoir.)	
7000 grains	,, 1 lb. (avoir.).	

CAPACITY (LIQUIDS)

4 gills	make 1 pint	(pt.)
2 pints	,, 1 quart	(qt.)
4 quarts	,, 1 gallon	(gal.)

1 gallon of pure water weights 10 pounds.
6¼ gallons make 1 cubic foot.
1 cubic foot of water weights 62½ pounds or 1000 ounces.

DRY OR CORN MEASURE

2 pints	make 1 quart	(qt.)
4 quarts	,, 1 gallon	(gal.)
2 gallons	,, 1 peck	(pk.)
4 pecks	,, 1 bushed	(bush.)
8 bushels	,, 1 quarter	(qrtr.)
4 quarters	,, 1 ton	(cargo).

LINEAR MEASURE

12 inches	make 1 foot	(ft.)
3 feet	,, 1 yard	(yd.)
22 yards	,, 1 chain	(ch.)
10 chains	,, 1 furlong	(fur.)
8 furlongs	,, 1 mile	(ml.).

Also,

6 feet	make 1 fathom	
5280 feet	,, 1 mile	
1760 yards	,, 1 mile	
80 chains	,, 1 mile	
5½ yards	,, 1 rod or pole	
4 poles	,, 1 chain	
100 links	,, 1 chain	

6080 feet make 1 nautical mile.
A **knot** is a speed of 1 nautical mile per hour.

AREA

144 square inches	make 1 square foot	
9 square feet	,, 1 square yard	
484 square yards	,, 1 square chain	
4840 square yards	,, 1 acre	
10 square chains	,, 1 acre	
640 acres	,, 1 square mile.	

Also,

30¼ square yards	make 1 square pole or perch	
40 perches	,, 1 rood	
4 roods	,, 1 acre.	

VOLUME

1728 cubic inches	make 1 cubic foot	
27 cubic feet	,, 1 cubic yard.	

PAPER

24 sheet of paper	make 1 quire	
20 quires	,, 1 ream	
480 sheets	,, 1 ream.	

rested in the afternoon.

Conditions of work were poor. There were no unions, and employees and assignees were very much at the mercy of their employers. Hard work was regarded as a virtue, and was expected of everyone. Many workers received board and lodging in return for their labour, and little in the way of actual money.

Recreation

People in the colony had to make their

own entertainment.

Ladies and Gentlemen read novels and magazines, played the piano or violin, sang folk songs and danced, and just talked for hours on end. Books and magazines were imported, and exchanged between friends. There were no lending libraries at that time, so new books and magazines were eagerly looked for.

Out of doors, ladies and gentlemen went for walks (promenades), went horse-riding or driving in gigs, went boating or for picnics, and attended horse races or cricket matches in Hyde Park.

In the evenings, sometimes they visited friends for dinner, went to the theatre (although performances were rowdy and often amateurish), or sometimes to a ball. Balls were formal occasions, and lasted all evening. Those who attended were expected to dance until dawn. The quadrille and waltz were popular dances. The quadrille was a lively dance with four couples arranged in a square. The waltz was brand new.

The Lower Classes spent their time differently. Many could not read or play musical instruments. They did not possess horses, gigs, or the money to hire these. They spent their time walking, visiting, drinking, gambling, fishing, etc. Many convicts and assignees had very little recreation at all. They knew only hard work and sleep.

Meals

In Macquarie's time, most people ate well enough. The land now fed its settlers. Fresh sea foods were popular: kingfish, mullet, mackerel, rock cod, whiting, schnapper, bream, flathead, mud-oysters, crayfish, lobsters, and prawns. Fresh meat, such as beef, mutton, and pork, was also available.

Fish and meat dishes were eaten with vegetables, fruit, bread, and butter. Tea and spirits were also served. Most people in the colony, especially men, drank porter, rum, gin, and other spirits, with their meals, from tankards or glasses.

Currency

People spoke of two currencies — British ('sterling') and Colonial ('currency').

British:

2 farthings   = 1 halfpenny (pronounced 'hay penny')
2 halfpennies = 1 penny (less than 1 cent)
12 pennies   = 1 shilling (about 10 cents)
20 shillings   = 1 pound (about 2 dollars)
21 shillings   = 1 guinea

£5.00 = five pounds. 2/- = 2 shillings. 3d = three pence.
£5.6.7½ = five pounds, six shillings and seven pence halfpenny.
£2.4.1¼ = two pounds, four shillings and a penny farthing.

Colonial:

1 holey dollar = 5/-
1 dump = 1/3d.

Music

Well-to-do people in the colony might have a piano, a harpsichord, or a violin. At this time, the piano was most fashionable. Many were small, square in shape and ornate, and had only a small keyboard. Classical music was popular. The works of Bach, Beethoven, Haydn, Handel, and Purcell were admired and played.

People also played music for dancing, and folk music. Some played folk instruments, such as button accordions, transverse wooden flutes, recorders, fifes, and even bagpipes. There were hundreds of folk songs imported from England, Scotland, Wales, and Ireland. At that time, Australian folk music had not yet developed.

English Folk Songs

These were some of the popular folk songs well known in Macquarie's time:

O Dear Twelve Pence

O dear twelve pence, I've got twelve pence,
   I love twelve pence as I love my life;
I'll grind a penny on't, and I'll end another on't,
   And I'll carry tenpence home to my wife.

O dear ten pence, I've got ten pence,
etc.

O Dear, What Can the Matter Be?

O! dear! what can the matter be?
Dear! dear! what can the matter be?
O! dear! what can the matter be?
Johnny's so long at the fair.

He promised he'd bring me a basket of posies,
A garland of lilies, a garland of roses,
A little straw hat to set off the blue ribbons,
That tie up my bonny brown hair.

Early One Morning

Early one morning, just as the sun was rising,
I heard a damsel to sing and to sigh,
Crying, O Cupid! O send my lover to me,
Send me my sailor, or else I shall die,

The Blue Bell of Scotland

O! where, and o! where does your Highland
   laddie dwell?
He dwells in merry Scotland, at the sign of the
   Blue Bell;
And it's o! in my heart, that I love my laddie
   well.
What clothes, in what clothes is your Highland
   laddie clad?
His bonnet's of Saxon green, his waistcoat of
   the plaid;
And it's o! in my heart, that I love my Highland
   lad.

Suppose, o! suppose that your Highland lad
   should die!
The bagpipes shall play over him — I'll lay me
   down and cry;
And it's o! in my heart, that I wish he may not
   die.

Sea Shanties

(At sea, these were sung only on merchant vessels.)

Haul Away, Joe

Solo: Way, haul, away, we'll haul away the bowline;
Chorus: Way, haul, away, we'll haul away, Joe!

Solo: Way, haul away, the packet is a-rolling;
Chorus: Way, haul away, we'll haul away, Joe!

Solo: Once I had a Spanish girl; she nearly drove me crazy;
Chorus: Way, haul away, we'll haul away, Joe!

Solo: Now I've got an Irish girl, and she is just a daisy;
Chorus: Way, haul away, we'll haul away, Joe!

Solo: King Louis was the King of France before the Revolution,
Chorus: Way, haul away, we'll haul away, Joe!

Solo: King Louis got his head cut off, which spoilt his constitution,
Chorus: Way, haul away, we'll haul away, Joe!

Blow the Man Down

(To 'blow' a man down meant to knock him down, so he could be 'pressed' or 'shanghaied'.)

As I was walking down Paradise Street,
With a Weigh Heigh! Blow the man down!
A pretty young damse! I chanced to meet,
Give me some time to blow the man down!

She was round in the counter and bluff in the
   bow,
With a Weigh Heigh! Blow the man down!
So I took in all sail and cried, 'Way enough
   now!'
Give me some time to blow the man down!

So I tailed her my flipper and took her in tow,
With a Weigh Heigh! Blow the man down!
And yardarm to yardarm away we did go.
Give me some time to blow the man down!

But as we were going, she said unto me,
With a Weigh Heigh! Blow the man down!

'There's a spanking full rigger, just ready for
sea,'
Give me some time to blow the man down.

But as soon as that packet was clear of the bar,
With a Weigh Heigh! Blow the man down!
The mate knocked me down with the end of a
spar,
Give me some time to blow the man down!

So I give you fair warning before we belay,
With a Weigh Heigh! Blow the down!
Don't ever take heed of what pretty girls say,
Give me some time to blow the man down!

A Convict Song

Farewell to Judges and Juries

Here's bad luck to you, Mr Justice Paley,
And also to you, Gentlemen of the Jury,
For seven years, you've sent me from my true
love,
Seven years, I'm transported, you know.

To go to a strange country don't grieve me,
Nor leaving old England behind,
It is all for the sake of my Polly,
And leaving my parents behind.

There's the Captain that is our commander,
The Boatswain and all the ship's Crew,
There is married men, too, and there's single,
Who knows what we transports do.

Dear Polly I'm going to leave you,
For seven long years, love, and more,
But that time will appear but a moment,
When returned to the girl I adore.

If ever I return from the Ocean,
Stores of riches I'll bring for my dear,
It's all for the sake of my Polly,
I'll cross the salt seas for my dear.

How hard is the place of confinement,
That keeps me from my heart's delight,
Cold chains and irons surround me,
And a plank for my pillow at night.

How often I wish that the eagle,
Would lend me her wings, I would fly,
Then I'd fly to the arms of my Polly,
And on her soft bosom, I'd lie.

Questions

(1) Who were the exclusives?
(2) Who were ticket-of-leave men?
(3) How did gentlemen dress during Macquarie's time?
(4) What were some of the forms of recreation during that time?
(5) How did the houses of the well-to-do differ from those of the poor settlers?
(6) What were conditions like for workers in the colony?
(7) What fresh food was available in New South Wales?
(8) Solve the following:

$$£ \ . \ s \ . \ d \qquad £ \ . s . d$$
$$15 \ . 16 . 7\tfrac{1}{2} \qquad 2 \ . 7 . 6$$
$$+2 \ . \ 0 \ . 2\tfrac{1}{2} \qquad -1 . 5 . 2$$

$$£ \ . \ s \ . \ d$$
$$1114 . 3 . 3\tfrac{1}{2}$$
$$\times 3$$

(9) What was the name of the colony's main newspaper?
(10) Name three classical composers who were popular at that time.

Research

Find out more about the following.
(1) Colonial architecture
(2) Fashions in dress
(3) Furniture
(4) Music
(5) Theatre.

Chapter 14

Changes in Colonial Government

Figure 14.1. Sir Thomas Brisbane.

Autocratic Governors

The first five governors of New South Wales (Phillip, Hunter, King, Bligh, and Macquarie) all enjoyed wide powers. They made laws, enforced their observance, and directed all administration. They answered to no one in the colony. They reported and answered only to the secretary of state for the colonies (or colonial secretary) in England and, through him, to the British Crown and government.

As we have seen, Commissioner Bigge criticized the powers enjoyed by Macquarie, and recommended that a council should share in ruling the colony. Because of Bigge's criticism of the governor's autocratic power, and because of social and economic changes in New South Wales, in 1823 the British government passed *An Act for the Administration of Justice in New South Wales and Van Diemen's Land*. Under the terms of this Act:

- The governor was given a council.
- The council was to consist of between five and seven members.
- Council members were to be chosen by the governor, and approved by the Crown. Earl Bathurst wrote to Thomas Brisbane, by then the governor of New South Wales, and suggested he include the colonial secretary (another colonial secretary, based in New South Wales), the lieutenant-governor, the chief justice, the principal surgeon, and the surveyor-general, on the council.
- The council had powers to make laws for the 'peace, welfare, and good government of the colony'. These laws were to be in keeping with British law and policies.
- The council could not initiate legislation. It could only pass laws proposed by the governor.
- If the governor proposed a new law, and a majority of the council opposed it, he could still appeal to the British government for support. With its support, he could still bring

the law into effect.

In 1828, two important changes were made to the Act:

- The number of council members was increased to 15, still chosen by the governor.
- The members of the council were given the right to veto any law proposed by the governor.

Exclusives vs Emancipists

The governors were duty bound to appoint high officials to their council. They also appointed favourites. These men were, at first, always exclusives. Naturally, this annoyed the emancipist class. As the population of New South Wales grew, more and more ordinary people began to want to have some say in the government of the colony.

At first, this did not happen. Governors Brisbane, Darling, and Bourke were placed in a difficult situation. Sometimes they quarrelled with the council and sometimes, in the line of duty, tried to protect the interests of the poorer class.

William Charles Wentworth

The emancipists found a capable leader in William Charles Wentworth (1790–1872). Wentworth was born in a small stone cottage on Norfolk Island. He was the son of D'Arcy Wentworth, a doctor, and Catherine Crowley, a convict. He was therefore an emancipist by birth.

Wentworth became one of the most dynamic men in the colony. He went on to become a grazier in New South Wales. With Gregory Blaxland and William Lawson, he was the first to find a way over the Blue Mountains. He also sailed to England and studied law. In England, he studied 'the excellence of the British Constitution'. He returned to Australia, determined to do all he could to procure 'a free constitution for my country'.

Figure 14.2. William Charles Wentworth.

Wentworth arrived back in New South Wales with Robert Wardell, another lawyer, in July 1824. The two men began to print and issue their own newspaper, *The Australian*. They did not ask permission to do this, and they were quite open in their political comment. They were not prepared to censor important news. They made it quite clear that they stood for freedom of speech, freedom of the press, and political reform. Their paper proved a powerful rival to the semi-official *Gazette*.

Wentworth attracted a large following, and soon he clashed with Governor Darling, who damned him as a 'demagogue' and a 'vulgar, ill-bred fellow'. In turn, Wentworth was very critical of the governor's rule, particularly his part in the Sudds and Thompson case.

Joseph Sudds and Patrick Thompson were two privates in the 57th Regiment, stationed in Sydney. They deliberately stole some cloth from a shop in order to

Figure 14.3 Gregory Blaxland.

Figure 14.4. Governor Darling.

get themselves convicted and expelled from their regiment. However, Darling was determined to make an example of them. The men were forced to wear yellow convict clothes, iron chains, and spiked collars, and were publicly drummed out of their regiment to the tune of the 'Rogues' March'. They were then sent to work on a road gang for seven years. Sudds, who was in a poor state of health, died shortly afterwards. The case aroused strong public feeling; Wentworth, Wardell, and Edward Smith Hall, another radical, exploited it to the full. Their attack on the governor was one reason for his recall in 1831. (Darling was cleared of all blame.)

Towards Representative Government

Bourke, who replaced Darling, was a more liberal man. In 1833, he wrote a letter to the colonial secretary suggesting that the governor's council should be enlarged to 36 members, with two-thirds elected by the colonists. This proposal was not accepted. The British government had grave doubts about allowing a democratic form of government in a penal colony.

In May 1835, Wentworth and his associates formed the Patriotic Association. One aim of this Association was to appoint a Colonial Parliamentary Advocate, who would live in London and communicate the wishes of ordinary people in Australia to the British government.

In 1836, the emancipists sent a petition to the British government, asking for more representation on the governor's council. They asked that the council be reformed as a 'Representative Legislature upon a wide and liberal basis'. Letters were also sent to important people in England.

In 1841, James Macarthur, son of John Macarthur, attempted to bring together the emancipists and the exclusives. If this could be achieved, he argued, the British government might be

Figure 14.5. Governor Bourke.

Figure 14.6. Governor George Gipps.

111

persuaded to act to establish a more democratic council. This would be in the interests of everyone.

In 1842, the British government gave way and granted representative government to New South Wales:

- The council was increased to 36 members.
- The governor was to appoint 12 members. Six were to be government officials, and were to include the colonial secretary. Six were to be private members.
- Twenty-four members were to be elected by freeholders (either householders or landowners).
- Members of the council had to own land valued at at least £2400 a year.

- The Port Phillip District was allowed six members of represent it. These were to represent freeholders there.
- Small district councils were also set up. (This was the beginning of local government.)
- The governor was allowed to retain control over the sale of Crown land.

These provisions of the Act meant that only people who owned property could sit on the council or vote. Many poor people were excluded from government.

The First Elections

The first elections for the new council

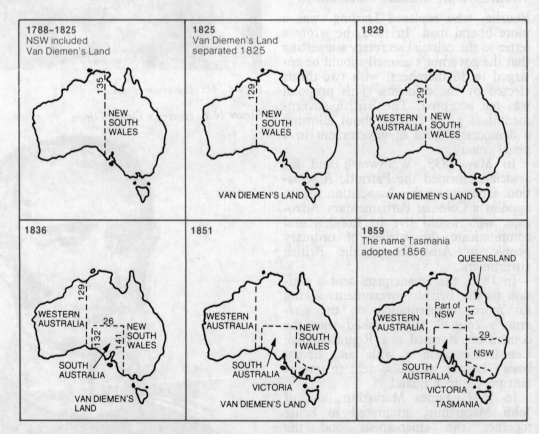

Figure 14.7. The formation of the Australian colonies. The numbers on the borders show latitude (east-west) and longitude (north-south).

were held in June 1843. They caused great excitement; indeed, there was almost a riot in Sydney. Governor George Gipps welcomed the new members with these words:

Gentlemen of the Legislative Council,
The time is at length arrived which has for many years been anxiously looked forward to by all: and I have this day the pleasure to meet for the first time the Legislative Council of New South Wales, enlarged as it has been under the statute recently passed by the Imperial Parliament for the Government of the Colony. I congratulate you very sincerely on the introduction of popular representation into our Constitution, and I heartily welcome to this Chamber the first representatives of the people.
The Council, gentlemen, is composed of three elements or of three different classes of persons — the representatives of the people — the official servants of Her Majesty — and of gentlemen of independence, the unofficial nominees of the Crown.
Let it not be said or supposed that these three classes of persons have separate interests to support — still less that they have opposing interests, or any interest whatever, save that of the public good. Let there be no rivalry between them save which shall in courtesy excel the other, and which of them devote itself most heartily to the service of their common country.

The Act of 1842 failed to satisfy many colonists. They wanted a truly democratic form of government, with less control from Britain. They also wanted control of Crown land taken away from the governor. Earl Grey, the Colonial Secretary, attempted to appease and satisfy the colonists by proposing a number of modifications which were, in the end, rejected by the British Government.

The Growth of Self-Governing Colonies

In Chapters 16–20, we will see how different colonies were established around the coast of Australia. The government of these colonies had to be considered, along with that of New South Wales.

In 1850, the British government passed the *Australian Colonies Government Act*. It was the brainchild of Earl Grey, and it sought to put an end to the problem of colonial government in Australia. It included these provisions:

- Victoria was to be separated from New South Wales.
- Queensland would be separated when petitions asking for this were presented.
- Legislative councils, based on the 1842 model, were to be set up in Victoria, South Australia, and Tasmania.
- A similar legislative council would be set up in Western Australia when at least two-thirds of its householders presented a petition asking for this.
- All colonies would be allowed to devise their own constitutions, whenever they wished. (This was a most important provision.)

Questions

(1) Who was governor of New South Wales in 1829?
(2) Who was governor in 1843?
(3) What were the provisions of the *Act for the Administration of Justice in New South Wales and Van Diemen's Land?*
(4) What changes were made to this Act in 1828?
(5) Did the council established by the above Act represent the people of New South Wales? Why? Give your reasons.
(6) What did William Charles Wentworth want to achieve in New South Wales?
(7) Why did Wentworth belong to the emancipist class?
(8) Who was Robert Wardell?
(9) Why did James Macarthur attempt to bring the emancipists and exclusives together?
(10) What were the provisions of the *Australian Colonies Government Act?*

Research

Find out more about the following:

(1) The governors who followed Macquarie

(2) The campaign for responsible government
(3) William Charles Wentworth
(4) Robert Wardell
(5) Earl Grey.

Chapter 15

The Squatters and the Governors

The Availability of Land

When white people came to Australia, they found an open country, with huge unfenced areas suitable for grazing and farming. It was only natural that in time they would turn their eyes to this land and want to settle on it.

As we have seen, the British authorities and the governors often made grants of land, usually for loyalty or service, or out of favouritism. In the case of convicts and ex-convicts, land grants were given for good behaviour. Land was also sold.

However, from the very beginning of

Figure 15.1. The squatter's run.

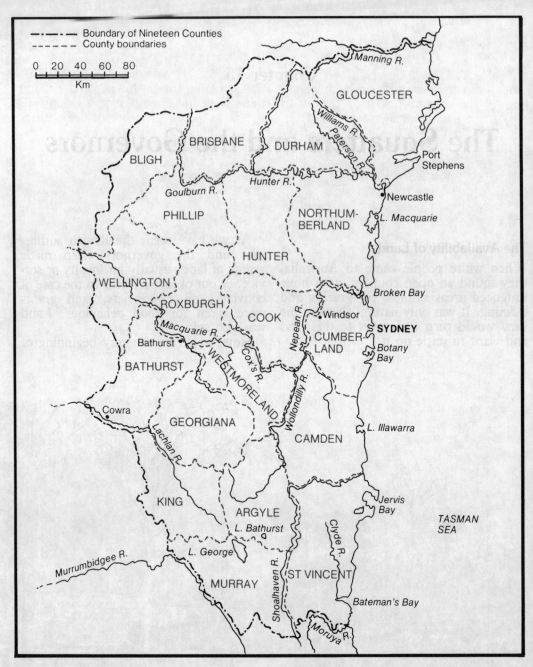

Figure 15.2. The Nineteen Counties.

settlement, squatters and squatting posed a problem.

Squatters and Squatting

The term 'squatter' was used in England and America to describe a person who settled on land without legal claim to it. In the early years of Australian settlement, a number of runaway convicts, emancipists, and others 'squatted' illegally in the bush around Sydney, Parramatta, and Hobart. They put up bark huts and tried to eke out a living from farming, distilling sly grog, or some-times even from making raids on neigh-bouring herds and flocks. Needless to say, these early squatters were held in contempt by the authorities and by soci-ety at large.

Soon, however, the term 'squatter' gained a wider meaning. A number of hardworking and enterprising men, some of them former army and naval officers, ex-officials, and 'gentlemen' im-migrants, began moving out, away from the settled districts, and establishing properties on Crown land. These were a new breed of squatter. They were in-terested mainly in building up large flocks or herds, and in making a quick profit.

Official Reaction: 'Limits of Location'

The early governors were instructed to prevent squatting if possible. Squatting violated the main principles of English law. It meant that authority was flouted. It meant a decreased control over settle-ment. It also meant that the Aborigines could not be protected.

In 1829, Governor Darling defined the 'Limits of Location' beyond which no one could go. A boundary line was drawn on the map around Sydney. It went from the Manning River in the north to Moruya in the south, from the east coast to the Lachlan River in the west. The boundary line encompassed an estimated 8 833 280 hectares. This area was divided into 19 counties. The plan was that, in time, these counties would be surveyed fully and developed. Anyone who crossed the Lachlan or the Manning opposed the government and broke the law. They also, incidentally, removed themselves from the protection of the government.

Crossing the Boundary

It was one thing to draw a line on the map. It was another to enforce its observance. The authorities found that they could not succeed. The boundary was too long, the bush was too deep, and there were not enough troops or officials to act as police. Macarthur and others had shown that there was money to be made from grazing, and there was no holding those intent on squatting. By 1836, the boundary had been crossed north, west, and south.

The squatters often acted as explorers. Often, too, they followed in the tracks of other professional explorers sent out by the government. Allan Cunningham led them north to the Darling Downs, to settle on the banks of the Gwydir, Dumaresq, and Condamine. Hume and Hovell led them south to the Murray, and on to the Port Phillip District. Sturt led them to the Darling River. Major Mitchell led them to the fertile Western District. And so it went.

Figure 15.3. Major Mitchell.

The Land They Found

The Licence System

Governor Bourke was advised by men of influence in the colony, for example Sir John Jamison and Captain Phillip King (son of Governor King), to introduce a system of licensing. This would control squatting to a certain extent.

Bourke agreed and, in 1836, passed an Act through his council:

- The Limits of Location were abolished.
- Reputable squatters were to be allowed to purchase a licence for £10 a year. This would allow them to graze over as much land as they pleased. They were not given ownership of the land, only grazing rights for the duration of the licence.
- Commissioners were appointed to issue and check on licences. They were also to define roughly the areas to which licences applied and to set-

tle disputes between rival squatters. A variable tax on stock was added to the licence fee in 1839. Bourke's Act legalized squatting and the spread of settlement.

Further Squatter Demands

Now that they had gained recognition, the squatters complained that they had no guarantee of tenure of their land. Why spend money making improvements if they could be asked to move on?

Governor Gipps gave squatters the right to purchase at least 129.6 hectares every eight years, at £1 per acre, until they owned their whole run, or as much of it as they needed. The squatters objected strongly to this suggestion, on the grounds that they were already paying a yearly licence fee and tax.

Figure 15.4. Squatters made long journeys to find land suitable for establishing a run.

Figure 15.5. Provisions were often carried on drays drawn by bullocks.

Eventually a compromise was reached. Squatters were sold leases to the land they held, with the right to purchase whenever they wished.

In 1852, the British government surrendered all control over Australian lands. This seemed to satisfy the squatters for the moment.

Establishing a Run

Establishing a run took money, time, and effort. Sound planning was necessary.

First the squatter had to find his land. Often he would make an exploring trip on horseback, carrying light provisions and a musket for defence. He looked for water, good soil, grass, and timber for building.

Water was most important. If a squatter settled on the bank of a creek, and that creek dried up, he would be ruined.

When he found the land he wanted, the squatter marked out the boundary by chopping or cutting blazes (marks) on trees, hammering in pegs, or piling up stones as markers. Then he returned quickly to civilization and made arrangements to move onto this land.

The squatter purchased a squatting licence or lease, bought stock and provisions, and hired men. He then transported provisions and goods on bullock-drawn drays or horse-drawn wagons. Often he hired a driver and off-sider to transport his goods. Transport was slow, and often drays and wagons became bogged in mud or stuck in creeks or on difficult ground.

The squatter bought sheep and cattle in town at salesyards, and drove them out to his run, or bought them from his nearest neighbours. Often he preferred the latter method, since neighbours were

Figure 15.6. A simple slab hut with a roof of bark sheets held in place by saplings.

more likely to be honest, as they had to live with him for years to come.

Some squatters went out searching for land with their stock and provisions, and began settlement as soon as they picked out the land they wanted.

Building

As soon as he had found his property, the squatter had to begin constructing a shelter.

While he was doing this, he would sleep in a tent, or bark hut.

Most early squatters made their homes and outbuildings from natural bush materials to hand. Sometimes they would hire a carpenter to help with the building.

The slab hut was a common form of shelter. The squatter felled straight timber and trimmed it with an axe or

Figure 15.7. The squatter's home comprised one room that was sparsely furnished.

adze, sawed it into lengths, split it with wedges and mallets into slabs, and used the slabs to construct walls. He filled the spaces between the slabs with clay or mud. He cut sheets of bark or, better still, shingles to cover the roof. He built a chimney from stones and mud (not river stones — they exploded when heated) or bricks. He made the floor out of hard earth, or slabs. Very few log cabins were built.

As the squatter prospered, he built a more substantial home of brick, weatherboard, and slate. A few squatters could afford to have good-quality building materials transported to their properties. Some even had prefabricated homes delivered.

For furniture, poor squatters constructed tables and chairs from bush materials and other odds and ends. The richer squatters brought their furniture with them. Often, bush furniture was built ingeniously. Parts of packing cases, canvas and bush limbs were used to create tables, chairs, and beds.

Figure 15.8. Shearing by hand.

Developing and Working the Property

Once the squatter had a roof over his head, he had to turn the bushland around him into a viable farm.

Sheep grazed in flocks of several hundred on open pastures, watched over by a shepherd who might be an emancipist or an assignee. At night, the sheep were herded into a special sheep pen formed by setting up 'hurdles' or temporary barricades. This stopped sheep wandering and protected them from 'warrigles', 'dingoes', or wild dogs. In cold weather, or at night, the shepherd (watchman) sat in a portable wooden 'watchbox'.

During the spring it was lambing season, and the squatter had the chance to increase his flocks. He had to take care to preserve as many lambs as possible.

During the shearing season, the squatter washed the sheep in a creek or dam, allowing them to dry overnight, and then sheared them with hand shears.

The squatter tried to have drafting yards and a shearing shed built by this time. Sometimes, however, this was not possible. Wool was pressed into bales in a wool press, and carted by bullock dray into market.

As flocks increased, the squatter had to employ shearers for the shearing season.

The squatter allowed cattle to wander and feed in the nearby bush, watched over by mounted stockmen. Fat cattle were mustered and driven to market for killing every season.

While sheep and cattle were grazing, squatters planted small orchards, cultivated vegetable gardens, and fenced off, cleared, and ploughed a paddock or paddocks for wheat. Once the squatter had a good supply of wheat, he could make his own flour. Oats, for horses, could also be grown.

Figure 15.9. Sawing wood for building materials.

Most farmers used ploughs pulled by one or two horses.

Fences were built with slip-rails instead of gates. There were few fences at first. They were used only to protect crops and to pen animals.

Equipment for Squatting

Before setting off for the bush, the squatter needed to draw up a list of what he required. Here is one such list:

1 ton flour.
Enough meat for the journey: on arrival beasts for slaughter can be purchased of neighbours.
4 or 5 cwt salt (approx. 203 or 254 kg).
1 cwt soap (or ½ cwt) (approx. 50 or 25 kg).
2 chests tea (1 chest).
7 or 8 cwt sugar (4 cwt) (approx. 355 or 406 kg).
3 cwt tobacco (1 cwt) (approx. 152 kg).

2 frying-pans.
1 dozen tin quart pots.
1 dozen tin pint pots.
Several iron pots.
1 doz pocket knives.
1 doz tin plates.
½ doz tin dishes.
1 doz blankets.
Bed-ticking.
3 or 4 doz check shirts.
2 or 3 doz woollen ditto.
2 or 3 doz pair of boots.
Jackets, of sorts.
Trousers, of sorts.
Needles, thread, pipes.
3 cross-cut saws: a 6 ft, a 6½, a 7 ft (approx. 1.8 m, 2 m, and 2.1 m).
1 pit saw, fine space, 7 ft plate (approx. 1.8 m).
Tiller and box for ditto.
Cross-cut and pit saw files.
½ doz best falling axes.
2 lopping axes.
2 mortizing axes.

1 broad axe.
1 heavy adze.
1 light ditto.
Chest of carpenter's tools.
Grindstone and frame.
½ doz padlocks, hasps, and staples.
Several bags of nails of sizes (100 lbs, of sorts) (45 kg).
Firearms, powder and ball.
4 or 5 buckets.
30 or 40 fathoms of good ½ in rope (12.7 mm).
A small churn.
½ doz spades.
½ doz heavy breaking-up hoes.
A small but very strong plough and tackle (may be left till second load).
½ doz reaping hooks (ditto).
1 doz sheep-shears (ditto).

Wool-bagging, and packing needles and twine (ditto).
A good tarpaulin.
Paper, pens, ink, etc.

Problems and Dangers

The squatters faced many problems and dangers:

- In summer, there was always the risk of **bushfire**, which could appear with little warning and spread in a blaze across a property, destroying buildings, fences, stock — even human life.
- In winter, in some areas, there was

Figure 15.10 Squatters needed fences to protect their stock.

The Land They Found

Figure 15.11. A dog was often the squatter's only company.

Figure 15.12. Life could be very lonely for those squatters who lived further out in the bush.

even attack the squatter, his family, and employees. Some squatters knew no rest until their area was more fully settled, and the Aborigines driven off.

- **Dust storms** in dry regions were uncomfortable and tried a squatter's patience.
- **Accidents** were always a worry. They could not be avoided when men were involved in clearing, building, and working with animals. For instance, falls from horses were common, and often resulted in broken bones.
- **Illness** was a problem, as usually there was no doctor available, and a squatter or his wife had to give as much aid as possible. Squatters kept a good supply of castor oil for 'stomach upsets'.
- Many early squatters and their hired workers were single men, and **loneliness and boredom** were other problems to be faced. Mem became very attached to their friends, or 'mates', and to their dogs and horses.

Entertainment

Squatters made their own entertainment. They sang folk songs, played musical instruments, danced, or just sat by the fire in the evening and talked for hours on end. Men smoked pipes or chewed tobacco. There were books and magazines to be read. In more settled areas, picnic race meetings would be held, and whole families would attend to meet with neighbours and friends, share a luncheon, and match horses. The actual races themselves were rough affairs, ridden over dirt tracks.

Dances were also sometimes arranged in local halls. Young people dressed up in their finery and rode horses or drove sulkies or carts for kilometres to attend.

The church and local hall, once established, became the centre of much social life. Further out, however, the squatter's life was much more lonely. There were

always the risk of **flood**. Rivers and creeks could swell very quickly, burst their banks, and sweep away stock and ruin buildings. Rising water also isolated squatters from the outside world, and from one another.
- The **Aborigines** were sometimes hostile. They would spear stock, and

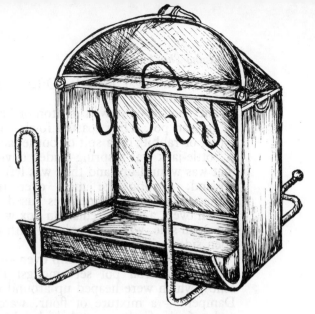

Figure 15.13. Safe for hanging meat (top left).

Figure 15.14. A Dutch oven (above).

Figure 15.15. Cooking pots (below).

Figure 15.16. Butter churn (bottom left).

no race meetings and dances, and even visitors were rare.

Cooking

The squatters did their cooking in the fireplace. For their tea they boiled water from the creek or tank in a black iron kettle or billy, suspended from a hook over the flames. They sweetened the tea

with brown sugar crystals. Often they had no milk.

They boiled or stewed mutton or beef in an iron pot. They roasted fowl, wild birds, or rabbits on a spit or bottle-jack. A bottle-jack was a spring-loaded device that was wound up, and then was left to unwind, turning the meat over the flames. Squatters sometimes used a Dutch oven, a semi-circular tin box with one open side, which was placed with its open side facing the flames.

Baking was done in a camp oven — a three-legged iron pot set amongst the ashes, which were heaped up around it. Damper — a mixture of flour, water, and a pinch of salt — was baked right in the hot ashes. The cook blew off the hot ash or wiped it off when the damper was cold.

Squatters did their own slaughtering of mutton, beef, and pork, and grew their own vegetables and fruit. They grew potatoes, peas, pumpkins, apricots, peaches, apples, oranges, figs, grapes, and watermelons. Occasionally, the squatter would enjoy a fruit cake, boiled sweets (such as black-and-white striped humbugs), or hard toffee, bought from a store in town.

Recipes of the Squatting Era
Kangaroo-Tail Soup

Cut two tails into joints, and fry brown in butter. Slice three carrots and three onions and fry them also. Put tails and vegetables into a stewpan with a bunch of herbs, a pound of gravy beef cut in slices, salt and pepper, and three quarts of water. Allow to boil, then simmer for four hours. Take out the pieces of tail, strain the stock, thicken with flour, and add a little colouring if not brown enough. Then put back the pieces of tail, and boil up for another ten minutes before serving. Season with salt, pepper, and parsley.

Roast Wallaby

In winter the wallaby may hang for some days, but in summer it must be cooked very soon after it is killed. Cut off the hind legs at the first joint, and after skinning and paunching let it lie in water for a time to draw out the blood. Make a good veal forcemeat, and after well washing the inside of the wallaby fill it with the forcemeat, and skewer or sew it up. Truss like a hare, and put it down to a bright, clear fire, keeping it some distance off when first put down, then nearer, and roast from one-and-a-half hours to an hour and three quarters, according to size, basting well all the time with milk and butter. When nearly done, dredge with flour and butter till nicely frothed.

Plum Pudding

Take a pound of stoned muscatel raisins or prunes, one-and-a-half pounds of sultanas or currants, a pound of moist sugar, half a pound of bread crumbs (from bread two days old), a pound of suet skinned and finely chopped, two ounces of sweet almonds blanched and pounded, a quarter pound of mixed candied peel sliced, an ounce of ground nutmeg, an ounce of ground cinnamon, the rind of a fresh lemon, eight eggs broken separately and well beaten, and half a pint of brandy. Mix all the dry ingredients the night before, and next morning add only the eggs and the brandy. Mix all well together. Spoon the pudding into a buttered, well-floured cloth, and tie it close. Place in a saucepan of boiling water and keep it boiling for eight hours. Plunge into cold water for a second just before dishing.

If this is to be served at Christmas, stick some slips of blanched sweet almonds liberally all over the surface of the pudding, and in the middle stick a sprig of berried holly or evergreen. Sprinkle over the whole some crushed loaf sugar and finally add burning spirits. For a brandy sauce, take three-quarters of a pound of finely sifted sugar, add slowly half a tumbler of brandy, and beat till well mixed. Alternatively, beat together sherry and sugar, slowly adding grated nutmeg and rose or vanilla extract.

Dora's Plain Cake

Beat the yolks of sixteen eggs to a cream with a pound each of butter and of sugar, and then add a pound of flour, half a pound of currants, one nutmeg grated, and half a wineglass of brandy, gradually mixing all together. Finally put in the whites of the eggs, which must be beaten up to a good froth. Bake in a moderate oven.

From Drought to Quagmire:
A Squatter's Journey Inland

From the *Report of an Inquiry into the State of the Public Lands and the Operation of the Land Laws, Sydney, 1882:*

Having in April, 1842, collected such of the herd as had survived the terrible three years of drought preceding the early part of 1841, and obtained a small flock of merino sheep, I commenced my journey for the Murray with two bullock-drays, cattle and sheep, with four white men and two black boys, which last decamped very soon after we started. Travelling was almost impossible through the boggy state of the roads, the drays getting continually stuck fast in the mud, until we reached the Breadalbane Plains.

The grass improving every day until we crossed the Murrumbidgee at Gundagai, where there was the most luxuriant crop of grass I had ever seen — about a yard high, and in thickness a dense mass. (Nine months afterwards, those grassy flats were bare as a ploughed field.)

In travelling down the Murray, heavy rain came on at Hillas Station; and when with much difficulty we reached Huon's Station the ground was so swampy that we had to leave the loading of one dray there; even the saddle horses could not carry their riders.

July 28: The natives killed a young cow in the night. The lagoons on the upper side of Mr Howe's station, beginning to fill from the overflow of the Murray. The country wet and the grass growing rapidly in the flats. Found the Edward River rising fast from the overflow of the Murray, causing great delay in crossing. Travelled on over a very low tract about three miles. The watercourses beginning to fill as we passed them; and came to Gulpa Creek, which greatly obstructed our progress.

August 8 to 15: Before we could extricate ourselves and the stock from this low tract, the blacks had killed two lots of sheep and a cow. At last we got everything across the Gulpa Creek, and on to the future Moira Station, glad to escape from the fast-flooding country, where we were being hemmed in by the water and the natives, even to an utterly barren though more elevated position, where there was absolutely nothing to indicate that there had been even a passing shower of rain for years! As the sheep were just beginning to lamb, we were compelled to halt there.

August 16: From the first, the blacks frequent-ly speared the cattle and scattered the herd in all directions. I had an early opportunity when collecting them together, usually twice a week, to see a very large extent of the surrounding country. The same appearance of intense drought and sterility pervaded the whole.

December 31: Blacks continuing spearing cattle. This month has been very hot and dry, with intolerable swarms of mosquitoes, forcing us to fill the huts with dense smoke every night.

1843:
February 4: The first soaking rain we have had since we came here last August. The whole station became a mere quagmire through the heavy rain, so that the horses could not carry their riders, nor the cattle escape from the natives.

July 7 and 11: Heavy rain; station a mere bog. Natives surrounded cattle. Threw spears at the stockman, who was on foot, and drove the cattle into a swamp, where they slaughtered eight of the finest of them.

August 31: Natives attacked the shepherd and the watchman, and plundered the tent, driving the whole of the sheep to the bank of the Murray to slaughter them there; in the midst of which, I came in sight and rescued the remainder of the sheep, which I left with the shepherd, and then returned to watch the blacks and prevent them from carrying away the slaughtered sheep over the Murray during the night. This I succeeded in doing, at some risk, for one light jagged spear, thrown at me just as the moon rose, stuck firmly in the ground close to my foot. The natives, finding that the carbines they had stolen from the shepherds were useless to themselves after they had fired them off and reloaded them with powdered fired them off and reloaded them with powdered charcoal and gravel — which of course proved a failure — brought the back over the river and left them leaning against a tree for me to take them away.

September 21: Mr John Clarke's people driven out by the natives from his station down the Murray.

September 23: A part of Messrs Gwynne's herd came here from the Edward, driven out by natives.

September 27: Attack on Moira by natives forestalled. A large number of natives came, some in canoes, who commenced parleying with me, while two other lots had landed at some distance and were endeavouring to make their way (unseen) to the back of the huts. Others were making their way from tree to tree, with their long spears, through the swamp some 200 yards (185 m) from the building. One powerful native, carrying a very long spear, was approaching very stealthily to get within reach of a young man who was quietly digging some ground for a garden near the edge of the swamp, and to whom I made a sign to come away. At this moment, when it was evident that the blacks were about to make a rush upon the station, a sergeant of the Border Police, who had been watching their movements from his place of concealment in the kitchen, came out and fired at the native alluded to. The ball fell short, but near the black, who made his escape with all speed. A panic at once seized the whole of the natives. Those who were to have attacked the station from the back were seen tearing down the high bank to escape to their canoes in the swamp, which were loaded with spears, and in their haste raising dust like that of a mob of cattle. We endeavoured to capture some of the canoes, but found them too far away in the water for us to reach them. The canoe belonging to the native who had done the parleying we did not give him time to take away; in it we found a portion of a freshly killed sheep. We tried very hard to capture the black, who was, I have no doubt, the author and planner of this most formidable attack upon the Moira station, but what with diving and swimming, he managed to get clear away into the deep water and reed beds of the lake.

Questions

(1) Who were the first squatters in Australia?
(2) Why did later squatters select large runs on Crown land?
(3) Why were the authorities not, at first, in favour of squatting?
(4) Which governor defined the 'Limits of Location'?
(5) Which governor first introduced squatting licences?
(6) What were some of the squatters' grievances?
(7) How were these grievances resolved?
(8) How were the squatters' first buildings constructed?
(9) What dangers and difficulties did the squatters face?
(10) Describe how squatters cooked their meals.

Research

Find out more about:
(1) Early exploration in New South Wales
(2) The squatting problem
(3) Early recipes
(4) Early building and carpentry
(5) Life in the bush.

Chapter 16

Early Days in Tasmania

Figure 16.1. Nicolas Baudin.

Reasons for Settlement

The British government and Governor King both issued orders to plant settlements in Tasmania. Why did they issue such orders? There were at least two strong reasons:

- They were afraid that the French would settle in Tasmania, and wanted to forestall this.
- They felt a need to protect the whaling and sealing industries around the Tasmanian coast.

Fear of the French

Previous chapters have shown that the French had been interested in the Pacific Ocean for some time. La Pérouse's voyage of exploration had caused concern to the British government. In 1792–93, Bruni d'Entrecasteaux made an extensive survey of the Derwent River, and in 1802 Nicolas Baudin, in his ships *Géographe* and *Naturaliste*, made an extended survey of the Tasmanian coast. Baudin named Freycinet Peninsula after his second-in-command. Peron, the expedition's leading scientists, collected plant and animal specimens, and wrote a long account of the Tasmanian Aborigines.

Was the French government interested only in scientific inquiry? Or was it interested in settlement? King, in Sydney, had his doubts. Baudin sailed to Sydney to rest his crew, many of whom were suffering from scurvy. He then returned south to continue his exploring and charting. King heard that some French officers, while drinking with his officers, had let it slip that their government had ideas about settling Tasmania. All of King's worst fears seemed confirmed. If the French attempted to plant a colony in Tasmania, they would be invading British territory, since Tasmania was officially a part of New South Wales. It had been claimed by Phillip. A French base in the south would also be a menace to ships sailing past Tasmania on their way to Sydney.

It therefore seemed essential to settle Tasmania before the French, and so avoid future trouble.

Whaling and Sealing

Every year, hundreds of whales called the Right or Back whale swam into the mouth of the Derwent River and other inlets around the Tasmanian coast to breed. Bay whaling, as it was called, was a profitable investment. Obviously it was in Britain's interest to have secure access to the Derwent.

King was also a friend of the Enderbys, who were in the whaling business. Some have suggested that they influenced him to secure the Derwent for whaling.

Great numbers of seals also bred on the shores of the Bass Strait islands, and sealing was also a profitable investment at that time. In 1802, some 200 men were working in sealing gangs in the Strait. They were employed by the Sydney merchants, Campbell, Kable and Underwood, and Simeon Lord. The Americans were also sealing in the Strait, so British interests had to be protected.

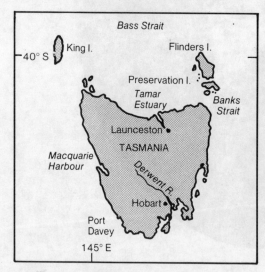

Figure 16.2. Tasmania and the Bass Strait islands.

At that time, King thought that the young colony had found a staple in seal-skins (for the wool industry was not yet established). He wrote, 'Sealskins are the only staple yet discovered there'. A settlement in the Strait would therefore protect sealing interests.

King Island Claimed

Before attempting to settle Tasmania, King sent Lieutenant Robbins in the *Cumberland* to chase after Baudin and claim King Island for Britain. On 23 November 1802, Robbins caught up with the French in Sea Elephant Bay on the island. Robbins landed his men, hoisted the British flag on a tree, and formally claimed the island for King George. He and his small party waited until the French left before sailing back to Sydney.

Settlement in Southern Tasmania

In 1803 King sent Lieutenant John Bowen, RN, a young naval officer, with a small party of convicts, marines, and some free settlers to establish a settlement on the Derwent.

Bowen's party arrived in the Derwent on 12 September 1803, sailing up into the river's cold waters, under the massive beauty of Mt Wellington. Bowen chose Risdon Cove as the site for a settlement. There was a stream of fresh water there, and the soil was good. The *Lady Nelson* dropped anchor, and the party went ashore to begin the hard work of clearing and building. Bowen was keen enough on the job, but his soldiers and convicts were lazy.

One month later, Lieutenant-Colonel David Collins (who had been judge-advocate in Sydney) entered Port Phillip Bay, Victoria. He had come from England under orders from the British government to establish a penal colony on Bass Strait under the control of the governor in Sydney. Collins landed at Sorrento, 13 km inside the bay. He soon

Figure 16.3. Lieutenant-Colonel David Collins.

decided, however, that the spot was unsuitable. The soil was too sandy, and the tides were difficult for shipping. He wrote to King, and King advised him to settle at Port Dalrymple, at the mouth of the Tamar River, on the north coast of Tasmania. Port Dalrymple had been discovered previously by Flinders. From there, he could keep a watch on the Strait, and his settlement could be used by sealing vessels.

However, Collins was not impressed by the Tamar, and he decided to join Bowen on the Derwent. In so doing, he deliberately ignored his orders from Britain to place a settlement on Bass Strait.

Collins began reloading his ships and sailed south, down to the Derwent. He arrived at Risdon Cove on 16 February, and was not impressed by the location or the progress of Bowen's settlement.

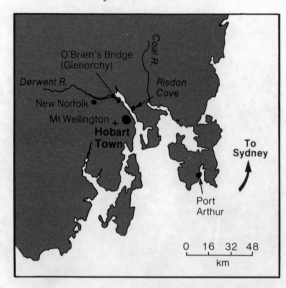

Figure 16.4. The site chosen for the settlement of Hobart Town near the mouth of the Derwent River in southern Tasmania.

Instead, he chose to settle his party at Sullivan's Cove, on the opposite side of the river, further downstream, under Mt Wellington. There was a small plain there, and a rivulet of fresh water that flowed from the mountain into the Derwent. This settlement was named Hobart Town, after Lord Hobart, the colonial secretary.

Bowen then returned to Sydney, and the Risdon Cove settlement was abandoned in favour of Hobart Town. Collins afterwards became the lieutenant-governor of southern Van Diemen's Land.

Settlement in Northern Tasmania

When war with France began again in May 1803, the British government sent orders to King to place a settlement on the southern shores of Bass Strait. It took almost a year for these orders to reach King. When he did receive them, he promptly sent Colonel William Paterson, with a small party, to establish a settlement at Port Dalrymple.

Paterson's party included a number of settlers and convicts from Norfolk Island. The British government was concerned at the expense involved in maintaining this island outpost, which had failed to live up to expectations. King felt that many of the people on Norfolk Island could be used much more satisfactorily at Port Dalrymple.

Paterson's party landed at Outer Cove, later called York Cove, just inside the Tamar Heads, where George Town is now situated.

Soon Paterson decided to transfer the settlement to York Town, on the opposite side of the river, at the head of the

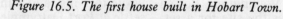

Figure 16.5. The first house built in Hobart Town.

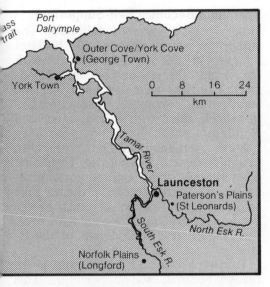

Figure 16.6. Launceston was settled at the head of the Tamar River where the meeting of the North and South Esk Rivers provided a permanent supply of fresh water.

West Arm. Here there were creeks, and better timber for building.

Unfortunately the creeks at York Town ran low in summer, and in 1806 the settlers moved again, this time to the head of the Tamar River, where the North and South Esk rivers meet. The site was also at the foot of the (then) crashing Cataract Gorge. The new settlement at Launceston had a permanent supply of water (from the North and South Esk rivers) and had wider pastures to the south.

Two Different Settlements

The northern and the southern settlements in Tasmania were at first independent of each other. Deep bush and mountains separated the two for some time, and communication between them could be made only by ship around the coast. Paterson was lieutenant-governor in the north, Collins lieutenant-governor in the south. Both answered to the governor of New South Wales, in Sydney.

(However, Paterson was lieutenant-governor of New South Wales, and so had authority over Collins in the south.)

The north-east was called the Shire of Cornwall, the east and south-east the Shire of Buckingham, and the island was still known by its Dutch name of Van Diemen's Land.

An overland trip between the two was not made until 1807 by Thomas Laycock. The island was not combined under one government until 1812. After that, the lieutenant governor in Hobart was responsible for the whole island.

The two settlements developed different characters. Many free settlers and businessmen settled in the north, while the southern settlement boasted mainly convicts, soldiers, public servants, and whalers.

Difficulties of Settlement

The early Tasmanian settlers faced again most of the problems that had been faced by the First Fleeters at Sydney Cove. The land was hard. Farming implements and tools were inferior. Soldiers were discontented. Convicts were lazy. Some convicts escaped, to become bushrangers. Provisions had to be brought in by ship from Sydney or Britain. If ships were delayed by storms, or were wrecked, supplies ran low. When this happened, the settlers hunted kangaroo and emu and boiled 'Botany Bay Greens' (from a plant *Atriplex*, related to saltbush) which grew on the tidal flats.

The settlers lived in wattle-and-daub and bark huts until more permanent structures could be built. In the north, the settlers made bricks with clay from the lake beds. At first, these bricks were poorly fired. Settlers in the south had plenty of sandstone for building. At first, however, there were not enough architects, builders, and stonemasons.

Free Settlers from Norfolk Island

Hobart and Launceston were begun as

convict settlements, but free settlers wanted to take up land. During 1807–8, about 200 more Norfolk Islanders arrived. They were free settlers — retired guards, their wives and children, together with some convicts who had worked off their sentences or had been emancipated, and their wives and children. The British government had obliged them to leave Norfolk Island and help build up numbers in Van Diemen's Land, as a defence against the French.

The new settlers received small grants of land, as compensation for the loss of their island. Some made homes for themselves in Hobart. Others went to the Derwent, and settled at New Norfolk. Some took up land at Norfolk Plains, on the South Esk River, near Launceston (now called Longford). These Norfolk Islanders were among the first free settlers to help develop Tasmania.

Tasmania Becomes Self-Supporting

Other free settlers soon followed. The authorities promised them 400 hectares for every £1000 of capital brought with them, plus the labour of assigned convicts. Convicts were 'assigned' for the length of their sentences. The settler had to provide them with shelter, food, and clothing.

Some settlers chartered, or even bought, vessels to sail to Tasmania. They brought their families, equipment, stock, and furniture with them. Free settlers became owners of much of the good plain and open forest country in the eastern, less rugged half of the island.

Hobart Town and Launceston eventually became self-supporting. This happened more quickly in the north, where there was good agricultural and grazing land at Paterson's Plains (now St Leonards) and White Hill. Farms were

Figure 16.7. A convict plough gang at Port Arthur.

established in the south at New Town and O'Brien's Bridge (now Glenorchy). Pittwater (now called the Coal River Valley) eventually became very productive, and supplied the whole island with wheat and flour. Some was even sent to Sydney.

Eventually a land company, called the Van Diemen's Land Company, was formed in England to develop land in north-western Tasmania. Free land grants continued in Tasmania until the early 1830s. After that, free settlers had to buy their land.

A Tasmanian Tragedy

Tragically, the settlement of Tasmania led to the complete extinction of the Tasmanian Aborigines as a full-blooded race.

The natives had been treated kindly enough by explorers in the past, but early settlers were not so kind. One of the first incidents occurred at Risdon Cove. One of Lieutenant Bowen's officers ordered his men to fire a round of grape and canister at some Aborigines who were hunting near by. (Grape and canister consisted of small lead pellets which spread out when fired. The effect was similar to that of a modern shotgun.) Several Aborigines were killed. Afterwards, the officer argued that he had acted in defence of the small settlement. Witnesses, however, declared that he was drunk at the time.

Not only did white people take the Aborigines' land but they also shot and drove off their game. When an Aborigine speared a settler's sheep for food, the white settler responded harshly, and outside the law. The settlers hunted down and killed Aborigines, whether they were guilty or not. At the same time, sealers raided Aboriginal camps for women and children. Women were used to hunt seals on the Bass Strait islands, and children were used as black servants.

After such treatment, the Aborigines fought back. They united under the

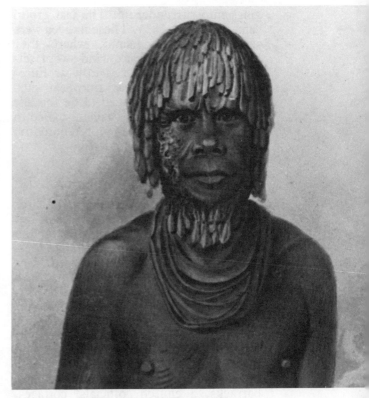

Figure 16.8. A Tasmanian Aborigine. The settlement of Tasmania by Europeans brought an end to the Aboriginal race on the island.

leadership of Musquito and, later, Black Tom. They killed white settlers who were caught unguarded, and burned houses and crops. For a time the settlers could speak of a 'Black War'.

In 1828, Lieutenant-Governor Arthur was forced to declare martial law. In 1830 he tried organizing a 'Black Line' to capture all the Aborigines. Soldiers, convicts, and hundreds of volunteers advanced in a long, straggling line through the bush, converging on East Bay Neck. Two Aborigines were shot dead, and one woman and a boy were captured. The rest escaped.

Eventually gentle persuasion won where warfare had not. George Robinson, a missionary and adviser on Aboriginal affairs, was able to talk the Abori-

The Land They Found

gines into surrendering. The last group came in during 1834. These natives were sent to Flinders Island, where they pined away in a bleak, wind-swept settlement, and were forced to wear European clothes and follow European customs. Truganini, believed to be the last of her race resident in Tasmania, died in 1876. She was the widow of Wooreddy, chief of the Bruny Island tribe.

A Convict Hell — Port Arthur

For many years, Tasmania received large numbers of convicts, many of them difficult men who had committed further crimes after arriving in Australia. Macquarie Harbour, on the rugged west coast of the island, was established as a place of secondary punishment.

In 1830 this was replaced by Port Arthur, on the Tasman Peninsula, which was much closer to Hobart. At Port Arthur a whole penal settlement, or township, slowly developed. It included cell blocks, a hospital, a court house, barracks, a church, officials' cottages, and offices. Escape from Port Arthur was extremely difficult. Prisoners were locked up in stone cells in the evening, and guarded closely by day. If a convict escaped, he was surrounded by deep, rugged bush and freezing waters. To reach Hobart, he had to cross Eaglehawk Neck, a narrow, sandy land bridge guarded by savage guard dogs and sentries.

Convicts who misbehaved were tied to a triangle and flogged with a cat-o'-nine-tails, or shut up in pitch darkness in a solitary confinement cell. Convicts who committed serious crimes were tried at Port Arthur. If they were found guilty, they were taken to Hobart by ship, and hanged in public. Convicts who died at Port Arthur were ferried out to a small offshore island, the Isle of the Dead, and buried with quicklime in an unmarked grave.

Questions

(1) Why was Tasmania settled?
(2) Who ordered the settlement?
(3) Where did Collins settle on the Derwent?
(4) Why did Paterson move his settlement to Launceston?
(5) Who governed Tasmania in 1805?
(6) What difficulties did the early settlers face?
(7) Why were many Norfolk Islanders obliged to settle in Tasmania?
(8) Why did other free settlers go to Tasmania?
(9) What caused the Black War?

Figure 16.9. The convict jail at Port Arthur.

(**10**) Where did the authorities settle the last of the Tasmanian Aborigines in Bass Strait?

Research

Find out more about the following.

(**1**) John Bowen

(**2**) David Collins

(**3**) William Paterson

(**4**) The war between Britain and France during the early 1800s

(**5**) The geography of Tasmania and the islands in Bass Strait.

Chapter 17

Victoria: The Squatters' Colony

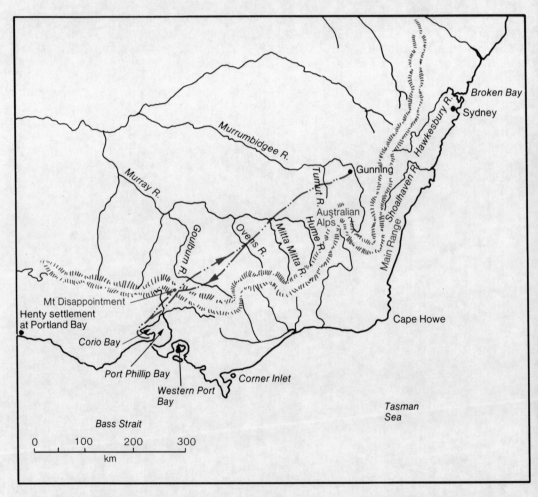

Figure 17.1. The overland journey to the Port Phillip District made by Hume and Hovell in 1824–25.

Early Visitors

Victoria, as we know it today, began as part of New South Wales. It was called simply the Port Phillip District.

The explorers Bass and Flinders visited the Victorian coast between 1797 and 1802. In 1802 both Flinders in the *Investigator* and John Murray in the *Lady Nelson* explored Port Phillip Bay.

One early attempt at colonization failed miserably. We saw in the last chapter how David Collins stayed only a short time at Sorrento before leaving for the Derwent River. By 1804 everyone had left the settlement.

In 1824 Hamilton Hume and William Hilton Hovell made an overland trip from Gunning, near Goulburn, to Port Phillip Bay. They were impressed by the good supply of water and fertile soil in the general area, and they reported on these when they returned north. However, their discovery did not lead to a northern attempt to settle the Port Phillip District.

In 1826 Captain Wright established a military and convict station at Western Port Bay to forestall the French. This settlement was abandoned in 1828.

For years afterwards, the area was visited by only a few whalers and sealers. Some of these men were escaped convicts or former convicts who had made a temporary home for themselves on some of the Bass Strait islands. A rough bunch of men, they became known as the 'sea rats'.

Early Interests in Settlement

Settlers living in Tasmania had heard good accounts of the Port Phillip District from visiting whalers and others. They saw an opportunity to obtain good land across Bass Strait.

In January 1827, John Batman and Joseph Tice Gellibrand, two Launceston men, wrote to the governor of New South Wales asking for grazing land at Western Port Bay. Bourke refused this request. He had orders to contain the spread of settlement in Australia.

Figure 17.2. A wool store owned by the Henty family. The Hentys introduced the first sheep and cattle into Victoria.

Figure 17.3. The Hentys' whaling station at Portland Bay.

The Henty Family at Portland

The Henty family decided to look for land across Bass Strait. This family had come to Tasmania aboard a chartered vessel, the *Caroline*. Originally, the Hentys had planned to live in Western Australia, but they had been disappointed with the area, and had decided to settle in Tasmania instead. They had arrived in Tasmania just after the free land grants ceased, so they could not acquire a property.

Now the Hentys hoped to make up for their disappointments by obtaining land in the Portland Bay area. The family asked for the help of Lieutenant-Governor Arthur in Hobart, but he was not allowed to help them settle illegally in New South Wales.

The Hentys made their move before the governor of New South Wales could stop them. Edward Henty, with Henry Camfield and four servants, left Tasmania in the *Thistle* in October 1834. The small party sailed across to Portland Bay, and landed on 19 November. The *Thistle* then returned to pick up more members of the family and supplies.

The Hentys cleared the bush, built homes, barns, and fences, and intro-

duced their merino sheep and cattle to pasture. Frank Henty opened the first sheep run, at Merino Downs. Stephen Henty's son, Richmond, was the first white settler born in the Port Phillip area.

The Hentys put money into whaling, as well as agriculture and grazing, and by 1838 they employed some 70 whalers in six or seven boats. Stephen Henty managed that side of the business. However, the Portland area was slow to develop because Portland Bay was a poor harbour and the spot was very isolated. Later, the Hentys had to fight to keep the land they had settled without permission.

John Batman at Port Phillip Bay

John Batman, who was living in Launceston, still had not given up his plans to settle in the Port Phillip district. He formed an association of 15 men, including himself, later called the Port Phillip

Figure 17.4. John Batman.

Association. This Association had two aims:

- To explore new country across Bass Strait
- To 'purchase' suitable land for settlement from the Aborigines.

Batman was just the man to carry out these aims. He had been born in Parramatta, and was a capable farmer, bushman, and explorer. Also, he had spent considerable time with the Aborigines, and knew their ways.

On 10 May 1835, he set sail in the *Rebecca*, a schooner. With him were three servants, James Gumm, William Todd, and Alexander Thompson, and seven New South Wales Aborigines as interpreters. Storms delayed the ship, but on 29 May Batman dropped anchor off Indented Head, at the entrance to Corio Bay. He then explored the Geelong area.

Next he moved his vessel to the mouth of the Yarra River estuary, and explored the Salt Water River estuary, and explored the Salt Water River (now Maribyrnong River) area. On 6 June, on the banks of the Merri Creek, he met eight elders of the Dutigallar tribe and entered into a highly profitable, and also highly illegal, contract with them. The Aborigines, three of them called Jagajaga, and the others Cooloolock, Bungarie, Yanyan, Moowhip, and Mommarmalar, agreed to sign over a total of some 600 000 hectares of land in return for an annual payment of blankets, knives, tomahawks, looking glasses, pairs of scissors, handkerchiefs, shirts, and flour. The Aborigines knew nothing about contracts, and signed this 'treaty' with a cross. Batman's servants acted as witnesses.

Batman returned to the Yarra, and decided to settle on the spot where Melbourne now stands. He wrote in his diary:

The boat went up the large river I have spoken of, which comes from the east and I am glad to state about six miles (10 km) up found the river

Figure 17.5. *The Port Phillip Bay area, which Batman explored in the schooner* Rebecca *in May 1835.*

all good water and very deep. This will be the place for a village.

Batman left his men at Indented Head and returned to Launceston on 14 June to pick up his family and make arrangements with his business associates to exploit his recent purchase of land. He wrote to Lieutenant-Governor Arthur, saying that he hoped the British government would honour the treaty he had concluded, and would give him every support and encouragement.

Lieutenant-Governor Arthur wrote to the British government on Batman's behalf, recommending that a large grant be made. The colonial secretary, however, would not confirm such a grant. In the eyes of the officials, Batman was a trespasser and nothing more.

John Pascoe Fawkner

Meanwhile, another party of squatters prepared to cross Bass Strait. John Pascoe Fawkner was a restless businessman and ex-convict. Fawkner hoped to make

Figure 17.6. *Boom-Bul-Wa and Quar-Tan-Grook, his wife, two Aborigines of the Port Phillip*

Figure 17.7. *Batman's house on the Yarra. The land on which it stood was part of that obtained in his 'contract' with the Aborigines.*

a first landing with his small party in July or August 1835, but could not because he had to remain in Launceston to answer a debt claim.

Fawkner's party left George Town in July and sailed across to Western Port Bay in the *Enterprise*. After rejecting the area as unsuitable, they sailed into Port Phillip Bay and found their way to the Yarra. The *Enterprise* anchored below a ridge of small falls (the Yarra Yarra proper) at the bottom of what is now William Street. Fawkner's men were most impressed with the spot. The land was green and fertile and perfect for settlement. They unloaded horses, pigs, provisions, seed, fruit trees, grog, etc, and began building. They turned over two hectares and planted them with wheat and vegetables on the slope of a small hill (which is now the corner of Spencer and Flinders Streets).

Fawkner arrived on 11 October with his family.

Figure 17.8. John Pascoe Fawkner.

Batman and Fawkner

Batman returned to Indented Head with his wife Eliza and seven daughters. From there, the party moved across to the Yarra. They settled on the hill above Fawkner's plot of wheat and vegetables. This hill was later called Batman's Hill.

Batman looked on Fawkner and his settlers as trespassers, and asked them to move on. Fawkner did not want to move on. Eventually the two men reached a compromise. Batman and his people took the north bank of the river; Fawkner and his people the southern bank. This meant that Fawkner had to abandon his two hectares of wheat and vegetables, which Wise and Gilbert had worked on. Batman paid him £5 for this. The later wheat harvest was said to be about 100 bushels (3.6 cubic metres).

Batman built a wooden house with a brick chimney. The chimney was built by William Buckley, a convict escaped from the earlier Sorrento settlement, who had lived with the Aborigines as a 'wild white man', and had walked into

Figure 17.9. William Buckley — the 'wild white man'.

143

Batman's camp at Indented Head. Batman lived in this house for the rest of his life with his wife and family. He died in 1839, at the age of 39, and was buried in Melbourne's Old Cemetery, where the old Victoria Market now stands. However, his grave had no headstone, and is now lost. Batman's widow and family eventually had to leave their home, because the New South Wales government would not recognize their claim to the land they had settled on. Batman's house was used as government offices. Much of the colony's business was done in what was once the kitchen.

Eventually Fawkner moved across the Yarra, to live in an inn built on the south-east corner of William Street and Flinders Lane. There he took in lodgers, opened a library, sold imported newspapers, established the first printing press in the settlement, and produced the newspaper *The Port Phillip Patriot and Melbourne Advertiser*.

The Spread of Settlement

In the years that followed, more and more settlers arrived in the Port Phillip area. At first, most of them came from Tasmania. Soon settlers began to arrive overland from the Sydney district. Finally, free settlers began to arrive by ship from Britain.

The population began to rise steadily and the colony developed rapidly. Houses and other buildings were constructed. The little 'village' of Batman and Fawkner began to grow in size, and rural development fanned out from the Bay for hundreds of hectares.

At first, no one could agree on what the village should be called. Fawkner's group had favoured Pascoevale. Batman's group favoured Batmania. Many favoured the name Dutigallar (Doutta Galla) after the local Aboriginal tribe. Some, who saw an opportunity to make a lot of money out of the area, nicknamed the town El Dorado. For many years, the village was straggling, unplanned and evil-smelling. In the streets, one rubbed shoulders with many different types of people: graziers, shopkeepers, Aborigines, whalers, sealers, sailors, and ex-convicts.

Official Recognition

Batman's land purchase was not recognized by either the British or New South Wales governments. But what could they do? Expel all settlers? Fine them for trespassing? This was not practical.

Eventually, some sort of recognition of the settlement had to be made. Law and order had to be established, and taxes collected. In 1836, Governor Richard Bourke sent Captain William Lonsdale to act as resident magistrate, to administer and guide the settlement. He arrived aboard HMS *Rattlesnake*, bringing with him his family, three constables, 30 soldiers, and 30 convicts. He moved into a newly built house near the corner of Spencer Street and Little Collins Street, near Batman's house. For a

Figure 17.10. Captain William Lonsdale.

Figure 17.11. Lonsdale's house stood near the corner of Spencer and Little Collins Streets, not far from John Batman's house.

short time, he and Batman were neighbours.

The following year, Bourke visited the settlement aboard *Rattlesnake*. He gave the township the name of Melbourne, after Lord Melbourne, the British prime minister. He laid down plans for a new, cleaner, more regular township. Melbourne would be rectangular, one mile (1.6 km) in length, parallel with the Yarra, and half a mile wide. The streets would be one-and-a-half chains wide (about 30 m) and would cross at right angles, one-eighth of a mile (0.2 km) apart. Nine streets would run back from the river. Four larger ones would cross these at right angles, thus forming four-hectare blocks. The plans included little streets to enable carts to service back entrances. The streets would all be named after members of the Royal Family, Australian explorers,

Figure 17.12. Plans for the township of Melbourne drawn up in 1837. Governor Bourke ordered that the township be rectangular in design.

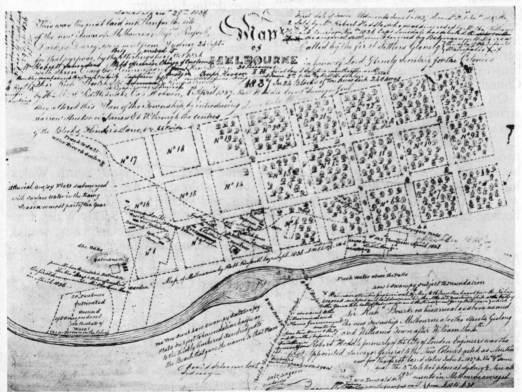

Figure 17.13. Charles Joseph La Trobe.

and famous men of the time. (Elizabeth Street was one exception.) Allotments went up for auction — the average lot fetching £35. Old houses and other buildings in the way were demolished. Convict labour was used to make the new streets. Free brickmakers came from Sydney and Hobart Town to build permanent brick buildings. A local brownstone was quarried for St James's Church.

On 1 October 1839, C. J. La Trobe arrived as the first superintendent. He was sent by Governor Sir George Gipps. La Trobe brought his wife, daughter, two servants, and a portable wooden house, which he established on a small hill overlooking the Yarra. This house was called Jolimont. William Lonsdale became his sub-treasurer.

A New Colony

Inevitably, the settlers in the Port Phillip district wanted to have some control over their own affairs. They became angry at their lack of power in a new legislative council set up for New South Wales in 1842. In this new council, Melbourne Town had only one representative, and the Port Phillip District as a whole had only six members. Three of these six members resided in Sydney. The three representatives from the district itself had little power.

Residents also resented the money they paid in taxes going to Sydney, and they resented efforts to begin a penal colony in Melbourne. In 1849, two transports arrived carrying a total of 500 convicts, but the locals refused to allow the convicts to land, threatening violence if they did so. The convicts later went to Sydney.

The residents of the district sent petitions to Queen Victoria and the colonial secretary. However, these documents were returned to the governor of New South Wales. He passed them back to Superintendent La Trobe. Fortunately, however, some British politicians did see the need to change the situation.

In 1850 the *Australian Colonies Government Act* was passed, creating a new colony called Victoria, after the Queen, from the first day in 1851. Its boundaries were defined clearly:

The territories now comprised within the district of Port Phillip, including the town of Melbourne, and bounded on north and north-east by a straight line drawn from Cape Howe to the present source of the River Murray, and thence by the course of that river to the eastern boundary of the colony of South Australia, shall be separated from the colony of New South Wales . . .

The governor of New South Wales would no longer have control over Victoria, and Victoria would cease to return members to the New South Wales legislative council. A supreme court would also be set up in Victoria.

Advanced Civilization in Melbourne

The Port Phillip Patriot and Melbourne Advertiser, Monday, 7 October 1839:

The present position of Australia Felix is a very peculiar one — her career of prosperity having

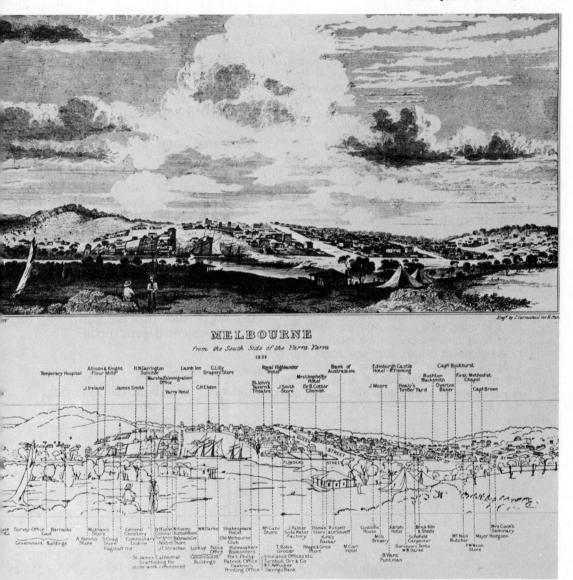

Figure 17.14. Melbourne, from the south side of the Yarra in 1839. Already it was a flourishing town with a growing number of small businesses and public buildings.

been hitherto quite unparalleled in the annals of British Colonization; and this not only without any efficient aid from the Mother Country, but we might even add, without her knowledge.

It now scarcely exceeds four years since a few enterprising individuals from Van Diemen's Land first landed in this district. These at once discovered the advantages of the country, and as soon as those became known settlers from all the neighbouring colonies crowded to it.

Already Melbourne, which eighteen months ago possessed only three brick houses, is a flourishing town, with a population of between two and three thousand souls, and containing most of the appendages of an advanced civilisation. It has five places of worship of different denominations of Christians — a Court of Justice, two schools, two banks, one club with sixty members, a fire and marine assurance company, and two newspapers are efficiently supported. Of the learned professions there are six clergymen, twelve medical men, and five lawyers.

Such is the present state of Melbourne, and with reference to the back country of Australia Felix, it may be said, that this, for upwards of one hundred and eighty miles, is covered with flocks and herds, and there are now stations along the whole line of road to Sydney. Of wool, our staple commodity, there was exported in 1837, sixty thousand five hundred and twelve pounds (27 500 kg); — in 1838, two hundred and thirteen thousand two hundred and thirty-three pounds (96 924 kg); — in 1839, eight hundred and six thousand eight hundred and seventy-seven pounds (366 762 kg) — independently of large quantities shipped coastwise to Sydney; and it is estimated that the clip about to be made will amount in value to upwards of one hundred thousand pounds sterling.

With such evidences of progressive prosperity, it is quite certain that Australia Felix must soon have become one of the most important possessions of Britain, had she been merely suffered to remain on a footing of equality with the other Crown Colonies of Australasia; we regret, however to say, that this has not been the case . . .

Questions

(1) Why were Tasmanian squatters interested in the Port Phillip district?
(2) What interests did the Hentys develop at Portland Bay?
(3) What was the name of the Aboriginal tribe living in the Melbourne area?
(4) Name some of the elders of that tribe.
(5) Who decided first to build a settlement on the banks of the Yarra?
(6) Why did Melbourne and the Port Phillip district develop so quickly?
(7) Why did the settlers want to see the Port Phillip District separated from New South Wales?
(8) In which year did separation occur?
(9) Who was the new colony named after?
(10) What did the prosperity of the settlement depend upon?

Research

Find out more about the following.
(1) The Henty family
(2) John Batman
(3) John Pascoe Fawkner
(4) Captain William Lonsdale
(5) Superintendent C. J. La Trobe.

Chapter 18

Early Settlement in Queensland

Oxley and the Moreton Bay Settlement

Queensland, like Victoria and South Australia, was once a part of New South Wales. Also, like Victoria, it was first planted with a convict settlement.

Commissioner Bigge had recommended that further penal settlements should be set up for troublesome con-

victs. Governor Brisbane, who was Macquarie's successor in Sydney, hoped that a new, northern convict settlement would take pressure off Port Macquarie, established in 1821. It would also remove convicts from Sydney, and therefore please the exclusives. Therefore, Brisbane commissioned John Oxley, the surveyor-general, to check the northern

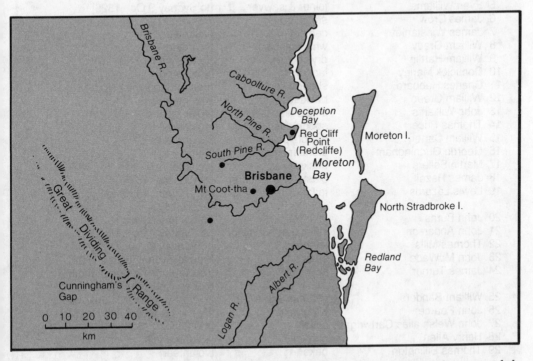

Figure 18.1. Map of Moreton Bay. In 1823 John Oxley surveyed this coastline and recommended that the settlement of Brisbane be made on the banks of the Brisbane River.

coast of what is now New South Wales and the southern coast of what is now Queensland for a suitable site.

Oxley sailed north in the *Mermaid* and explored Port Curtis and Moreton Bay. He decided upon Red Cliff Point (now Redcliffe) in Moreton Bay. Brisbane then instructed Oxley and Lieutenant Henry Miller of the 40th Regiment to found a settlement at Redcliffe.

The small party sailed north in the brig *Amity*, and landed at Redcliffe on 24 September 1824. Many of the convicts were volunteers. They began to build quarters for the staff, soldiers, and themselves.

However, the site did not last long. Oxley began to explore the nearby Brisbane River to find its source. He was impressed by its breadth, many reaches, and surrounding timbered hills. On 28 September he landed on what is now North Quay, and recommended that it was a better site than Redcliffe.

In December, Chief Justice Forbes inspected the new site, and approved Oxley's choice. That same month, Lieutenant Miller and his party moved from Redcliffe to the new site. The remains of the Redcliffe site became known to the local Aborigines as Humpybong — the place of dead, or empty, houses.

The Convicts aboard the 'Amity'

1	Robert Humphries	labourer	[died 4 Nov. 1825]
2	Thomas Warwick	sawyer	[volunteer]
3	William Francis Jun.	sawyer	[volunteer]
4	Robert Butler	carpenter	[free to Sydney 9 Jan. 1826]
5	Evan Williams	joiner & sawyer	[to Sydney 9 Oct. 1826]
6	James Crow	stable boy	[volunteer]
7	James Winstanley	cabinet maker	[volunteer]
8	William Grady	whitewasher	[volunteer]
9	William Hartlin	dry cooper	[run 12 Jan. 1826]
10	Dominick Marley	labourer	[volunteer]
11	Charles Hubbard	shoemaker	[free to Sydney 13 Mar. 1826]
12	William Green	bricklayer	[volunteer]
13	John Williams	ship's blacksmith	[volunteer]
14	Thomas Price	spoon driss [*sic*]	[volunteer]
15	William Carter	marble polisher	[volunteer]
16	George Gunningham	stone mason	[volunteer]
17	Martin Sellers	brickmaker	[volunteer]
18	James Hazell	plasterer's labourer	[run 12 Jan. 1826]
19	Lewis Lazarus	tailor	[run 12 Jan. 1826; to Sydney 4 Feb. 1832]
20	John Burns	labourer	[to Sydney 6 Jan. 1827]
21	John Anderson	sailmaker and tailor	[to Sydney 6 Jan. 1827]
22	Thomas Mills	seaman	[to Sydney 6 Jan. 1827]
23	John McWade	seaman	[free to Sydney 9 Jan. 1826]
24	James Turner	sailor	[run 12 Jan. 1826 and another 6 or so times until about 1837]
25	William Sanders	seaman and smith	[to Norfolk Island 21 July 1827]
26	John Pearce	waterman	[free to Sydney 9 Jan. 1826]
27	John Welsh alias Cartwright	sailor	[run 23 Oct. 1825]
28	Henry Allen	gunsmith	[volunteer]
29	Thomas Billington	baker	[volunteer]

Oxley's Advice to Governor Brisbane

10 January 1824:

Should it be deemed expedient to establish a settlement in Moreton Bay, the country in the vicinity of Red Cliff Point offers the best site for an establishment in the first instance; it is central in the Bay, and there is no difficulty in effecting a landing at all times of tide, though the soil immediately on the sea shore is but indifferent. A communication can easily be opened with the interior; it is about 10 miles (16 km) to the north of the entrance into Brisbane River, and must be passed by all vessels intending to enter it. Red Cliff Point must, however, be viewed as being better adapted for a military post and depot for stores than as the site of a principal settlement; the Brisbane River presents so many superior situations that, although a post here may be indispensable, I think a permanent settlement would be most advantageously formed on the west side of the River at the termination of sea reach.

Governor Brisbane's Instructions to Lieutenant Miller

27 August 1824:

As soon as you land, you are to place a military guard over (the) stores, which you are to continue at all times; and you are to keep regular accounts of all receipts and disbursements of provisions, slop clothing, tools and implements. Shortly after your disembarkation you are to establish a signal station on some height seen from the offing from whence early notice is to be given to you of every sail that heaves in sight. You are to use every effort to prevent the introduction of spirituous liquors. None but Government vessels are to be permitted to hold intercourse with your establishment. Yet in the very improbable event of any vessel happening to anchor in distress you are to afford her such relief as your circumstances admit, but the moment her damages are repaired you must order her away, taking care to search her strictly upon her departure. All letters or parcels coming to the settlement for convicts are to be delivered to yourself, and you are hereby required to give them over to the person to whom they are addressed after having opened and read them in his presence, and all letters addressed by them must before they are forwarded be also read by yourself. The soldiers will receive their military allowance of provisions. The ration to be issued to each convict is to consist of four pounds (1.8 kg) of salt meat and ... flour, but you will be entitled yourself to draw a treble allowance. The hours of morning labour will be from daylight till eight, when one hour and a half will be given for cleanliness and breakfast. Work will be resumed from half past nine until twelve. Two hours will then be allowed for dinner, and labour will afterwards continue from two o'clock until sunset. On Sunday mornings the convicts are to bathe, and when perfectly clean to be mustered for Divine Service, which is to be performed by yourself. A chronological register according to the accompanying form of all the convicts received at the settlement, with a number affixed to every name, and an alphabetical index at the reverse end of this record, is to be kept with the most exact care. No other dress will be allowed to be worn at the settlement than that which is furnished by Government. The yearly allowance to every convict is to be two shirts, two frocks, two pairs of shoes and two pairs of trousers, and the number affixed in the register before mentioned to the name of every convict is to be marked upon each article.

The overseers are prohibited from striking or pushing the convicts, but are to report to you the offences they commit. A due attention on your part to minute faults, and the occasional augmentation of labour with solitary confinement upon bread and water, will be far more effectual in the correction of offences than corporal punishment. But in the event of the commission of any serious crime, you will take the informations that are necessary in writing but not upon oath, will cause them to be read to the several witnesses, and then signed with their names or marks. Upon which evidence you will award such sentence as the case may appear to deserve, recollecting that you have not the power to inflict a greater punishment than fifty lashes.

Brisbane: A Cruel Outpost

On 15 August 1826, Governor Brisbane officially proclaimed the new site a penal settlement. Both the river and the new settlement were named after him. Forbes had wanted the settlement called Edinglassie, but this was rejected.

Brisbane began as a convict settlement and, for many years, was regarded as a cruel outpost where difficult and

Figure 18.2. Allan Cunningham.

troublesome convicts were sent. Wooden and stone buildings were constructed, and the settlement was developed. From Brisbane, commandants sent out parties to explore south and west, and along the Brisbane River valley. Coal and lime were discovered at Ipswich. The general area was seen as good for grazing and agriculture, but free settlers were at first excluded.

Allan Cunningham and the Darling Downs

Allan Cunningham was a botanist and explorer. He came to Australia in December 1816. In June 1827, he discovered about 1 500 000 hectares of rich land 160 km west of Moreton Bay. The soil was rich and black. Volcanic basalt had weathered for millions of years to produce it. It was perfect for grazing and agriculture. Cunningham named the area the Darling Downs, after the governor, Sir Ralph Darling.

The following year he discovered a pass (Cunningham's Gap) through the ranges to Moreton Bay. He then hurried back to Sydney with his exciting news. He worked hard to 'sell' his discovery to squatters. Many of them were moving north to the New England area of New South Wales, and to other areas near Brisbane.

It was 12 years before anyone took any notice of what Cunningham had to say about the Downs. Patrick and George Leslie eventually listened. They assembled drays, horses, sheep, and servants and set out, pioneering a trail into the Downs. They settled at Toolburra Station, near Warwick, in 1840.

Other settlers soon followed, marking out properties for themselves. Tradesmen and businessmen followed. They set up small, bark shops at a place called The Springs. This settlement lay beside a bullock track which linked Ipswich with Moreton Bay. Mr Thomas Alford, with his wife and two daughters, arrived in 1842, and renamed the settlement Drayton, after a parish in Somerset, England. Today Drayton is a suburb of Toowoomba, the capital of the Downs.

Cunningham's Gap provided the means of communication between the Downs and the Brisbane settlement. There was a demand for labour, for shepherds and hut keepers, and the Brisbane settlement was able to supply some of this labour. The Brisbane convicts were regarded as hardened rogues, but the settlers felt that bad labourers were better than none at all.

The Darling Downs

From Cunningham's journal:

These extensive tracts, which I have named Darling Downs in honour of His Excellency, are situated in or about the mean parallel of 28°8′, along which they extend 18 miles (30 km) to the meridian of 152°. On the north side they are bounded by a rise of lightly wooded ridges,

Figure 18.3. The Moreton Bay settlement in 1835. Despite its beginnings as an outpost for the more hardened convicts, Brisbane soon began to attract free settlers.

skirted on their opposite margin by a level forest of box and white gum. A chain of deep ponds passes along the central lower portion throughout its whole length and falls westerly into the Condamine River; their breadth varies... Grasses and herbage were of the same species in similar situations in the southern country; no plant appeared more striking than the rib-grass (*Plantago struthionis*), the leaves of which measured 12–15 inches (30–38 cm) in length. From these lower grounds, downs of a rich black and dry soil, clothed with abundance of grass... stretched on an east and west line, constituting a range of sound sheep-pasture convenient to water but beyond the reach of floods.

Cunningham's Gap First Sighted

11 June:

Had the day continued fine and clear, I should have endeavoured... to have gained the highest ridge... about 2 miles (3 km) distant... it would have enabled me in taking a survey of

this... mountainous land to have observed how far a passage over these lofty ranges could be effected by which the... country passed over could become accessible from the shores of Moreton Bay or Brisbane River. We, however, noticed from the station to which we had climbed a very deeply excavated part of the main range heaving from us about NNE two or three miles (3–4 km), to the pitch of which there appeared a tolerably easy rise along the back of a forest ridge from the head of Millar's Valley. So remarkable a hollow in the principal range I determined not to leave unexamined, since it appeared... it might prove to be a very practicable pass from the eastern country to the Darling Downs and thus form the door of a very considerable grazing country.

14 June:

On 14 June Cunningham sent his men ahead to explore the pass before them.

(Cunningham's men) ascended a narrow ridge

153

Figure 18.4. The Darling Downs, the fertile
farming land discovered by Cunningham in
1827. This recent aerial photograph shows the
cultivation of the Downs for grain crops.

Figure 18.5. Cunningham's Gap. Allan
Cunningham discovered this pass to the Darling
Downs in 1828. It provided a means of
communication between the Downs and the
Brisbane settlement. Today a modern highway
takes the place of the trail pioneered by horses
and drays.

by which they rose gradually seven miles
(11 km) to a distance of about one mile (1½ km)
from the highest pitch of the Gap, when the
difficulties appeared to consist of the rugged-
ness of the large masses of rock that had fallen
from the heads into the hollow and the brush
with which these boulders were covered. On
ascending the south head they observed a
rather easier passage over the range where a
road could be constructed, the acclivity from
Millar's Valley being by no means abrupt and
the fall easterly from the range to the forest
ground at its foot appearing exceedingly moderate.

A Friend of the Aborigines

(From *Tom Petrie's Reminiscences of Early Queensland*):

On first coming, nearly forty-five years ago, to
North Pine, which is sixteen miles by road from
Brisbane, the country round about was all wild
bush, and the land my father took up was a
portion of the Whiteside run. The blacks were
very good and helpful, lending a hand to split
and fence and put up stockyards, and they

154

would help look after the cattle and yard them at night. For the young fellow was all alone, no white man would come near him, being in dread of the blacks. Here he was among two hundred of them, and came to no harm.

When with their help he had got a yard made, and a hut erected, he obtained flour, tea, sugar, and tobacco from Brisbane, and leaving these rations in the hut, in charge of an old aboriginal, went again to Brisbane, and was away this time a fortnight. Fifty head of cattle he also left in the charge of two young blacks, trusting them to yard these at night, etc. and to enable the young darkies to do this, he allowed them each the use of a horse and saddle. On his return all was as it should be, not even a bit of tobacco missing! And those who know no better say the aborigines are treacherous and untrustworthy! Father says he could always trust them; and his experience has been that if you treated them kindly they would do anything for you.

On the occasion just mentioned during his absence, a station about nine miles (15 km) away ran short of rations, and the stockman was sent armed with a carbine and a pair of pistols to see if he could borrow from father. Arrived at his destination, the man found but

blacks, and they simply would give him nothing until the master's return. The hut had no doors at the time, and yet they hunted for their own food, touching nothing.

Another time, while out riding in the bush, my father heard a great row, and a voice calling, 'Round them up, boys!' And on galloping up he came upon a number of poor blacks — men, women, and children — all in a mob like so many wild cattle, surrounded by the mounted black police. The poor creatures tried to run to their friend for protection, and he inquired of the officer in charge what was the meaning of it all. The officer — a white man, and one, by the way, who was noted for his inhuman cruelty — replied that they merely wished to see who was who. But father knew that if he hadn't turned up, a number of the poor things would have been shot. Can one wonder there were murders committed by the blacks, seeing how they were sometimes treated? This same police officer (Wheeler, by name), later on was to have been hanged for whipping a poor creature to death, but he escaped and fled from the country. It is possible he is still alive. His victim was a young blackfellow, whom he had tied to a verandah post, and then brutally flogged till he died.

Figure 18.6. A settler and a group of Aborigines in the early pioneering days of Queensland.

Development and Separation

In 1839, the penal settlement at Brisbane was abandoned. By that time, fewer convicts were being sent to Australia, and Port Arthur was developed to handle difficult convicts. The convicts at Brisbane were taken back to Sydney and, shortly afterwards, Brisbane became a centre of free settlement.

In 1841, the country around Brisbane, officially called the Northern District of New South Wales, was thrown open for selection at 12/- per acre. Many settlers bought land, and settled the banks of the Brisbane River. The Reverend J. D. Lang, and others, encouraged free settlers to settle in the north. By 1851, there were some 10 000 settlers, spread over a large area.

In 1854, the settlers asked Britain to make the Northern District into a separate colony. The British government was prepared to do this. It agreed to the creation of a new colony in 1856. However, it was 1859 before the necessary steps were taken. The new colony that came into being was named after the Queen.

In December 1859, Sir George Bowen arrived as governor of the new colony. By now there were 25 000 people in the colony. Brisbane had 7000 inhabitants. As yet, there was no other real centre of population.

Questions

(1) Why was a convict settlement established in Queensland?
(2) Why did Oxley suggest Redcliffe as a site for settlement?
(3) When was the move made from Redcliffe to Brisbane?
(4) What was the derivation of the nickname 'Humpybong'?

Figure 18.7. The first house built in Brisbane.

156

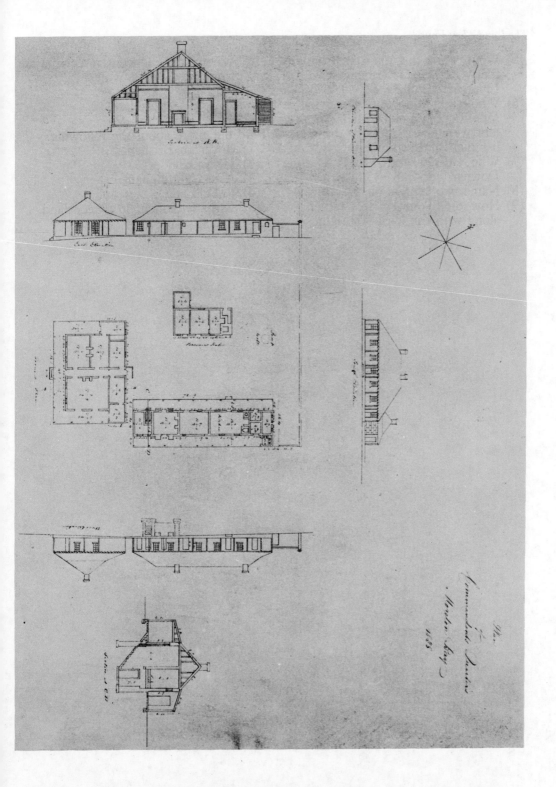

*Figure 18.8. Elevation plans of the Commandant's cottage, kitchen wing, and prisoner's hut.
(From the Moreton Bay Plans, 1838.)*

(5) What were the main instructions that Governor Brisbane gave to Lieutenant Miller?

(6) What skills did the first convicts at Moreton Bay possess? How important were these skills to the establishment of a settlement?

(7) Who discovered the Darling Downs?

(8) Name two settlers on the Downs.

(9) How did Tom Petrie's father get along with the local Aborigines?

(10) When did Queensland separate from New South Wales?

Research

Find out more about the following.

(1) Governor Brisbane
(2) John Oxley
(3) Alan Cunningham
(4) J. D. Lang
(5) Early settlement in Queensland.

Chapter 19

Western Australia:
The Swan River Colony

Figure 19.1. Captain James Stirling.

Figure 19.2. Dumont d'Urville.

The Settlement at Albany

The coastline of West Australia, or New Holland, had been known for centuries, but was considered too arid for settlement. Several ships continued to make contact with the coast. Captains Vancouver, Flinders, and King all sailed along it.

Fear of French settlement in the West finally prompted the British government to take action. A French expedition commanded by J. Dumont d'Urville was exploring the waters around Australia and New Zealand, and the British government feared that the French might plant a settlement on the remote west coast to menace British shipping. In March 1826, Earl Bathurst, the colonial secretary, wrote to Governor Darling in Sydney, ordering him to forestall the French by sending soldiers and convicts to Shark Bay.

On 11 March, Bathurst suggested an alternative site, King George Sound, 1100 km south of Shark Bay. It was a good habour, the climate was milder than that at Shark Bay, and the soil was

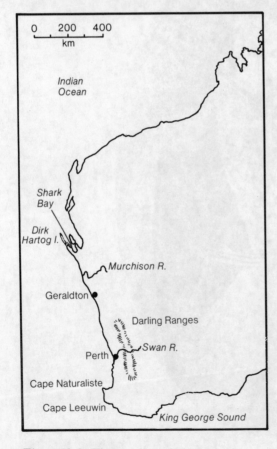

Figure 19.3. The coastline of Western Australia.

Figure 19.4. Major Edmund Lockyer.

160

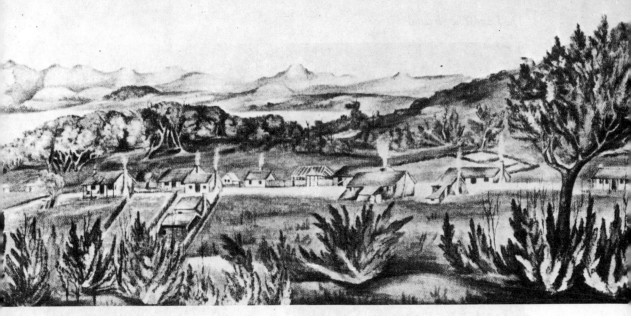

Figure 19.5. The settlement at King George Sound 1827, painted by Major Lockyer.

promising. It was also in a better position to protect ships sailing to or from Van Diemen's Land and Sydney.

Major Lockyer received command of the expedition and landed in the Sound on 25 December 1826. A small, military-convict station was begun at Albany. The members of the party put up huts, dug fortifications, and developed gardens. Supplies were shipped around from Sydney. Unfortunately, this proved difficult and expensive, and the Albany settlement was eventually abandoned. Eventually it became part of the Swan River Colony.

Stirling and the Swan River

Lockyer was followed around to Western Australia by Captain James Stirling, RN. He had orders from the British government to crush piracy in the Timor Sea, and to shift a small base which had been set up on Melville Island.

Stirling decided to avoid the summer monsoons by exploring part of the west coast between King George Sound and Shark Bay and, in particular, the Swan River, which had been discovered originally by the Dutch voyager Willem de Vlamingh in 1697. The river had been named after its black swans. In March 1827, shortly after Lockyer had landed in King George Sound, Stirling reached the river. He explored about 80 km upstream, and was impressed with the area's potential for settlement. The area was not as arid as other parts of the coast. Stirling found a plain covered with red gums, stretching towards hills to the east. And there was water. Fraser, a botanist serving with Stirling, was enthusiastic about the soil and vegetation. Obviously, a settlement could be founded on the banks of the river. Perhaps settlers could trade with China, India, Mauritius, and the East Indies. Such a settlement would command the trade routes of the Indian Ocean. The mouth of the river made a good harbour, and was being used already by whalers and sealers. The river itself could be used as a highway.

Stirling dreamed of a new, thriving colony, set up by him, to be called Hesperia, because it would face Hesperus, the evening star. Dreaming was one thing; it was another thing to persuade the British government to approve of the scheme. Governor Darling persuaded

Figure 19.6. Stirling's bivouac on the banks of the Swan River.

Stirling to travel to Britain to try to find supporters for the new colony.

Thomas Peel

The British government had become wary of establishing another colony in Australia. Each colony had always proved expensive to establish and maintain.

However, Britain would give its approval for a new colony if businessmen were prepared to finance its establishment. Stirling found that the British East India Company was not interested.

Other businessmen were interested, however. One was Thomas Peel, second cousin of Sir Robert Peel, the future British prime minister. Peel joined with two other investors to form a syndicate,

and approached the government. Peel's syndicate would convey 10 000 emigrants to West Australia and settle them on land with stock and equipment, at an estimated cost of £30 per head, in return for a grant of 4 000 000 acres (1 600 000 hectares), valued at one shilling and sixpence (1/6d) per acre, which would repay them for their investment.

However, the government agreed only to a grant of 1 000 000 acres (400 000 hectares) and this only on certain conditions:

- Peel's syndicate would not be allowed a monopoly.
- Any settler would be allowed to purchase land at a rate of 1/6d per acre, the 1/6d invested in stock and equipment.
- Two hundred additional acres

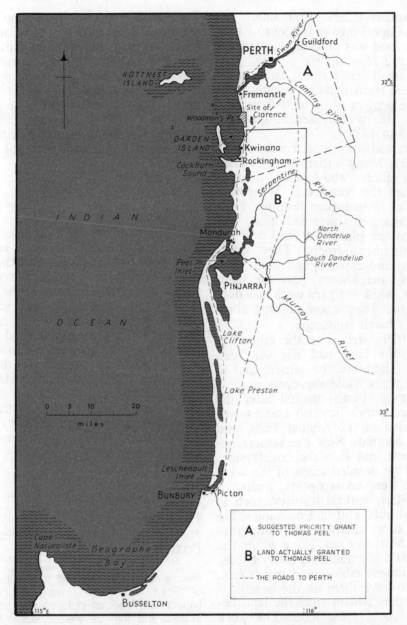

Figure 19.7. The Swan River settlement, showing the area of land granted to Thomas Peel.

(80 ha) would be granted for each labour taken out to the new colony.
• The land had to be developed within 10 years of arrival.

When they heard this, Peel's associates withdrew from the scheme. But Peel re-mained committed to it and invested £50 000.

Difficulties of Settlement

In 1829, a warship, HMS *Challenger*,

under Captain C. H. Fremantle, was sent from Cape Town to the Swan River, where the land was officially claimed for Britain (on 2 May 1829).

Soon a small fleet arrived, carrying the first settlers from Britain. Stirling came with these settlers as the first lieutenant governor. (He was lieutenant governor from 1829 to 1839.)

Peel arrived shortly afterwards with 300 settlers. Many settlers were ex-army and naval officers who had lost their incomes when the Napoleonic Wars ended. Most of them lacked farming skills. Many gentlemen imagined that they would acquire plenty of land and become gentlemen-farmers. They would hunt, fish, and explore, and their wives would visit neighbours, play the piano and cards, while the hard work was done by servants. They knew nothing about Australia's harsh landscape.

The settlers arrived in the rainy season, and the land had not yet been surveyed. Therefore the settlers had to shelter in tents while surveyors made a rough survey. Perth, named after the colonial secretary's Scottish home town, was founded on 12 August 1829, and land was allotted. Now the settlers began to move out into the countryside. They had no detailed maps of the area, and there were no signposts, roads, or bridges. Many natural features, such as creeks and hills, still had no names. No one was sure whether the Aborigines would be hostile or not. For a while, the settlers could not transport heavy goods, such as pianos, tables, and wardrobes, and had to leave them on the beach.

The settlers had to clear the land before they could grow food. The work was not easy — it was blistering and back-breaking, and some tools and implements were inferior. More settlers continued to arrive. Because there were few surveyors, land could not be surveyed fast enough.

Rich men purchased large holdings, for an investment if not for farming, and poorer settlers and later arrivals had to accept land further away from Perth.

The small population became widely scattered and difficult to administer. Also, settlers on the outskirts were attacked by Aborigines. Servants and others did not want to risk farming.

The colony had a shortage of currency, and no one wanted to employ men on public works, such as roads, bridges, and buildings. The British government did not want to employ them either.

Disappointment

The land soon proved a disappointment. The coastal soils of limestone and sand were poor, wheat failed, and the native grasses failed to nourish the colony's sheep and cattle. In winter, the ground flooded. In summer, it was scorched, and crops withered. To the east, the Darling Ranges contained good patches of soil, but were covered in dense forest, which had to be cleared. To the south there was hardwood forest, which was very hard to clear.

Not surprisingly, many settlers became discouraged, and left for the eastern colonies, hoping for more success there.

Not a Garden of Eden

Lieutenant-Governor James Stirling's opinion of the first settlement near Perth:

People came out expecting to find the Garden of Eden and some ... were astonished at finding hard work an indispensable preliminary to meat and drink. All were in fact in a state of disappointment ...

The plan which was adopted in the formation of this settlement may be viewed as an experiment in colonisation on a new principle. The expenses incurred in the transport of settlers to their place of destination, in the operations of agriculture, and in every other branch of industry, were to be defrayed out of their own funds, the Government having given no other pledge than that a small civil and military establishment should be provided for protection, and for the despatch of public business, and that land should be distributed on the most liberal terms.

It so happened that these inducements, co-operating with the novelty of the undertaking and the misrepresentations, and amplifications of interested individuals, were quite sufficient to attract a large body of emigrants to the shores of the new colony. Of those who came, a certain portion were efficient people of respectability and means, but many were adventurers without conduct, capital or industry, and a large number of indigent families were induced to embark for a settlement where no provision had been made for their maintenance by those who were interested in getting them out of England.

. . . Had the settlers been all equally industrious and well provided, as the best of them, there were enough to have accomplished rapidly and successfully the establishment of a colony . . . But so small a proportion of the community being fit for the task which they had undertaken, it has been only partially successful, the credit of which is due alone to those whose industry, intelligence and means have enabled them at this moment to consider themselves not only established but secure in a great measure of the reward of their exertions. All others except that class have suffered severely.

. . . The truth is that very few persons can imagine previously the difficulties and irretrievable losses which are met with in all such enterprises. But even where there is spirit and resolution to overcome all these, there is incurred in establishing an emigrant in a new country a long continued outlay before any return can be looked for, during which period if the settler's means fail, all his exertions are lost and his property ruined. His unfinished house or half-cultivated grounds cannot be sold, for the want of capital is the pervading want of the community and while the necessaries of life and labour are high, all that is not absolutely necessary has no marketable value.

E. G. Wakefield's View of the Swan River Settlement

The following is from the evidence of E. G. Wakefield before the Select Committee on the Disposal of Lands in the British Colonies, London, 1836:

What do you consider the most striking practical case of evil resulting from too great a profusion in granting land?:

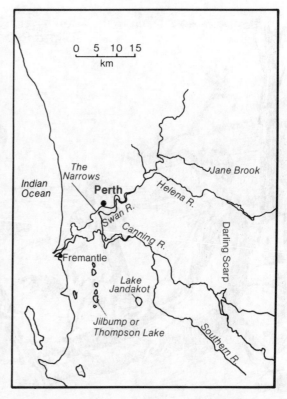

Figure 19.8. The first settlement near Perth on the Swan River.

The most striking because it happens to be the last, is the new settlement of Swan River in Western Australia.

In what way is that the most striking?

That colony which was founded with a general hope in this country, amongst very intelligent persons of all descriptions, that it would be a most prosperous colony, has all but perished. It has not quite perished, but the population is a great deal less than the number of emigrants; it has been a diminishing population since its foundation. The greater part of the capital which was taken out (and that was very large) has disappeared altogether, and a great portion of the labourers taken out (and they were a very considerable number) have emigrated a second time to Van Diemen's Land and New South Wales. The many disasters which befell this colony (for some people did actually die of Hunger) and the destruction of the colony taken out the Swan River, and the second emigration of people who went out, appear to me to be

Figure 19.9. 'Flourishing State of the Swan River Thing.' An unknown artist's impression of the poor conditions awaiting hopeful immigrants.

accounted for at once by the manner in which land was granted. The first grant consisted of 500 000 acres (200 000 ha) to an individual, Mr Peel. That grant was marked out upon the map in England — 500 000 acres were taken round about the port or landing-place. It was quite impossible for Mr Peel to cultivate 500 000 acres, or a hundredth part of the grant; but others were of course necessitated to go beyond his grant, in order to take their land. So that the first operation in that colony was to create a great desert, to mark out a large tract of land, and to say, 'This is a desert — no man shall come here; no man shall cultivate this land'. So far dispersion was produced, because upon the terms on which Mr Peel obtained his land, land was given to others. The Governor took another 100 000 acres (40 000 ha), another person took 80 000 acres (32 000 ha); and this

dispersion was so great that at last, the settlers did not know where they were; that is, each settler knew that he was where he was, but he could not tell where anybody else was; and, therefore, he did not his own position. That was why some people died of hunger; for though there was an ample supply of food at the Governor's house, the settlers did not know where the Governor was, and the Governor did not know where the settlers were.

Then, besides the evils resulting from dispersion, there occurred what I consider almost a greater one; which is, the separation of the people and the want of combinable labour. The labourers, on finding out that land could be obtained with the greatest facility (and despite that they were under contracts which assured them very high wages if they would labour during a certain time for wages) immediately laughed at their masters. Mr Peel carried out altogether about 300 persons, men, women, and children. Of those 300 persons, about 60 were able labouring men. In six months after his arrival he had nobody even to make his bed for him or to fetch him water from the river. He was obliged to make his own bed and to fetch water for himself, and to light his own fire. All the labourers left him. The capital, therefore, which he took out, viz., implements of husbandry, seeds and stock, especially stock, immediately perished; without shepherds to take care of the sheep, the sheep wandered and were lost; eaten by the native dogs, killed by the natives and by some of the other colonists, very likely by his own workmen; but they were soon destroyed; his seeds perished on the beach; his houses were of no use; his wooden houses were there in frame, in pieces, but could not be put together, and were therefore quite useless and rotted on the beach. This was the case with the capitalists generally.

The labourers, obtaining land very readily, and running about to fix upon locations for themselves, and to establish themselves independently, very soon separated themselves into isolated families, into what may be termed cottiers, with a very large extent of land, something like the Irish cottiers, but having, instead of a very small piece of land, a large extent of land. Everyone was separated, and very soon fell into the greatest distress. Falling into the greatest distress, they returned to their masters, and insisted upon the fulfilment of the agreements upon which they had gone out; but then Mr Peel said, 'All my capital has gone; you have ruined me by deserting me, by breaking your engagements; and you now insist upon my observing the engagements when you yourselves have deprived me of the means of doing so'. They wanted to hang him, and he ran away to a distance, where he secreted himself for a time till they were carried off to Van Diemen's Land, where they obtained food, and where, by the way, land was not obtainable by any means with so great a facility as at Swan River.

There are some settlers remaining at the Swan River. Have they taken means to secure labour in the way of slaves?:

They have not attained that object but they have sent a deliberate petition to the Government here, praying that one of the conditions under which the Swan River colony was founded, namely, that convicts should never be sent there, might be (changed) in their favour; that they might be favoured with the services of convicts from England; for that unless that were

granted to them, it was quite impossible for them to do any good in the colony.

One Settler Who Was Determined to Stay

The following letter was written by a settler, Mr W. L. Brockman, to a Mr T. Du Boulay, of Shaftesbury, Dorset, in 1833. Brockman had lost his house in a fire, and Mr Du Boulay, a relative, had placed £200 to his credit with English agents, and was prepared to lend him another £300 if necessary:

Woodbridge, 30 January 1833

Dear Du Boulay,

... The money you have so opportunely placed to my credit in my agent's hands will enable me to build myself a comfortable house at Herne Hill, which I should not otherwise have been able to complete.

... I was obliged to make some sacrifice in my breeding stock last winter in consequence of my loss, it being next to impossible to borrow money here even at the enormous rate of 30 per cent; but my crops of corn have turned out so well that I hope soon to be able to replace them. My growth of wheat this year I expect will yield about 900 bushles (33 cubic metres) ...

... We suffer much inconvenience here from the want of a bank. Any capitalist starting a banking establishment on a liberal scale would be certain of realising a large fortune, and the Colony would be most materially benefited by it.

... The climate of this country I should think as fine as any in the world; the spring, autumn and winter are delightful; the summers perhaps a little too hot; the nights however cool, and seldom many very hot days in succession.

As to the land, we have as poor, and as rich soils, as any perhaps in the world, but plenty of the latter for all our purposes, and ... this year, if the Government encourage the growth of corn by making contracts with the settlers, there will be sufficient, or nearly so, grown for the consumption of the Colony.

... Left as we have been to fight our way unassisted through innumerable difficulties, this Colony has made most rapid strides, and its success is now complete ... Our exports are mahogany and wool. I am paying great attention to the latter, and hope next season to have a good specimen to send home. Hitherto I have sold my wool in the Colony, being determined to send none home in my own name till I can spend such as will do me credit.

... Believe me, very truly yours
(*Signed*) W. L. Brockman.

Arrival of the Convicts

By 1844, the price of land had risen to £1 per acre, people were continuing to leave the colony, and there was a labour shortage. In that year, the colonists were compelled to ask the British government to send convicts to the settlement. Convicts could be used as a cheap labour force, and the British authorities would have to spend money on their upkeep. This would benefit the colony.

The British government was willing to send convicts to the colony, and the first shipload arrived on 1 June 1850. At first, these men lived in rented lodgings, sheds, and stores. Fortunately, they were well-chosen men, and there was little trouble. Convicts sent to Western Australia were fortunate in that they were not treated as brutally as convicts in New South Wales and Van Diemen's Land. A jail was finished in Perth in 1856, and in Fremantle in 1857.

Before long, the convicts had built a new government house, pensioners' barracks, town hall, and marketplace. There were no more labour problems, and finance was more readily available. Convicts and ex-convicts and guards all required food, which was supplied by the farmers. The results were as hoped for.

The End of Transportation

Between 1850 and 1870, the population of Western Australian increased fivefold. By 1870, there were 25 000 people in the settlement.

By the late 1860s, convicts made up a large percentage of the population. These convicts were all males, since no female convicts were sent to Western

Australia. Many free settlers had misgivings, fearing that the moral tone of the colony would be lowered. Also, the colony could not have responsible government while transportation continued. (Responsible government had been granted to the other colonies during the 1850s.)

The attitude of the British government changed, and it was now less in favour of transportation, which had become expensive and did not relieve pressure on British jails. Therefore transportation ceased in January 1868.

The discovery of gold in 1886 brought in miners, and ensured the success of the colony.

Questions

(1) Why was Western Australia first settled?
(2) Who established the military-convict station at Albany?
(3) Why did Stirling think the Swan River was a good site for a settlement?
(4) Why was the British government at first reluctant to settle the Swan River?
(5) What was Peel's plan for settlement?
(6) Who claimed Western Australia for Britain?
(7) When did the first settlers arrive at the Swan River?
(8) Describe some of the difficulties faced by the early settlers.
(9) Why were convicts sent to Western Australia?
(10) What effects did transportation have on the development of Western Australia?

Research

Find out more about the following.
(1) J. Dumont d'Urville
(2) Captain James Stirling
(3) Thomas Peel
(4) Early settlement
(5) Convicts in Western Australia.

Chapter 20

Wakefield and South Australia

Figure 20.1. Edward Gibbon Wakefield.

Figure 20.2. Captain Charles Sturt.

Charles Sturt's Discovery

New South Wales suffered a bad drought in 1829, so many settlers were keen to find water and fresh pastures. Captain Charles Sturt left Sydney in that year with a small party. They wanted to find water, pastures, and the directions of the rivers west of the Blue Mountains.

Sturt and his party sailed down the Murrumbidgee River in a whaleboat, and turned into the unexplored Murray. The party then followed the Murray downstream for more than 2500 km. The men camped at night on the banks, keeping a lookout for hostile Aborigines and noting good farming and grazing land.

Finally Sturt emerged at Lake Alexandrina, at the mouth of the Murray, in 1830. When he returned to Sydney, he reported that he had found good land for settlement. This news was carried back to Britain.

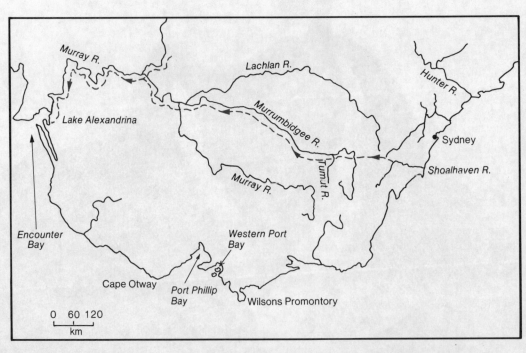

Figure 20.3. The journey made by Sturt and his party in 1829.

Edward Gibbon Wakefield and the Systematic Colonizers

While Sturt was exploring the Murrumbidgee and the Murray, a number of theorists and writers in England were turning their attention to the matter of colonization. In England, Scotland, and Ireland, there was not enough land and too many workers. Overseas, however, there were new, wide lands, sparsely inhabited by natives, waiting to be settled. This land should be developed, and the natives should be taught 'civilization'. Colonies like New South Wales and Van Diemen's Land had a shortage of labourers. The problem was how to transplant workers from one side of the world to the other, effectively and economically, to benefit both Britain and the colonies.

In 1827, Edward Gibbon Wakefield was sent to Newgate Prison, London, to serve a three-year sentence for the abduction of a young heiress. While he was in jail, he wrote and published a small book entitled *A Letter From Sydney*. This book was serialized in the London *Morning Chronicle*, and widely read.

In the book, Wakefield outlined his plan for the settlement of Australia:

- Land should not be granted free to settlers, nor should it be sold cheaply to them.
- Labourers should have to work hard in the colony, and save their money, before they could afford to buy land.
- Land should be sold at a 'sufficient price' to settlers who could afford it.
- The money raised from such land sales should then be placed in a fund, and used to bring out labourers from Britain to work for the landowners.
- Settlers should be chosen carefully. They should be young, have skills, and be keen to make a success of their life in Australia.

Wakefield also believed that much could be learned from the early difficulties of colonists in Western Australia. Selling land at a 'sufficient price' would mean that men with a large amount of capital could not purchase large estates, and therefore force out the poorer settlers beyond the reach of markets. Also, Wakefield was not in favour of convict labour, which had ruined the eastern colonies.

Wakefield attracted a number of theorists to his ideas. One was Robert Gouger, a religious dissenter and political radical, who edited Wakefield's book. Charles Buller was another theorist who was prepared to follow Wakefield.

Some influential men even became interested — men like Lord Durham, Lord Howard, Sir William Molesworth, and the Earl of Ripon. The followers of Wakefield and Gouger came to be called the Systematic Colonizers. They began a National Colonization Society in London.

The South Australian Land Company

At this time came the news of Sturt's discovery of the Gulf St Vincent area in South Australia. Here, surely, was a place to begin an experimental colony, putting into effect the new ideas of Wakefield and Gouger. This colony would be far removed from the convict settlements of New South Wales and Van Diemen's Land.

Because of his term in prison, Wakefield found himself eased out of polite society, and Gouger had to carry on in his name. In 1831, he submitted three plans for settlement to the colonial office. He also became secretary of a specially formed South Australian Land Company.

The colonial office was suspicious of the plans. How much would all this cost the government? Were Wakefield and his associates interested only in making a profit for themselves?

The South Australian Association

The South Australian Land Company folded late in 1833. It was followed by a

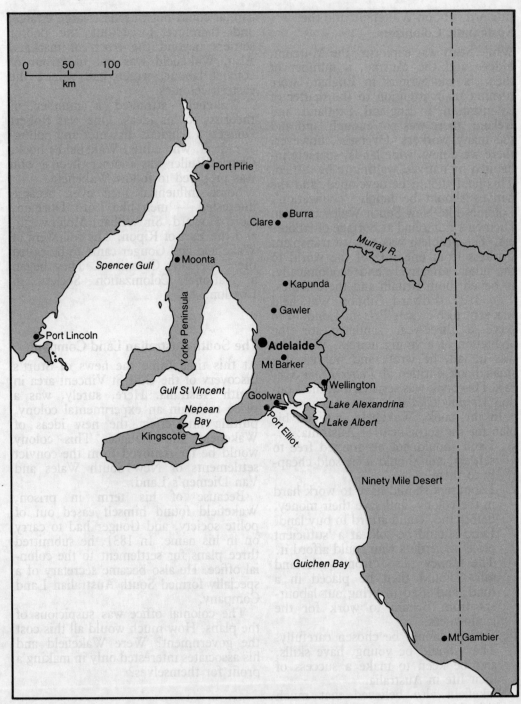

Figure 20.4. The coastline of South Australia. Gulf St Vincent was the site chosen for the first settlement.

new South Australian Association, led by Gouger and George Grote, who was a scholar and parliamentarian.

The new association managed to convince the government to try its plan.

The result was the *South Australia Act* of 1834. Under this Act:

- There would be dual control of the colony. The colonial office would appoint a lieutenant-governor, and a

BY ORDER OF THE

Colonization Commissioners

FOR HIS MAJESTY'S PROVINCE OF

South Australia

Notice is hereby given, that from and after the 15th Day of July next, the Commissioners will

SELL ORDERS

FOR

Town and Country Sections

OF LAND,

Entitling the holders to priority of choice; and will receive applications from such intending Settlers as may wish to have Servants or Labourers conveyed to the Colony Free of Cost by means of the

Emigration Fund.

The GOVERNOR, COLONIAL COMMISSIONER, and other CHIEF OFFICERS, will depart about the beginning of the month of SEPTEMBER next, or as soon as the preliminary arrangements shall be completed.

Copies of the Regulations for the Disposal of Public Land and the Emigration of Labourers, may be obtained at the Office, *No. 61, Lincoln's Inn Fields,* where persons desirous of purchasing Land are requested to apply, & where a Register of such applications will be immediately opened, & continued in the order of application.

By Order of the Board. ROWLAND HILL, *Sec.*

MARTIN & CO. Lithographers & Printers, 26, Long Acre.

Figure 20.5. The official land sale notice issued in England to settlers intending to migrate to South Australia.

Figures 20.6 to Figure 20.13. Early settlers who arrived aboard HMS Buffalo in 1836. These eight Adelaide citizens were only young boys when they landed in South Australia with their parents in 1836. The photographs were taken at a banquet in 1871 to celebrate the opening of the Adelaide Town Hall.

Figure 20.6. Samuel Chapman.   *Figure 20.7. Sir James Hurtle Fisher.*

Figure 20.8. William Langley.   *Figure 20.9. James W. Adams.*

Figure 20.10. John Harris.

Figure 20.11. William Thompson.

Figure 20.12. Robert Frazier Russell.

Figure 20.13. James Cronk.

Figure 20.14. Governor George Gawler.

the price of land was too low. It was not, he argued, a 'sufficient' price. He was disillusioned and felt powerless, and so he refused to have anything further to do with the scheme.

Meanwhile, John Hindmarsh, a naval officer with considerable experience, was appointed as governor. J. H. Fisher was appointed resident commissioner. Speculators and investors came forward to found the South Australian Company.

The new company was dominated by George Fife Angas, who was a Baptist and a businessman. The company was prepared to invest in whaling, real estate, and banking. Its capital gave a great boost to the whole project. Members of the company also assisted the authorities to select settlers and labourers. Many who asked to go to South Australia were philosophical radicals in politics and religion. Many also had high standards of culture and education.

resident commissioner would be appointed by a board of commissioners in London. The commissioner would be responsible for land sales and immigration.

- Land would be sold in South Australia at a minimum price of 12 shillings per acre. The money would be used to pay the costs of administration, and to bring out labourers.

- No convicts would be sent to the colony.

- Responsible government would be granted when the population of the colony reached 50 000. In the meantime, the lieutenant governor would be assisted by a nominee council.

Preparing to Settle South Australia

Wakefield hoped to be offered a place on the board of commissioners, and was annoyed when he was not. He also felt

Problems of Settlement

In 1836, 546 settlers arrived in South Australia. They arrived at different times, in the *Duke of York*, the *John Pirie*, the *Lady Mary Pelham*, the *Sarah and Elizabeth*, the *South Australian*, the *Rapid*, and HMS *Buffalo*.

The *Duke of York* arrived first, on 29 July. At first the passengers settled on Kangaroo Island. They found they were not the first white settlers there. A few whalers, sealers, and wallaby-skin hunters had squatted on the island. The settlers pitched tents ashore, began to build shelters, cleared some land, and planted some vegetables. Some of the early squatters helped them.

On 20 August 1836, the surveyor-general, Colonel Light, arrived in the brig *Rapid*. He brought with him a number of assistants, including Lieutenant Field, RN, Messrs J. S. Pullen, W. Hill, W. Jacob, G. Claughton (all surveyors), together with Dr Woodford, Mr A. Baker, mate, and other survey hands. Light set about his work before the governor, Hindmarsh, arrived. Hindmarsh did not arrive until 28 December, in HMS *Buffalo*.

Colonel Light examined Kangaroo Island and the mouth of the Murray, and decided that both were unsuitable for settlement. He then examined the eastern shore of Gulf St Vincent, and decided that Port Adelaide Inlet and Holdfast Bay were most suitable. They were good anchorages.

By March 1837, Light and his assistants had surveyed the site of Adelaide, naming the future city after the wife of King William IV. However, by this time tempers had become frayed. The strict, religious dissenters objected to the immoral behaviour of some of the other settlers. A number of questions were also asked. Why had the surveyors arrived so late? Why had the governor arrived so late? Hindmarsh and Fisher quarrelled over the site of the settlement. In fact, Hindmarsh seemed to quarrel with nearly everyone.

So far, no land had been surveyed for the settlers in the country. Light needed more helpers, and wrote to the commissioners in England, asking for assistance. The commissioners misunderstood the problem, criticized and censured him for not doing enough, and Light resigned in protest. When he did this, his staff resigned as well.

Settlers continued to arrive in great numbers, but little land was surveyed in the country. They had to wait around Adelaide and could not go straight to work.

Governor Gawler

In October 1838, both Hindmarsh and Fisher were recalled. They were replaced by George Gawler, who was to act as both governor and resident commissioner.

By now, there were 5000 settlers in Adelaide, the land outside the settlement was still unsurveyed, there were no main roads, bridges, or public buildings, men could not work, and salaries were unpaid. Many men of capital had invested their money in town lands, in order to speculate on rising prices. They had no intention of developing farms in the countryside. Settlers began leaving for the eastern colonies, where they could buy land more easily and cheaply. The new colony, in fact, seemed to be facing disaster.

Gawler went to work. He increased the number of surveyors and set them to work in the country. He engaged the unemployed in public works, including much-needed roads and new buildings.

Like Macquarie, Gawler spent a good deal of money. He drew bills on the board of commissioners, which eventually ran out of funds. In August 1840, the board went bankrupt. The colonial office could not afford this. The colony could not be abandoned, but spending could be cut back. The government paid some

Figure 20.15. An early sketch of the road to Adelaide.

Figure 20.16. Governor George Grey.

Figure 20.17. Lashbrook Farm, South Australia.

outstanding debts, deprived the board of commissioners of power, and appointed a new governor with instructions to reduce government expenditure and increase revenue.

Governor George Grey

Grey was ruthless in carrying out his instructions. He dismissed officials. He stopped public works. Immigration stopped. He reduced the wages of men on relief works. Labourers were expected to work long hours, from 6 a.m. to 6 p.m. He increased taxes all round.

As a result, government expenditure fell from £170 000 in 1840 to £30 000 in 1843. Revenue during the same period fell from £30 000 to £24 000.

Hundreds of men were thrown out of work, and Grey became very unpopular. Petitions were sent to Britain pleading for his recall. A model of him was burned in the street, and some men marched on Government House, threatening to attack him.

Two years later, however, it became apparent that things would improve:

- Grey had made things so uncomfortable in the city that many people moved out on to the land. Many who had been thrown out of work in the

Figure 20.18. Adelaide and its villages in 1845.

By the end of 1842, there was almost no unemployment.

- In 1842, Bull and Ridley invented an automatic harvester, which greatly assisted harvesting.
- Between 1841 and 1845, silver, lead, and copper were discovered and mined at Glen Osmond, Kapunda, and Burra.
- Immigration began again in 1844.

Grey left the colony in October 1845.

The Wine Industry

Between 1838 and 1839, some 500 German farmers from Silesia settled at Klemzig and Hahndorf. These people had come to Australia to escape religious persecution at home. They established farms and became self-supporting. Others followed, and by 1860 their numbers had increased to about 8000. They were active in establishing a wine-making industry in South Australia, especially in the Barossa Valley. They also helped to develop agriculture elsewhere in the colony.

Figure 20.19. Wine-making in South Australia. The Auldana Cellar.

city found jobs as agricultural labourers. Thus labour was cheap, and assisted the farmers.
- Farms prospered, and more land was taken up and developed. Food became cheaper.
- Unemployment decreased gradually.

179

Was Wakefield's Scheme a Success?

To be fair to the man, his scheme was never put into practice as he had wished. He did not understand Australian conditions, or the problems involved in developing a pastoral industry. Neither did the first settlers. Wakefield is important because of his influence. He inspired men to try to found a colony that was not based on convict labour.

Questions

(1) Who discovered Lake Alexandrina?
(2) What 'problem' did English colonizers seek to solve in 1830?
(3) Outline Wakefield's plan for the successful colonization of Australia.
(4) Who were some of the people who supported Wakefield?
(5) Outline the provisions of the South Australian Act of 1834.
(6) Who was appointed first governor of South Australia?
(7) Describe some of the difficulties encountered by these early settlers.
(8) Name some of the early settlers of South Australia.
(9) Why was Governor Grey unpopular?
(10) Name five villages close to Adelaide in 1845.

Research

Find out more about the following.
(1) Wakefield and his theories.
(2) Hindmarsh
(3) Fisher
(4) Gawler
(5) Grey.

Chapter 21

The Rush for Gold

Early Finds

Australia is a land rich in minerals. As Australia's population increased slowly, more land was explored and settled, and convicts, explorers, bushmen, and others began to discover gold:

- **James McBrien** found gold on the Fish River, 24 km east of Bathurst, in February 1823.
- **Count Strzelecki** found gold near Hartley, near Lithgow, in 1839. La-

Figure 21.1. 'The Argus Flat Gold Mining Company Claim, Forest Creek.' The discovery of gold brought with it not only new prosperity, but also dramatic changes in the social and political life of the colonies.

ter he found more gold at Bathurst.

- **The Reverend W. B. Clarke** found gold, again in the Lithgow area.
- In 1848, **McGregor** found gold quartz at Wellington. It assayed in London at 800 grams to the tonne.

However, these early discoveries did not provoke a gold rush. Different reasons have been given for this. It has been suggested that the authorities were afraid of the trouble that a gold rush might cause. For instance, there might be convict riots. When Clarke showed Governor Gipps samples of the gold he had found, Gipps is supposed to have told him: 'Put it away, Mr Clarke, or we shall all have our throats cut'.

It is more probable that, at that time, no one knew much about gold mining. All gold and silver that was found belonged to the government. Prospectors could not keep the gold they found. The best they could hope for was a reward. Also, gold was not found in large amounts.

Edward Hammond Hargraves

Hargraves is important because he helped to create the first gold rush in Australia.

Figure 21.2. Edward Hammond Hargraves.

He was born in England, and worked in Australia at various occupations before travelling to the goldfields of California in July 1849. He had fair success on those fields.

One of the things he learned was how to identify country where gold was likely to be found. He realized that country of a similar nature existed in New South Wales. Eventually, he left the Californian fields and sailed back to Australia, arriving in Sydney on 7 January 1851.

In Sydney, Hargraves borrowed money to buy a horse and provisions, and then rode over the Blue Mountains to the rugged valleys beyond Bathurst. There he teamed up with a young bushman, John Lister, and taught him the skills of prospecting, using pan and cradle. They washed their first pan of gold in the junction of the Summer Hill and Lewis Ponds Creeks, at Ophir, some 32 km north of Bathurst. Later, Lister and William Tom found more gold, and gave it to Hargraves.

Hargraves went back to Sydney and bargained with the authorities. He would disclose the location of the gold finds, for a reward of £500. Deas Thomson, the colonial secretary, was not in a bargaining mood, however. He told Hargraves he must trust to the government's generosity. Hargraves then named the localities.

The New South Wales Gold Rush

The rush was now on. The authorities were bewildered, and could do nothing to stop it. Men from all walks of life were struck suddenly with gold fever, and left their jobs for Ophir. Within three months, about 400 miners were camped there. By the end of the year, this number had increased to 2000.

Some miners sought to escape paying a licence fee of 30 shillings by moving north to the Turon River. Gold was then discovered on this river, and another field sprang up. By the end of 1851, Sofala had become the main centre, with 4000 miners.

The £500 reward was paid to Hargraves, he was appointed a Commissioner of Crown Lands and, in October 1853, he was granted a further sum of £10 000 by the New South Wales government. Later, the Victorian government paid him £2381 because his efforts had stimulated a search for gold in Victoria.

Gold Discoveries in Victoria

The gold rushes in New South Wales attracted a number of people from Victoria. This concerned Melbourne businessmen, who put pressure on the government. Victoria, now an independent colony, needed to retain its population. If gold were discovered in Victoria, it would gain increased population and prosperity. A Gold Discovery Committee was formed, and a reward of 200 guineas was offered to anyone finding payable gold within 320 km of Melbourne.

This reward was claimed the very next day (10 June 1851). One claimant was William Campbell, who had found gold at Clunes in 1850 and kept quiet about it.

Another find followed. James William Esmond, who, like Hargraves, had been

Figure 21.3. James William Esmond.

to California, had found gold at Clunes, north of Ballarat, on 29 June 1851.

Gold was found next in the Buninyong Ranges, near Ballarat, in August 1851.

Then, in December, came news of a discovery at Bendigo.

By the end of 1851, the goldfields of Victoria were attracting more miners than those of New South Wales. They also promised to be richer fields.

The Land They Found

Social Upheaval

The discovery of gold had an immense impact on the cities, small townships, and the countryside during the first few years of the rushes. Here is an extract from the Bathurst *Free Press*, dated 17 May 1851. It describes some of the excitement which followed the discoveries of Hargraves, Lister, and Tom:

The discovery of the fact by Mr Hargraves that the country from the mountain ranges to an indefinite extent into the interior is one immense goldfield has produced a tremendous excitement in the town of Bathurst and the surrounding districts. For several days after our last publication, the business of the town was utterly paralyzed. A complete mental madness appears to have seized almost every member of the community — and as a natural consequence there has been a universal rush to the diggings. Groups of people were to be seen early on Monday morning at every corner of the streets, assembled in solemn conclave, debating both possibilities and impossibilities and eager to pounce on any human being who was likely to give any information about the diggings. People of all trades, callings, and pursuits were quickly transformed into miners, and many a hand which had been trained to kid gloves, or accustomed to wield nothing heavier than the grey goose-quill became nervous to clutch the pick and crowbar or 'rock the cradle' at our infant mines. The blacksmiths of the town could not turn off the picks fast enough, and the manufacture of cradles was the second briskest business of the place. A few left town on Monday equipped for the diggings, but on Tuesday, Wednesday, and Thursday the roads to Summer Hill Creek became alive, literally alive, with new-made miners from every quarter, some armed with picks, others shouldering crowbars or shovels and not a few strung round with washhand basins, tinpots, and colanders.

'Roughest and Dirtiest Set of Vagabonds'

Florence Endershaw, a writer of the time, describes the new miners on the road:

From Sydney hundreds of parties were pro-

ceeding daily; each town upon the road, each farm by the wayside and every branch thoroughfare from the surrounding districts contributed its due proportion to the crowd that daily thronged the road to this newly reported El Dorado.

Gentlemen of no occupation, gentlemen of undoubted wealth, professional gentlemen, squatters, clerks, merchants, farmers, tradesmen, mechanics, and labourers, with old men, and even women and children, flocked in one continuous stream. In spite of the wide difference of character and habits, they looked the roughest and dirtiest and habits, they looked the roughest and dirtiest set of vagabonds I almost ever beheld. Blue shirts, red shirts, and striped shirts, belts like a brigand's, boots like a Spanish muleteer's, and hats in inconceivable variety . . . their outfits and equipment were very nearly all alike; the same complement of picks, cradles, shovels, tin dishes, and the like . . . along miles of deep and heavy sandy road and over mountains rough and steep. Then, too, when night came on and camping became necessary, were to be seen thousands of persons who had never passed a night out of their beds in their lives, now lining the road and lying on the ground, in every conceivable state of discomfort and confusion.

Desertion of the Towns

The Victorian Lieutenant Governor, Charles La Trobe, reported to the British government:

Within the last three weeks, the towns of Melbourne and Geelong and their large suburbs have been in appearance almost emptied of many classes of their male inhabitants; the streets, which for a week or ten days were crowded by drays loading with the outfit for the workings, are now seemingly deserted. Not only have the idlers to be found in every community, and day labourers in town and the adjacent country, shopmen, artisans, and mechanics of every description thrown up their employments, and in most cases, leaving their employers and their wives and families to take care of themselves, run off to the workings, but responsible tradesmen, farmers, clerks of every grade, and not a few of the superior classes have followed . . .

Cottages are deserted, houses to let, busi-

Figure 21.5. A miner's hut at Forest Creek.

ness is at a stand-still, and even schools are closed. In some of the suburbs not a man is left, and the women are known for self-protection to group together to keep house. The ships in the harbour are, in a geat measure, deserted; and we hear of instances, where not only farmers and respectable agriculturalists have found that the only way, as those employed by them deserted, was to leave their farms, join them, and form a band, and go shares, but even masters of vessels, foreseeing the impossibility of maintaining any control over their men otherwise, have made up parties among them to do the same. Fortunate the family, whatever its position, which retains its servants at any sacrifice, and can further secure the wonted supplies of their households from the few tradesmen who remain, and retain the means of supplying their customers at any augmentation of price. Drained of its labouring population, the price of provisions in the towns is naturally on the increase . . . Both here and at Geelong all buildings and contract works, public and private, almost without exception, are at a standstill.

Life and Works on the Diggings

Once they had arrived on a gold field, miners put up white calico tents or bark huts for shelter. A few stayed in boarding houses or hotels, once they were built. If they had not brought equipment to the field, they had to buy it there. Miners needed a pan, pick, shovel, hoe, crowbar, a puddling tub, cradle, axe, as well as general camping equipment and stores. Often miners formed small partnerships to defray expenses and share the workload. Licences were bought and claims staked. Claims were four metres square. This area was not large, but it could contain considerable alluvial gold.

At first a miner dug a shaft straight down, through the alluvial top strata, into old pipeclay and slate beds underneath. In some areas, this shaft could go down to a depth of 50 metres. From this

Figure 21.6. Deep-shaft mining at Ballarat.

Figure 21.8. Washing Out a Good Prospect. (*A contemporary photograph by Antoine Fauchery.*)

Figure 21.7. Puddling machine.

main shaft, miners dug out horizontal shafts called 'drives' or 'cross cuts'. (Miners sometimes tunnelled into one another.) A windlass of bush timber was erected over the top of the shaft.

One miner worked down the shaft, filling up buckets of 'washdirt'. A second miner winched the buckets to the top of the shaft.

This dirt had to be washed to see if it contained any gold. The miner first 'puddled' the dirt in a large tub, using a spade to swirl the dirt around in the water. This process got rid of the sticky mud, which floated out into the water, leaving only sand, gravel, and — he hoped — gold at the bottom.

He shovelled this residue into the 'hopper', or top part of his cradle, poured water through the hopper, and rocked the cradle at the same time. Fine sand and — again hopefully — gold would pass down into the receiver below.

The miner checked the gravel that was left in the hopper for gold nuggets, then threw it away. Then he placed the sand in a tin dish and washed it at the edge of a creek or pool. The sand swirled away slowly out of the dish. If there were any gold in the sand, it remained as small, glittering specks in the bottom of the dish. The miner lifted these out with his thumb and fingers, and added them to this pouch.

The mining process was slow and painstaking, and it went on all day, from dawn till dusk, six days a week. (Miners rested on Sundays.)

Before long, miners could pay to have their wash dirt carted to a creek or pond for washing. Puddling machines were also introduced onto the goldfields. Some of these were powered by horses. Owners of these machines made a living by puddling the washdirt of miners for a small charge. The owners of the dirt would watch closely, and finish the process themselves.

186

Figure 21.9. The story of gold at Pegleg Gully, Victoria.

Not all gold was alluvial (surface gold able to be washed out in water). Reef or lode gold was embedded in veins of quartz. To retrieve this gold, the miner had to crush the quartz. Some of the quartz was pounded and crushed by hand in a 'dolly' — a stout iron or steel pot which acted as a mortar. Eventually, miners carted their quartz to a battery — a crushing machine — and paid to have their quartz crushed beneath the machine's steam-powered stampers.

Miners kept some gold dust or nuggets for use in an emergency, and sold the rest to the government. It was taken, under trooper escort, to the city. A trooper escort was needed because sometimes bushrangers attempted to hold up shipments.

When some of the miners had gained enough gold, they would go on a spending spree, either on the field, in a nearby town, or in the city. Some miners made and lost a small fortune overnight. Some miners made a tidy sum and returned home. Many miners struggled to survive on the field, then turned to other employment. Most miners did not 'strike it rich'.

A Lucky Find

Two extremely lucky miners were John Deason and Richard Oates. They arrived in Melbourne from England in 1854. They spent some time mining around Bendigo, with little success, then decided to settle on the land. They took up a block of land at Moliagul about 12 km north of Dunolly, in central Victoria. They decided that they would work the land for a living, and search for gold in their spare time. Several small nuggets had been found in the area, and they hoped they might still find payable gold. They found a small, alluvial deposit and worked this for seven years.

On 5 February 1869, Deason went to work their claim, while Oates worked in a paddock close by, hand-threshing wheat. Deason decided to remove four loads of washdirt for puddling. He removed three, and was working on his fourth when his pick struck something hard just under the surface of the earth. At first he thought that his pick had struck a boulder, and he began to prise it out of the earth. In so doing, he broke the handle of his pick.

He took another pick, prised up the boulder, and was surprised to find that his boulder was really a large gold nugget, covered with soil and gravel. The nugget measured about 61 cm long, and more than 30 cm wide.

Deason and Oates buried the nugget until nightfall, then carted it to Deason's house and hid it in the fireplace, behind the fire. The next day, they concealed the nugget in a box and took it to the bank in Dunolly, where they deposition it on the floor of the manager's office. Everyone present was amazed at its size. When they attempted to weigh the nugget, they discovered that the bank's scales were not large enough. Archie Wells, the local blacksmith, had to break it up so that it could be weighed.

Deason and Oates had finally struck it rich. Their find was the largest alluvial nugget found in the world, and was nicknamed the 'Welcome Stranger'.

Gold Miner's Song

With My Swag All On My Shoulder

When first I left old England's shore, such yarns as we were told,
As how folks in Australia could pick up lumps of gold!
So, when we got to Melbourne Town, we were ready soon to slip
And get even with the captain; all hands scuttled from the ship!

Chorus:
With my swag all on my shoulder, black billy in my hand,
I travelled the bush of Australia like a true-born naive man!

We steered our course for Geelong Town, north-west to Ballarat,
Where some of us got mighty thin, and some got sleek and fat!
Some tried their luck at Bendigo, and some at Fiery Creek;
I made a fortune in a day — and spent it in a week!

For many years I wandered round as each new rush broke out.
And always had of gold a pound, till alluvial petered out.
'Twas then we took the bush to cruise, glad to get a bite to eat;
The squatters treated us so well, we made a regular beat.

So, round the lighthouse* now I tramp, nor leave it out of sight;
I take it on my left shoulder, and then upon my right.
And then I take it on my back, and oft upon it lie,
It is the best of tucker tracts, so I'll stay here till I die.

Chinese Miners

News of the gold discoveries in Australia spread quickly around the world. Many nationalities were attracted to the diggings — including the Chinese. Chinese miners came to Australia either directly from China or from the Californian diggings.

The first arrivals landed early in the 1850s. They formed themselves into small parties, each of which included experienced miners, and made their way up country to the diggings. A contemporary writer describes their appearance:

They presented a curious appearance to European eyes when seen on the road — their singular-looking garments hanging loosely upon them — slippers turned up at the toes, umbrella-like hats of basket-work — and long bamboos on their shoulders from each end of

* Station homestead generous with food handouts.

188

Figure 21.10. A Chinese joss house. A modern reconstruction at Sovereign Hill, Ballarat.

which were suspended their goods and chattels consisting of tent, blankets, rice-bags, and in some instances, a gold washing cradle. Marching as they did, in Indian file, they presented the appearance exactly of figures on an old tea chest.

Once they reached the gold field, the Chinese established their own camp and went to work. They worked extremely hard. They worked down old abandoned mine shafts. They worked back through tailings and mullock heaps, searching for payable specks that other miners had missed. They stood for hours up to their knees, or even waists, in cold water, scooping up gravel and sand from river or creek beds — while other miners preferred to keep to the edge of the bank.

Unfortunately, the Chinese made no attempt to mix with other miners. They did not try to learn English, or adopt European habits and customs. They isolated themselves and, by so doing, made themselves targets for criticism and hostility. European and colonial-born miners complained about their low standard of living, their opium-smoking, the fact that they were not Christians, the fact that they sent most of the gold they found back to China, the fact that they wasted water, and so on.

There were anti-Chinese riots at Bendigo (1854), Buckland Valley on the Ovens River (1857), Lambing Flat near Young (1861), and at Clunes (1873). During these riots, Chinese property was destroyed and Chinese miners had their pigtails cut off. Two were killed at Lambing Flat.

Eventually, some colonial governments passed legislation restricting the entry of the Chinese. The federal *Immigration Restriction Act* of 1901 restricted 'non-white' entry of migrants to the whole of Australia.

By this time, many Chinese had returned to China. Others had turned to labouring work, such as building

Figure 21.11. The interior of a Chinese gambling house.

Figure 21.12. A gold licence.

railways, market gardening, and laundering. A few became prosperous merchants.

Chinese Immigration

You doubtless read the papers,
  And as men of observation,
Of course you watch the progress
  Of Chinese immigration —
For thousands of these pigtail chaps
  In Adelaide are landing;
And why they let such numbers come
  Exceeds my understanding.

On Emerald Hill it now appears
  A Joss House they've erected;
And they've got an ugly idol there —
  It's just what I expected;
And they offer nice young chickens
  Unto this wooden log;
And sometimes with a sucking pig
  They go the entire hog.

Now some of you, perhaps, may laugh,
  But 'tis my firm opinion,
This colony some day will be
  Under Chinese dominion.

They'll upset the Australian Government,
  The place will be their own;
And an Emperor with a long pigtail,
  Will sit upon the throne.

Trouble on the Gold Fields

The gold fields were by no means quiet, peaceful places, and during the early 1850s a number of disturbances arose. Some of the reasons for these disturbances were:

(1) **The Licensing System.** The cost of administering the gold fields proved enormous. Commissioners and clerks had to be employed. Police had to be posted to keep law and order. Escorts had to be provided for gold shipments. Roads and bridges to the fields had to be built. Government camps and buildings had to be established.

In order to meet these costs, the colonial governments introduced the miner's licence. This cost 30 shillings per miner per month. The licence became extremely unpopular with the miners. Many

Figure 21.13. A licence search. This regular procedure was strongly resented by the miners.

could barely afford to pay 30 shillings each month. Many felt that the fee was unjustified because they had to pay the fee even if they did not find gold.

There were protests against the miner's licence. Four hundred miners staged a protest on the Turon field in New South Wales in February 1853. Soon afterwards, the New South Wales government reduced the fee to 10 shillings per month.

In the same year, in Victoria, there was talk about the possibility of actually increasing the licence fee. A movement called the Red Ribbon Movement was formed to oppose this. Fearing violent protest, the Victorian Government reduced the fee to 20 shillings (£1) per month, or £2 for three months.

In 1854, at Ballarat, miners went so far as to burn their licences. After that, and the Eureka Stockade incident, the Victorian government abolished the licence and replaced it with a much cheaper Miner's Right.

(2) Policing and Licence Searches. Miners objected to the quality of the police on the diggings. Many policemen were hardened ex-convicts from Tasmania, and often they were corrupt and brutal. Other police were just inexperienced. Miners in Victoria called all police 'traps' (or 'Joes', after the governor, Charles Joseph La Trobe).

Licence hunts carried out by these men became very unpopular, and the cause of much excitement and commotion. W. Kelly, a miner, describes one such search at Ballarat, in 1853:

Come up boys — come along quick, the game is started! And as I was being hoisted up I heard the swelling uproar and the loud chorus of 'Joes' (police) from every side.

As I gained the surface everybody was in commotion, diggers with their licences lowering down their mates without them; others with folded arms, cursing the system and damning the government, some 'stealing away' like hares when hounds are in the neighbourhood and several tally-ho'd, bursting for points where they could escape arrest while 'Joe! Joe! Joe! Joe! Joe!' resounded on all sides, the half-clad

Amazons running up the hill-sides like so many bearers of the 'Fiery-cross' to spread to the neighbouring gullies the commencement of the police foray. The police, acting on a pre-concerted plan of attack, kept closing in on their prey.

(3) Decline of Alluvial Gold. Alluvial or surface gold began to decline very rapidly. In 1853, the average earning of a miner was 154 g of gold a month. By 1854, this had fallen to 42 g. Miners had to sink deeper shafts, and work much harder for an income. Most earned approximately 30 shillings a week, and had to pay high prices for just about everything. Eggs cost a shilling each. Potatoes were 1/6 a pound, milk 4 shillings a quart. A bag of flour cost £5.

Given this situation, it was no wonder that miners objected to paying the licence fee. The future rested with the mining companies, who could afford deep mining for lode gold.

(4) Lack of Land. Many miners wished to turn from mining to settling

Figure 21.14. Sir Charles Hotham.

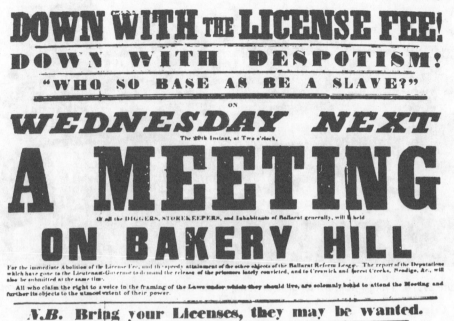

DOWN WITH THE LICENSE FEE!
DOWN WITH DESPOTISM!
"WHO SO BASE AS BE A SLAVE?"

ON

WEDNESDAY NEXT

The 29th Instant, at Two o'clock,

A MEETING

Of all the DIGGERS, STOREKEEPERS, and Inhabitants of Ballarat generally, will be held

ON BAKERY HILL

For the immediate Abolition of the License Fee, and the speedy attainment of the other objects of the Ballarat Reform League. The report of the Deputation which have gone to the Lieutenant-Governor to demand the release of the prisoners lately convicted, and to Creswick and Forest Creeks, Bendigo, &c., will also be submitted at the same time.

All who claim the right to a voice in the framing of the Laws under which they should live, are solemnly bound to attend the Meeting and further its objects to the utmost extent of their power.

N.B. Bring your Licenses, they may be wanted.

Figure 21.15. Public notice of the miners' meeting at Bakery Hill.

on the land. They could invest small amounts in developing small properties. However, this was difficult, because squatters held very large properties, and would not make room for small-time farmers. The squatters were in a powerful position because they were represented in the government. Miners felt that this was extremely unjust.

(5) **Political Radicals and Agitators.** Many miners came to Australia from Europe. A few came from America. Many of these men had radical political ideas. For instance, the English Chartists wanted a genuinely democratic government, under the British Crown. The six points of their famous Charter were:
- Every man to vote
- No property qualifications in order to enter parliament
- Members of parliament to be paid a salary
- Annual general elections
- Equal electoral districts
- Secret ballot.

The Republicans went further. They wanted a complete break with the British Crown and its representatives in Australia.

Some of these men were prepared to stir up trouble on the gold fields. They pointed out that miners had no political rights at all, despite the fact that they were contributing to the prosperity and development of the country. They argued that the whole situation should be changed. They were supported by many of the miners.

(6) **The Chinese.** As we have seen, the presence of the Chinese miners on the gold fields caused resentment among many other miners.

Trouble at Ballarat

In August 1854, Sir Charles Hotham succeeded La Trobe as lieutenant governor of Victoria. He toured the gold fields and found fields like Ballarat to be prosperous. He was determined to increase government revenue. There was a deficit. Obviously, many miners were

Figure 21.16. Troops from Melbourne arriving at the Government Camp, Ballarat, November 1854.

Figure 21.17. Peter Lalor.

not paying their licence fees. This was not good enough for Hotham. He therefore ordered police to conduct licence inspections at least twice a week.

Such an order was sure to provoke a bitter response from the miners, and it did. They felt that they were being suppressed tyrannically.

On 6 October, another infuriating incident occurred. Two miners, James Scobie and Peter Martin, went to the Eureka Hotel for a drink. Unfortunately they had already been drinking, and were drunk. Because of this, they were refused admittance. An argument followed. James Bentley, the hotel proprietor, his wife, and a friend were on one side. Scobie and Martin were on the other side. The two miners were set upon, and Scobie was killed.

Bentley, his wife, and his friend were all accused of the murder, but were acquitted by an inquiry. When this happened, the miners saw red. Bentley was an ex-convict, and was unpopular on the field. The miners suspected bribery and corruption.

On 17 October, about 4000 miners attended a noisy meeting outside the Eureka Hotel to discuss the matter.

They took up a collection to pay for information leading to the arrest and conviction of the person or persons responsible for Scobie's death. The presence of police and mounted troopers at the meeting did nothing to calm matters. The meeting got out of hand. There was shouting and yelling, and objects were thrown. The miners then rioted, and burned down Bentley's hotel.

On 11 November, another, larger meeting was called on Bakery Hill. It is estimated that 11 000 miners attended that meeting, where a Ballarat Reform League was formed. A committee of seven men was appointed to represent the miners. The League determined to work for an improvement in goldfields administration, and an abolition of the detested licensing system.

Bentley was then arrested, tried, and on 23 November found guilty of the manslaughter of Scobie. This pleased the miners. Here, at last, was some justice.

Shortly afterwards, however, three miners arrested after the hotel fire were found guilty of riot. They were McIntyre, Fletcher, and Westerby. The Ballarat Reform League sent three representatives to see the governor, and ask him to release the convicted miners. Hotham refused politely, but promised to investigate conditions on the gold fields and to appoint a miners' representative to the legislative council.

The next day, soldiers from Melbourne reached the gold fields. They were given a rough reception by the miners.

On 29 November, there was yet another meeting, and Frederic Vern, a German, proposed that miners burn their licences. This was done. A flag was also displayed. It had white stars forming a cross on a blue field.

About 500 men swore allegiance to their Southern Cross flag. Peter Lalor, an Irish miner, led them in a loyal oath, a musket in one hand, pointing to the miners' flag, atop a high flagpole, with the other. The oath went: 'We swear by the Southern Cross to stand truly by each other and fight to defend our rights and liberties. Amen.'

Commissioner Rede now responded by ordering another licence check for the next day. His action is important. If he had not ordered such a check, at that time, perhaps a clash could have been avoided.

When the police began rounding up miners who had no licences, there was violent protest. Again there was shouting. Again, stones were thrown. This time, shots were fired, and the Riot Act was read.

Members of the Ballarat Reform League hastily met at Diamond's Store, where they elected Lalor to take command of the situation.

The Eureka Stockade

The miners began to build a rough stockade, which was completed by 2 December. They also acquired muskets, pistols, and pikes, and drilled to fight with them.

2 December was a Saturday so, when the day finished, most miners abandoned the stockade. It was felt that the authorities would not think of attacking the stockade on the sabbath.

Unfortunately, the police, troopers, and soldiers from Melbourne not only decided to attack on the sabbath, but also decided to attack at three o'clock in the morning. The few miners in the stockade were taken by surprise and were defeated quickly. The fighting lasted about 20 minutes.

Later, Lalor described the attack in the *Argus* newspaper (19 April 1855):

About three o'clock on Sunday morning, the alarm was given that 'the enemy' was advancing and I believe that one or two signal shots were fired by our sentries. On discovering the smallness of our number we would have retreated, but it was then too late, as almost immediately the enemy poured in one or two volleys of musketry, which was a plain intimation that we must sell our lives as dearly as we could. There were about 70 men possessing guns, 20 with pikes, and 30 with pistols. But many of those with firearms had no more than one or two rounds of ammunition. Notwithstanding all these deficiencies, I cannot speak too highly of the conduct of the men present . . . when it is considered that the odds were three to one against us . . . and that we were really surprised. As the inhuman brutalities practised by the police are so well known, it is unnecessary for me to repeat them. About 10 minutes after the beginning of the fight . . . I received a musket ball (together with two other smaller bullets) in the left shoulder which shattered my left arm and from the loss of blood I was rendered incapable of further action . . .

Fourteen miners were killed outright during the attack on the Eureka Stockade, and eight died later of wounds. Twelve were wounded, and about 100 taken prisoner. Some of the police ran amok at the close of the battle, and two bystanders were killed. The government lost Captain Wise, the commanding officer, plus five privates. Some property (such as miners' tents) was destroyed.

Victory in the End

The miners lost their battle, but their grievances were heard eventually. A Melbourne public meeting condemned the assault on the stockade, and Foster, the colonial secretary, was forced to resign. A Royal Commission was appointed to examine the whole quesion of the gold fields, and W. C. Haines, the new colonial secretary, promised reforms.

The following year, 13 miners charged with high treason were acquitted. On 27 March, the Report of the Royal Commission was made known. A Miner's Right of £1 per year replaced the old licence, and the holder was given the right to vote.

Gold Discoveries Across Australia

By the end of the century, a large number of gold fields had been discovered and worked across Australia — with varying degrees of success.

Figure 21.18. Miners and soldiers meet in bitter combat during the storming of the Eureka Stockade on Sunday, 3 December 1854.

Effects of the Gold Rushes

The importance of the gold rushes in the course of Australian history cannot be minimized. Some of the far-reaching effects of the rushes were:

- **Increase in Population:** This was the most noticeable effect. The population increase was truly enormous. In 1850, there were about 400 000 people in the colonies. By 1861, there were almost three times this number. In New South Wales, the population almost doubled, while in Victoria it increased seven times over!
- **Changes in Society:** In the past, the squatters and other large landholders had enjoyed considerable privilege and power. Now they were greatly outnumbered by miners and ex-miners. These miners and ex-miners were mostly free spirits. They were not convicts. They held democratic political views. They were impatient about the traditional form of society. They wanted land and the opportunity to invest in business.
- **Democracy within Colonial Governments:** The trend towards democracy had begun before the gold rushes, but the rushes speeded it up. In the first few years after the discovery of gold, democratic reforms included:
  — Manhood suffrage (the vote for all men)
  — Vote by ballot
  — Electoral redistribution
  — Triennial parliaments.
- **Increase in the Wealth of the Colonies:** Gold reserves were built up. More money was minted. More banks were built.
- **Business Boom:** The great increase in population meant an increase in demand for goods and services. Imports increased. Trade with Britain increased.
- **Benefits for People on the Land:** At first, these people complained because their shepherds and workers ran off to the gold fields. Soon they found, however, that they could do without most of them. Sheep, if fenced in, did not need to be watched 24 hours a day. Squatters also found a great new demand for their produce — wool, wheat, milk, eggs, and grain. Flocks increased in size, and more land was cleared and cultivated.
- **Improvements in Transport and Communications:** Roads and bridges were built. Stagecoach lines (especially Cobb & Co.) came into operation. Railways were built. Thousands of kilometres of telegraphic wire were strung to link Melbourne, Sydney, and Adelaide.

Figure 21.19. View of Melbourne from the south side of the Yarra River, 1858. It was already a centre of business growth with a steadily increasing population.

- **White Australia:** Australia's 'White Australia Policy' was prompted by anti-Chinese feeling during the gold rushes.

Supplying the Gold Fields

From a letter written by Alfred Joyce of Norwood, 12 December 1854:

Dear_____

You will no doubt blame me for not having written to you for so long a time, but the fact is I have been more occupied this last four months than ever I was before since I have been here. Shortly after I wrote to you last I had so much business on these new diggings [Maryborough] that I had to be in five days out of every six and to keep about half a dozen men at work at the head station and to make up the books and accounts every evening.

As it is some time now since I wrote to you it will be best for me to give a detailed account of the progress of affairs here since the date of my last letter. Just about that time, the beginning of September, having no fat sheep of my own, I purchased 500 off one of my neighbours and commenced to sell in small quantities to the butchers, but unfortunately, before I had been occupied a fortnight in this branch of trade, there came a glut of sheep on to the diggings, which, together with the ones I had purchased not turning out so well as I had expected, stopped my trade altogether, unless I had chose to sell for considerably less than they cost me. About this time, finding my hay (of which I had ten tons) did not sell very readily on the station, I commenced carting some of it to the diggings, and had not taken in more than two loads of it before I met with a purchaser for the whole of it. Having disposed of this, I commenced doing what I could for the disposal of the Plaistow stock (about twenty tons) of which not one ton had yet been sold. I soon met with purchasers for portions of it, and immediately proceeded to Plaistow to arrange for the carting of it up. The average price was £65 per ton. The delivery of the hay, which was being carted in simultaneously from both stations, kept me fully occupied for six or eight weeks. It afterwards turned out that I was not in the least too energetic in pushing it off, for by the time the last of it got on to the diggings, the people began to leave (for want of water to wash with) and I had

to submit to a slight reduction in the last ton or two. After I had been engaged selling the hay for about a month, I was induced from several circumstances to open a butcher's shop on the diggings for the sale of my own fat stock. As soon as I had decided upon it I sent an assistant or two to commence the erection of a place, but before it was completed (little more than a week) one half the people had left, so that the undertaking turned out a complete loss, and I took the first opportunity of breaking it up. Soon after I had commenced carting in the hay, I sent in with it several times on trial some milk and vegetables which, selling very well (the milk 2 shillings per quart and lettuces three for a shilling), I engaged a man expressly and sent in every day with a horse and cart all the milk, eggs, and vegetables we could spare. We were sending in at the first ten gallons per day, and the gross receipts, with the vegetables and eggs, was between £4 and £5 per day, but this like all the rest has fallen off very considerably lately, though I have not yet relinquished it nor yet have I omitted sending in for one day; but the receipts from it are not above one half what they were, as the price of milk has fallen to sixpence per quart and the cows give considerably less this dry weather. The supply of vegetables has ceased altogether from the extraordinary drought we are experiencing this year, and of which more anon. During the whole of this busy time I had to commence preparations for shearing, which, with all I could do, was unavoidably delayed for a full month, thereby causing a very considerable loss in the value of the wool and the condition of the sheep.

Questions

(1) Who promoted the first gold rush in Australia?
(2) To which field was the first rush made?
(3) Name five early gold fields.
(4) Why were some Victorians concerned about the New South Wales rushes?
(5) What effect did the discovery of gold have on many people in the cities and towns?
(6) Why was washdirt 'puddled'?
(7) Where was the 'Welcome Stranger' found?

(8) Why did most European miners object to Chinese miners working on the gold fields?

(9) Could the Eureka Stockade incident have been averted? If so, how?

(10) What were some of the important effects of the gold rushes?

Research

Find out more about the following.
(1) Old gold fields in your state
(2) Mining operations
(3) Chinese miners
(4) The uprising at Ballarat
(5) The effects of the gold rushes.

Chapter 22

1860–1901:
Towards a United, Democratic Australia

Important Changes

Important changes occurred in Australia between 1860 and 1901. Some of these changes were:

- Transportation of convicts ceased completely.
- The last British troops were withdrawn.
- Land was opened up to poorer settlers for selection.
- Trade unions and a national Labor Party developed to improve conditions and protect the interests of workers.
- Tariff barriers were established to protect Australian industries.
- Chinese and other 'coloured' people were excluded from immigrating, supposedly to protect the jobs of Australians.
- Education was provided for all children.
- A sense of nationalism developed.
- There was a great revolution in transport and communications (e.g. the railway and the telegraph). These helped to tie the different settlements together.
- The country was united eventually under one federal government.

An End to Transportation

Transportation to New South Wales, which then still included Queensland and Victoria, was officially ended by the British in 1840. Tasmania and Western Australia still received convicts. South Australia had never been a convict colony.

In the mid-1840s, William Gladstone, the colonial secretary, attempted to revive transportation to New South Wales. This action caused a lot of discussion and anger in the colony.

Anti-transportation groups formed to work for a complete end of the system. In 1851, Victorian and Tasmanian groups met in Melbourne, and an intercolonial Anti-Transportation League was formed. Members decided to refuse employment to convicts, and to fight for total abolition.

Transportation ended in the eastern colonies, including Tasmania, after opposition from members of the League and others, and the discovery of gold.

This left only Western Australia. The people of Western Australia had asked for convicts in the late 1840s, mainly for economic reasons, and the first convicts had arrived in 1850. Transportation to the West lasted until 1868. The system then came to an end throughout Australia.

It has been estimated that approximately 157 000 convicts were transported to Australia between 1787 and 1868. The exact number will never be known. Had the system been successful? Convicts had been removed from Britain, but that had not lessened the crime rate there.

Figure 22.1. A miners' meeting in the late 1890s. In the years following the gold rushes there developed a growing need to improve the conditions of the Australian worker.

The crime rate did decline eventually, but because of other factors. Convicts had supplied a labour force in Australia, but it had been an unwilling labour force. The transportation of convicts to Australia had, to a certain extent, corrupted and harmed emerging free society there.

The Withdrawal of British Troops

The last British troops were withdrawn from Australia in the second half of the nineteenth century. From then on, the colonies were expected to raise small forces for their own defence. The British Navy stood ready to protect shipping lanes and territorial waters.

Unlocking the Land

In the 1860s, most good land in Australia was in the hands of the squatters. These people held very large runs, on which they raised sheep and cattle. Both were profitable investments — especially sheep.

The rest of the land was Crown land, under the control of the various colonies' lands departments. We have seen that during the gold rushes the population of the country increased dramatically. Many miners found it difficult to make a living by mining, especially when alluvial gold began to decline. Many of these people wanted to turn to farming. As miners, they had lived an worked in the bush, and had come to love it. They

Figure 22.2. By the 1860s the squatters held most of the good land.

argued that Australia was a large country, with plenty of good land, and a lot of this land was not being used. In fact, many squatters had hardly developed their runs at all. It was unjust that a small number of pastoralists should hold so much land for themselves. If ex-miners, and others, were allowed to settle on small 'selections', the country would be developed more fully.

It was still believed that life in the country would make people good. They would be better off on their own small farms.

Demands were made to 'unlock' the land for everybody. Squatters, who had not purchased their land, should be made to sell some of it. Vacant Crown land should be thrown open at auction.

Of course, the squatters did not take

kindly to moves to deprive them of some of their land. They argued, through their politicians and newspaper editors, that they should be left to continue their good work. They had brought civilization to the outback. They had produced a staple (wool), which was sought by other countries around the world. The prosperity of Australia depended on them. They pointed out that they leased their land; that they did not hold it for nothing.

By the 1860s, the colonial governments had become more democratic. Many politicians wanted to pass laws to unlock the land. It was in their interests to do so. If they passed such Acts, the large number of people agitating for land would be satisfied, and silenced. Also, the squatters would be controlled to

Figure 22.3. A selector and his wife clearing land for settlement.

some extent. Many intelligent people of the time saw that change was necessary.

- **Tasmania** was the first colony to introduce legislation to unlock the land. Two Acts were passed, one for settled areas, and one for unsettled areas. In the settled districts, selectors could purchase 320 acres (129 ha) at £1 per acre (8/- per ha). In the unsettled districts, they could purchase up to 256 ha. Free land of up to 4000 ha was offered in rugged, mountainous country, but few accepted this.
- **Victoria:** The Nicholson Act of 1860 set aside 1.6 million ha of Crown land for selection. Selectors could purchase between 32 and 128 ha after it had been surveyed, at a rate of £1 per acre. If two selectors argued over the same land, the one offering the highest bid would be sold the

land. Improvements had to be made to the land, at a rate of £1 per acre, within two years. If this were not done, the selector would be forced to pay an extra 5 shillings per acre. The Duffy Act of 1862 set aside a further 4 million ha for selection.
- **New South Wales:** In 1861, the New South Wales government passed two Acts. These were the *Crown Lands Alienation Act* and the *Crown Lands Occupation Act*. These two Acts were also known as the Robertson Acts, after John Robertson, the Minister who introduced them. These Acts did not necessarily favour the selector. Rather, they aimed at achieving an even, just balance between the squatter and the selector.

The Crown Lands Alienation Act stated that anyone, male or female, of any age, could select between 16 and 128 ha of Crown land for £1 per acre. Prior survey was not necessary. One-quarter of the price had to be paid, as a deposit, and the balance paid off within three years. The selector had to live on his property and make improvements to it to the value of £1 per acre.

The Crown Lands Occupation Act stated that the squatter could keep his property by lease. In inner, developed areas, his lease was limited to five years. Rents were to be fixed by a Board of Commissioners. The squatter's property, however, could be thrown open to selection at any time. However, the squatter had the right to buy four times as many acres as he had spent pounds on improvements.

- **Queensland:** Selection was introduced in the 1860s in Queensland. Selectors were forced to live on their land and improve it. They received bounties on their crops. If a squatter gave up half his run, he was allowed a ten-year lease on the other half, plus the first right to purchase 1024 ha.
- **South Australia:** Selection Acts were passed in 1869 and 1872.
- **Western Australia:** The main regulation was passed in 1872. The maximum size allowed a selector was only 16 ha. This was too small an area for farming, and selection failed.

Squatters versus Selectors

For years after the passing of the Selection Acts, a contest was waged between the squatters and the selectors. The squatters tried every trick they knew to hold on to their land. They employed 'dummies' to pretend to be selectors and purchase parts of their runs for them. These dummies were friends, relations, stations hands, and even children.

Another underhead method was called 'peacocking'. Squatters purchased key points on their runs. Water, for instance, was essential. Therefore they bought land along their creeks and around their waterholes. Any genuine selector buying land on the run found it difficult to succeed without a good supply of water.

Squatters also took out mining leases on their land in strategic positions.

The squatters had the land, and the money, and the support of the banks, so they managed to survive. However, they did not have it *all* their own way. Dummies could, and did, stoop to blackmail, and opportunists purchased land for resale at a profit. Despite opposition, tens of thousands of selectors managed to carve out small farms for themselves across Australia, and squatters saw the size of their runs diminish.

For years, the selectors had a battle to survive. Many lacked a good knowledge of farming. Many lacked funds. Some grew crops like wheat, and found they could not afford to transport their grain long distances to market. Until railways were built, transport was an expensive business.

The Development of Trade Unions and a Labor Party

In early colonial society, there were no unions, and workers were exploited harshly. Later, small craft guilds developed to protect the interests of craftsmen and their families. The guilds were, in fact, similar to friendly or benefit societies. Membership was small. Members were not militant.

During the gold rushes, many men with European trade union experience came to Australia. At the time, many factories were built and businesses established. Workers began to form unions and agitate for shorter hours and better working conditions. An Eight-Hour Day Movement was formed to campaign to reduce the normal ten-hour day. This movement was eventually successful.

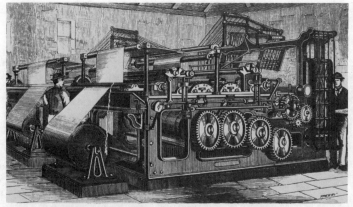

(a) Newspaper printing: The Age *Victory machines.*

(b) Geelong Paper Mill.

(c) Australian Glass Company's works, Richmond.

Figure 22.4. A growth of factories and small businesses led to the development of trade unions.

Figure 22.5. The 1890 Maritime Strike.

From the late 1870s onwards, a new type of unionism began to develop. Unions for semi-skilled and unskilled workers were formed. They were relatively easy to join, as there was a low joining fee. They were highly organized, and they were quite militant. If members could not get better hours, conditions, and pay by negotiation, they were prepared to strike.

The new unions used newspapers such as *The Boomerang* and *The Worker* to communicate with their members and the public. Important intercolonial trade union congresses were held between 1879 and 1898. At these congresses, members determined to work for such things as the exclusion of Chinese labour, a basic wage, and ways and means of sending representatives to the colonial governments.

The Australian economy went through a boom in the 1880s, but there was a depression during the 1890s. Many small businesses collapsed and workers lost their jobs. Owners and bosses tried to limit wages and weaken unions, and this led to a number of bitter strikes.

The greatest strike of the time was the so-called Maritime Strike, which began in August 1890. Officers on ships, members of the Association of Marine Officers, wished to affiliate with the Melbourne Trades Hall Council as from March 1890. Common seamen were affiliated with the Council already. The shipowners feared this might lead to trouble, such as discipline problems. They joined together, raised a fund of £20 000 to fight the officers, and demanded they not affiliate with the Council. The officers refused and walked off their ships, followed by their crews. The miners at Broken Hill, and 16 000 shearers, also went out on strike in sympathy.

However, there was considerable unemployment at the time, and no shortage of strike breakers, or 'scab' labour (called 'scabs', after a disease in sheep). Police and soldiers were called in to protect non-union labour, union funds began to run out, and the strike collapsed.

The following year there was a strike of Queensland shearers, forcing the closure of most shearing sheds in that colony. Union leaders were arrested and imprisoned, and the strike collapsed in June of that year.

In 1892, the miners at Broken Hill went out on strike again, over a variation in their pay allowance. Many of the men became destitute and were forced to leave the mining town. Again leaders were arrested.

There was yet another strike in Queensland and northern New South Wales in 1894.

These strikes all failed, however, because of a shortage of strike funds to pay strikers, because the governments, banks, and newspapers were against the men, and because non-union labour could be found and used. Some small unions disintegrated under the pressure of the strikes, and many men had to return to work on the bosses' terms. Unionism was not destroyed, however. It had made its presence felt.

From 1890 onwards, unionists turned from strike action to political action. The Australian Labor Party was formed. The members began campaigning for votes in the different colonies for seats on the colonial governments. The first members were returned in New South Wales in 1891. Of the 48 who stood for parliament, 35 won seats — to the surprise of many.

In 1899, Australia saw its first Labor government — in Queensland. These men fought to improve conditions for Australian workers.

Tariff Barriers

The Australian colonies were a part of the British Empire. Their trade was dictated by Britain. They supplied British industry with raw materials, such as wool and whale oil, and also served as markets for British manufactured goods.

By the mid-nineteenth century, the official trade policy within the Empire was that of laissez-faire, or free trade. This meant that goods could be moved from one country to another, with no restrictions save small duties. These duties were levied in order to raise revenue for governments. In 1850, the *Australian Colonies Government Act* gave some of the colonies the right to raise such revenue.

In Australia, local industry was developing slowly. This industry was small and vulnerable. Often imported goods could be sold for a profit more cheaply than locally made goods. In order to protect local manufacture, some businessmen and politicians argued that a protective tariff, or tax, should be placed on imported articles. This would raise the price of the import so that it would have to compete with local manufacture. Tariffs, they argued, could help boost Australia's economy.

A Tariff League was formed in 1860, and David Syme, the owner and editor of Melbourne's *Age* newspaper, made the concept a political issue. In 1866, the Victorian government introduced a low protective barrier, based on the 1850 Act.

Victorian tariffs were increased as time went by. By 1877, the tariff had risen to 40 per cent. South Australia, Tasmania, and Queensland all followed Victoria. They feared their economic would suffer if they did not.

However, New South Wales was against tariff protection, and pursued a policy of free trade until 1892. Henry Parkes championed free trade in his state. New South Wales may have been more interested at that time in her expanding primary industries and land legislation than in manufacturing.

Protection and free trade were important political issues for decades. Great rivalry developed between Victoria and New South Wales. Each colony had to establish customs barriers, and smugglers tried to avoid these. Such problems were not resolved until federation.

Figure 22.6. A cartoon depicting the tariff problem. In the early 1860s Victoria favoured a policy of protection for her industries. Later, Queensland, Tasmania, and South Australia followed Victoria's lead, leaving New South Wales pursuing a policy of free trade.

Historians find it hard to judge how effective protection was.

A White Australia

Australian settlers were in the main racist. They looked down upon the Aborigines and Chinese miners as inferior and uncivilized. Nothing, they believed, could be done with the Aborigines, and the Chinese were a race of heathens. The Aborigines posed no real threat: indeed, they were fading from the scene. However, the Chinese did pose a problem. They had come to Australia to mine gold, and there was no guarantee that many more would not arrive in the future. Unionists were particularly concerned that the Chinese would always work for low wages, under poor conditions. They would continue to lower working and living standards — standards they were trying to raise.

In 1855, the Victorian government imposed a poll (head) tax on Chinese who landed in the colony. Later, South Australia, New South Wales, and Queensland passed laws restricting entry of Chinese miners.

In 1888, all colonies except Western Australia introduced heavy poll (head) taxes to keep out Chinese immigrants. When the ship *Afghan* tried to land 100 Chinese in Sydney, there was an anti-Chinese demonstration. Henry Parkes hurried an Act through the New South Wales parliament prohibiting Chinese immigration to that colony. All the other colonies passed similar legislation shortly afterwards.

In the second half of the nineteenth century, a new people appeared in Australia. These were the kanakas, or South Sea Islanders. These tall, brown, frizzy-haired people came from New Guinea, the Solomon Islands, New Britain, the New Hebrides, and Fiji. They were recruited roughly and deceitfully by contractors (called 'blackbirders') and shipped to Queensland to work in the cotton and sugar industries. (Robert Towns brought in the first of these people in 1863 to pick cotton on his property outside Brisbane.) It was kanaka labour that built up the sugar industry around Cairns, Townsville, Mackay, and Bundaberg.

Again unionists were alarmed. They did not wish to see a belt of cheap labour established in the north. This was unacceptable on humanitarian and political grounds. Others feared that the use of kanaka labour would make social integration in Australia all the more difficult.

In 1901, the new Commonwealth government passed an Act that prohibited the recruiting of kanakas after 1904. In the same year, the *Immigration Restriction Act* was passed, aimed at keeping out all non-Europeans. Potential immigrants had to pass a dictation test in any European language. Those who failed this test were not allowed to enter Australia. Needless to say, this test effectively barred most non-Europeans.

Education for All

Early colonial schools were run by the church, or by private individuals. State schools were set up later. This led to a dual system of education in the colonies. There were church or private schools,

Figure 22.7. Kanakas working in a field in Queensland, 1891.

and there were state schools. There was some competition between the two systems in opening new schools and providing education for the public.

There was also competition between the different denominations. English Anglicans, Scottish Presbyterians, and Irish Catholics all competed in furthering their particular interpretation of Scripture.

Many children could not gain an education, and went to work at an early age. Only the children of well-to-do parents enjoyed the benefits of a good education.

Education improved greatly after the gold rushes. The colonial governments aimed at providing state schools that were 'free, compulsory, and secular'. That is, parents did not have to pay fees, attendance was compulsory for all children below a fixed leaving age (between 13 and 15 years, depending on the colony), and no one faith could be promoted in the schools. Religious teaching

Figure 22.8. A Cobb & Co. coach leaving Bourke Street, Melbourne.

was limited to a fixed period each week, and was conducted by visiting clergymen. In theory, all children were to enjoy the benefits of a sound education. However, the church schools continued, and state aid to them became an important political issue. Should the colonial governments help maintain them? For a time, funds were cut off completely to both schools and churches. Funding was resumed later. Education was provided for all, but was still unequal.

Improvements in Transport and Communications

Until the middle of the nineteenth century, there was no fast means of transport in Australia. To get anywhere, you had to walk, ride a horse, drive a cart, wagon, or buggy, or travel in a boat or ship up river or around the coast. Roads were very bad, and bridges were narrow. Often there were no roads or bridges at all, and one had to travel through bush or over desert, fording rivers and creeks along the way.

Weather was an important factor. Rain could turn the ground into mud, and swell rivers and creeks. Storms could threaten ships at sea.

There were no telecommunications. People could communicate only by mail, and it took weeks for some letters to be delivered.

The second half of the nineteenth century saw great improvements in transport and communications. Stagecoach lines were developed. Railways were built to rival the stagecoach lines. Roads were improved. Ships became safer and faster. An overland, and then an overseas, telegraph was established. Mail was speeded up. These things all helped to bring Australians closer together, and to foster a sense of national identity.

Stagecoaches

The first coaches used in Australia were English. However, in 1853, four young

Americans arrived in Melbourne. They were Freeman Cobb, John Murry Peck, James Swanton, and John B. Lamber. All were in their early twenties, and collectively referred to themselves as 'the body'. They were enterprising. They hoped to start up a carrying trade between the city and the gold fields. To do this, they founded the Cobb & Co. stagecoach line, using imported American coaches.

These coaches began running in January 1854, between Melbourne, Forest Creek, and Bendigo. Later, other lines were developed, both by Cobb & Co. and by other companies.

There was soon an enormous and rapid expansion of coach lines across Australia. Coach travel was to last in the north until 1924. Only railways, motor vehicles, and aircraft put an end to it.

Railways

The steam engine appeared in the eighteenth century in Britain. It was the brainchild of English and Scottish engineers like Thomas Savery, Thomas Newcomen, and James Watt. At first it was used to pump water out of flooded mine shafts, and to supply houses and gardens with water. Later it was applied to transport. Private railway companies came into being, offering smoky rail travel between cities and towns. Other countries adopted the steam engine. Eventually it was brought to Australia.

The first steam-powered railway ran in Victoria. The Melbourne and Hobson's Bay Railway Company was incorporated in 1853, and was granted a strip of land for tracks between Flinders Street, Melbourne, and the pier at Sandridge (at Port Melbourne). Approximately four hectares were also granted at Flinders

Figure 22.9. Port Melbourne was the terminus for the first steam-powered railway in Victoria.

Street, and 10 hectares at Sandridge, for terminuses. Work began in March 1953.

Four locomotives were ordered from Robert Stephenson and Co. of Newcastle-upon-Tyne, England. They were late in arriving, however, and the firm of Robertson, Martin and Smith of Melbourne was asked to build a locomotive. The firm did so, within ten weeks. This locomotive was small, with wheels arranged in three pairs (i.e. 2-2-2). Its cylinders developed a mere 30 hp. Unfortunately, it ran for only six days and then broke down. A makeshift locomotive was brought into service, made up of a pile-driver engine mounted on a ballast wagon! Eventually services had to be suspended, until two of the engines ordered from England arrived.

The first railways in Australia were all founded by private companies. These included the Geelong and Melbourne Railway Co., the St Kilda and Brighton Railway Co., the Melbourne and Essendon Railway Co., the Sydney Railway Co., the Hunter River Railway Co., and the Launceston and Western Railway Co. All of these companies were granted land in order to lay tracks and build stations and terminuses. All suffered financial problems, and were taken over eventually by the colonial governments.

Unfortunately, different companies and governments decided on different gauges (width between the rails), and this hampered rail travel throughout Australia. However, railways did speed up the transport of both passengers and goods (e.g. wheat). Goods could be carried comparatively cheaply, and this stimulated trade and manufacture.

Faster Ships

The steam engine was applied to sea transport as well as to land transport. In Britain, and later in Australia, steam was used to turn either paddles (amidships or in the stern) or screws (in the stern). Paddles worked well on rivers, such as the Murray, but not at sea, where heavy swells broke and immobilized them. At first, steam was used as a supplement to sail — that is, ships were fitted with both steam engines and masts and sails. Wooden hulls were also replaced with iron hulls.

Eventually, despite competition from fast 'clipper' ships, steam-powered vessels replaced sail altogether.

The Telegraph

The telegraph was an American invention. It was based on Morse Code, a series of short and long impulses transmitted along an iron wire which was strung on poles between telegraph stage offices. Morse Code was named after its inventor, Professor Samuel Morse. The first telegraph in America, 'Samuel Morse's Electrical Telegraph', was established in 1844.

The first telegraph in Australia was established in Victoria, between Melbourne and Williamstown, in 1854. This was just 10 years after the first American line was brought into service. This telegraph owed much to the work of Samuel MacGowan, an American who had studied under Professor Morse, and who arrived in Melbourne on board the *Glance* in May 1853 (the same year Cobb and his associates arrived in Melbourne). MacGowan brought with him two chests of 'apparatus' and a box of tools. The Victorian government accepted his tender to establish a line between Melbourne and Williamstown. After it was completed, MacGowan was appointed General Superintendent of Telegraphs.

Other telegraphs followed. A line was established between Hobart and Launceston in 1857. Two years later, Tasmania was connected to the mainland by an undersea cable. However, this cable lasted only a few months. A second, more successful cable came into operation in 1869. The first telegraph in New South Wales was established between Sydney and South Head in January 1858. Nine months later, this line was extended to Albury, and the extended

Figure 22.10. Planting the first post of the overland telegraph at Port Darwin.

line connected with a line from Melbourne. Sydney was connected to Brisbane in 1861, and to Adelaide in 1867.

And so it went, with the cities, towns, and small settlements being strung together slowly by thousands of kilometres of electrified wire, to become part of a growing system of improved communication. Many of the men who cleared the scrub, dug the holes, raised the poles, and strung the wire were examiners.

At this time, the only communication Australia had with the outside world was by ship. The Peninsula and Oriental Steam Navigation Company carried mail to and from Europe. In June 1870, the British-Australian Telegraphic Company agreed to establish a cable between Java and Port Darwin, if South Australia

Figure 22.11. Henry Lawson, one of the leaders of the nationalist movement.

built an overland telegraph north to Port Darwin. This would allow the Australian colonies to link up with telegraphic networks in Asia and Europe. The South Australian government agreed, allocating £120 000 for the task. Charles Todd, postmaster-general of South Australia, was put in charge of operations. He was given only 18 months to complete his task.

By 1872, Port Augusta on Spencer Gulf had been linked with Port Darwin. At first there was a 421 km gap in the wire between Daly Waters and Tennant Creek, but this was covered by a pony express, run by John Lewis and Ray Boucaut. The first telegrams were transmitted on 23 June 1871. Charles Todd later wrote proudly that 'the Australian colonies were connected with the grand electric chain which unites all nations of the earth'.

Nationalism

Nationalism is a love for one's country and people. It is a feeling that they are superior to others. For the first hundred years after settlement, the people of Australia did not think of themselves as being Australian or of Australia as a nation. They thought of themselves as Europeans living in a wilderness. They were there because they had been taken there (as convicts), because they had been posted there (as soldiers, sailors, or administrators), or because they hoped to make money there (as squatters and miners). The thought of returning 'home' to Britain was never far from the minds of these people.

However, towards the end of the nineteenth century, many people in Australia began to think of themselves as Australians, and of Australia as their home.

By the 1880s, many people had been born in Australia. So had their parents. They knew no other land or culture. Many others who were not colonial-born wanted to see an Australia that was independent of the old world. Distance from Europe was an important factor. Australians, like Canadians and Americans, began to feel that they had less and less in common with the ways of the 'old country'. People in Australia were very conscious of the fact that Australia was a 'new' country. Everything seemed to lie in the future. Australia seemed a land that promised much. There was no entrenched monarchy and aristocracy, no lord and peasant classes, as in Europe. Australia was not wracked by violent religious intolerance. She had no empire to feel guilty about. She was developing a distinctive culture of her own, and it was wrong to overlook this. Many did not wish to break the ties with Britain but, at the same time, they wished to be accepted as Britain's equal. Henry Parkes asked, 'Why should not the name of an Australian be equal to that of a Briton?'

The nationalist movement was led by, and had as its heroes, editors, writers, poets, cartoonists, and artists. Henry Lawson, Joseph Furphy, and Bernard O'Dowd wrote poems, short stories, and novels about Australians and their way of life. Some of their works have become Australian classics. The *Bulletin* of Sydney, edited by J. T. Archibald (founded in 1880) and the *Boomerang* of Brisbane, edited by William Lane (founded 1887) became notorious for their articles criticizing Britain, British imperialism, squatters, city life, and anything 'un-Australian'. Arthur Streeton, Tom Roberts, Charles Conder, and Frederick McCubbin painted new, impressionist studies of Australia and its people.

Federation

By the end of the nineteenth century, Australia was ready for federation. There were a number of reasons for this:

- The colonies were all very similar, and one could move from one colony to another without experiencing any great feeling of change.
- Australians were beginning to think of themselves as one people, not just as Victorians, South Australians, and so on.
- Most Australians were not prepared

Figure 22.12. Tom Roberts's painting The Breakaway.

Figure 22.13. Sir Henry Parkes.

There was growing worry about Australia's ability to defend herself against an invader. If Australia were attacked, it could hardly rely for defence on six small armies, backed by six different governments.

Was an enemy on the horizon? Many Australians thought so. The Germans and the French were showing an interest in the Pacific. The Germans, for instance, were interested in east New Guinea. To forestall them, the Queensland government annexed this area in the name of Queen Victoria, in 1883. However, the British government refused to recognize this action — a fact that worried many Australians. A military expert, Major-General J. Bevan Edwards, examined Australia's defences in 1889 and submitted a report criticizing their weaknesses. A federal government would be able to establish a strong navy and army.

to argue against the idea of federation. It seemed inevitable and a good idea.

- To many, it seemed ridiculous that six separate governments should speak for Australia on important domestic issues.
- Australia's commerce was weakened and made unnecessarily complicated by colonial borders and customs duties. Under a federal system, there would be fewer restrictions.
- The six colonies all had separate Acts relating to immigration. A federal government would impose a uniform policy on this.
- The six colonies all had separate Acts relating to the entry of Chinese into Australia. A federal government would impose a uniform policy against such entry.

Fighting for Federation

The first, definite step towards Federation began at Tenterfield, New South Wales, in 1889, just after Bevan Edwards's report. On 24 October, Henry Parkes made a famous after-dinner speech, in which he declared that 'all great questions of magnitude affecting the welfare of the colonies' would be solved by 'a Parliament of two Houses, a House of Commons and a Senate'.

In 1891, the First Constitutional Convention met in Sydney, and its delegates worked on a constitution. Because of the 1890s depression, the different colonial governments temporarily put to one side the matter of Federation.

After that, a number of ordinary people who were not politicians became interested in Federation.

In 1897–98 a Second Constitutional Convention was held, in Adelaide, Sydney, and Melbourne. A new constitution

Commonwealth of Australia

Gazette.

PUBLISHED BY AUTHORITY.

No. 1.]	TUESDAY, 1 JANUARY.	[1901

By the QUEEN.

A PROCLAMATION.

VICTORIA R.

WHEREAS by an Act of Parliament passed in the Sixty-third and Sixty-fourth Years of Our Reign intituled, "An Act to constitute the Commonwealth of *Australia*," it is enacted that it shall be lawful for the Queen, with the advice of the Privy Council, to declare by Proclamation, that, on and after a day therein appointed, not being later than One Year after the passing of this Act, the people of *New South Wales*, *Victoria*, *South Australia*, *Queensland*, and *Tasmania*, and also, if Her Majesty is satisfied that the people of *Western Australia* have agreed thereto, of *Western Australia*, shall be united in a Federal Commonwealth under the name of the Commonwealth of Australia.

And whereas We are satisfied that the people of *Western Australia* have agreed thereto accordingly.

We, therefore, by and with the advice of Our Privy Council, have thought fit to issue this Our Royal Proclamation, and We do hereby declare that on and after the First day of *January* One thousand nine hundred and one the people of *New South Wales*, *Victoria*, *South Australia*, *Queensland*, *Tasmania*, and *Western Australia* shall be united in a Federal Commonwealth under the name of the Commonwealth of *Australia*.

Given at Our Court at *Balmoral*, this Seventeenth day of *September*, in the Year of our Lord One thousand nine hundred, and in the Sixty-fourth Year of Our Reign.

GOD SAVE THE QUEEN!

Figure 22.14. Proclamation of the Commonwealth of Australia in the Government Gazette, Tuesday, 1 January 1901.

was drafted, but only Victoria, South Australia, and Tasmania were prepared to go ahead and federate. Eventually, New South Wales and Queensland agreed to join the other colonies, after certain changes were made to the proposed constitution. New South Wales insisted that the new federal capital be located within its borders.

The new draft of the constitution was taken to England and presented to the British parliament. It was prepared to allow the colonies to federate — but was concerned that Western Australia would not be included.

In Western Australia, gold miners and others petitioned Queen Victoria to be allowed to join the other colonies. A referendum was held in the colony, and a majority voted for Federation.

After this, the British parliament passed a *Constitution Act*, granting Federation to Australia from 1 January 1901. Queen Victoria gave her royal assent on 9 July 1900.

The New Nation

A federal parliament was formed consisting of the British Crown, represented by a governor-general, a Senate, and a House of Representatives. The governor-general was given the right to summon and prorogue parliament. Both houses were to sit every year. Six senators were to be elected from each state, for a term of six years. Each senator had one vote, which meant that all states were equally represented. Elections for the Senate were to be held every three years, thus ensuring continuity and stability in the House. Senators were to choose a President. The Senate's main function was to review legislation proposed in bills in the lower house (the House of Representatives).

Members of the House of Representatives were elected in each state, according to the size of the population of that state. The total number of members was to be as near as possible to twice the number of senators, i.e., 72. Members had to be over 21, British subjects, qualified to vote, and resident in Australia for at least three years. Members were to elect a Speaker, and one-third of all members had to be present before any debate could take place. The Speaker could not vote, unless the numbers were equal. He then had the casting vote.

The new federal government assumed such important powers as trade and commerce, taxation, postal and telegraphic services, naval and military defence, civil and criminal courts, immigration, emigration, external affairs, lighthouses, beacons and buoys, quarantine, etc. The states retained control over education, police, rail transport, etc.

In parliament, the party with the most members elected formed a government, consisting of a prime minister, ministers, and backbenchers. Sir Edmund Barton, a lawyer, and son of a Sydney stockbroker and real estate agent, became the first prime minister (1901–03). Lord Hopetoun was appointed the first governor-general.

Questions

(1) When did transportation to Australia cease?

(2) Why were demands made to 'unlock' the land?

(3) What caused the Maritime Strike in 1890?

(4) What was meant by the term 'free, compulsory and secular'?

(5) What improvements were made in transport and communications in the second half of the nineteenth century?

(6) What effects did improvements in transport and communications have on Australians?

(7) Who was Samuel MacGowan?

(8) What were the characteristic features of Australian nationalism at the turn of the nineteenth century?

(9) Why did Federation occur?
(10) When did the Australian Commonwealth come into being?

Research

Find out more about the following people:

(1) Henry Lawson
(2) Tom Roberts
(3) Henry Parkes
(4) Alfred Deakin
(5) Sir Edmund Barton.

Chapter 23

Australians at War:
The Spirit of Anzac

Early Military Adventures

Australia was a part of the British Empire. As such, she was likely to be involved in Britain's imperial wars.

- **Khartoum.** When General Charles Gordon was killed in Khartoum by the fanatical followers of Muhammed Ahmed, the Mahdi (or Mes-

Figure 23.1. Troops leaving Sydney for Khartoum, 3 March 1885

siah), patriotic sentiment rippled through the colonies. Emotional accounts of the fighting, and poems, appeared in newspapers. William Dalley, acting premier of New South Wales, cabled London, offering a force of artillery and infantry. The contingent raised was small. Once it landed at Suakin, on the Red Sea, in 1885, it played no part in deciding the outcome of the war. The men who went there were more like mercenaries than regular troops. Their pay was five shillings per day and their duty was to shoot the enemies of Queen Victoria (in this case Arabs, Abyssinians, Egyptians, and Negroes).

- **The Boer War.** In 1899, the Boer War erupted in South Africa. Different colonies sent small contingents of cavalry and infantry to fight the Dutch guerrillas.

The first contingent left in 1899. A Commonwealth battalion, the Australian Commonwealth Horse, left Australia on 19 February 1902. The men who sailed believed they were going 'to protect British subjects from oppression and injustice'. Many, including Prime Minister Barton, feared that, if something were not done, the Cape of Good Hope would fall into enemy hands, and this would threaten Australia's sea lanes. Most of the Australians wished to impress the Mother Country with their courage and ability. They were young cubs of the British Imperial Lion.

More than 16000 men, all volunteers, served against the Boers between October 1899 and June 1902. Again, Australia played only a small, supporting role. The war ended in 1902, with the Peace of Vereeniging.

- **Boxer Uprising.** While the Boer War was being fought, Australia was involved in yet another imperial conflict. This was the Boxer Uprising in China. New South Wales sent a

ship, the *Protector*, and 260 naval volunteers, and Victoria sent 200 volunteers. These men did not take part in the famous defence of the foreign legations in Peking, but helped to police that city and Tientsin for nine months after the fighting. Many British troops were impressed with their loyalty to the imperial cause.

The Great War in Europe

The Great War (1914–18) began as a war in Europe, fought between Germany, Austria-Hungary, and the Ottoman Empire on the one hand, and Britain, France, and Russia (the Allies) on the other. Before long, other countries were involved. These included the countries of the British Empire — Canada, Australia, New Zealand, India, and South Africa. Russia withdrew in 1917, after the Bolshevik (Communist) Revolution. The United States of America then entered the War.

The war began when Germany attempted to invade and overrun France, and then turn on Russia. (This strategy had been worked out, years before, by General von Scholieffen.) The German armies never got any further than France, however. Two lines developed, one on the western front (across France and Belgium) and one on the eastern front (across Russia). For four years, the war was fought on these two fronts until Germany was defeated.

The war proved to be the bloodiest fought until then. More than 8 million men were killed. Thirty million were wounded, or captured, or disappeared without trace. Villages were destroyed. Farm land was laid waste. The economies of many countries suffered. The war bled Europe, and marked her decline in world affairs.

Historians still debate the causes of the war. It was undoubtedly the result of an arms race, especially between Britain

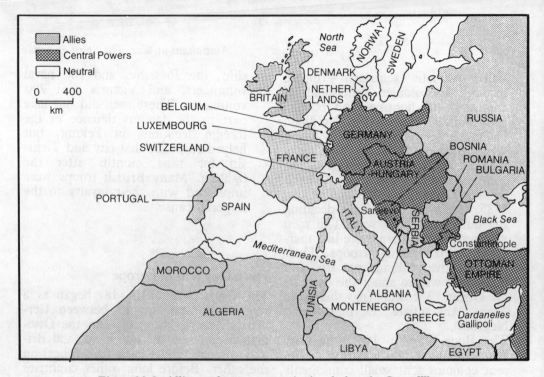

Figure 23.2. Alliances between countries just before the Great War.

Figure 23.3. Andrew Fisher.

and Germany. German aggression and a desire for empire cannot be overlooked. The Germans were jealous of the British Empire. The war was an imperial war, in that Germany and Austria tried to extend their control over other states. For instance, Hungary was forced to be a part of the Austro-Hungarian Empire. The Austrians hoped to extend their power further eastwards, and this resulted in the incident which sparked off the war.

Austrian forces went on military manoeuvres in the small, captured state of Bosnia. While visiting Sarajevo, the capital of Bosnia, the heir to the Austrian crown, Archduke Francis Ferdinand, and his wife, the Duchess Sophie, were assassinated by young freedom fighters from Belgrade University in Serbia. Austria-Hungary then moved against Serbia. A chain reaction followed, and battle lines were drawn.

The Call to Arms in Australia

Britain entered the Great War on 4 August 1914. Australia announced

222

her intention of supporting Britain, and declared war in the same month. The prime minister, Joseph Cook, announced that: 'Whatever happens, Australia is part of the Empire to the full. Remember that when the Empire is at war so is Australia at war.'

The Leader of the Labour Party, and a former prime minister (1908–09, 1910–13), Andrew Fisher believed his country should give total support to Britain. He promised, 'Australians will stand beside our own to help and defend her to our last man and our last shilling.'

Australians everywhere rallied to the cause. Everywhere people waited for the latest news from Europe. Crowds formed outside newspaper offices. The National Anthem and 'Rule Britannia' were sung in music halls, theatres, lecture theatres, and school halls. Composers and poets helped as well. W. W. Francis wrote the chorus:

Rally round the banner of your country,
Take the field with brothers o'er the foam;
On land or sea, wherever you be,
Keep your eye on Liberty.
But England, home and beauty, have no cause
    to fear;
Should auld acquaintance be forgot?
No! No! No! No! No! Australia will be there ...
Australia will be there.

Frank Johnstone, a *Bulletin* poet, wrote in *Sons of Australia:*

For Britain! Good old Britain!
    Where our fathers first drew breath,
We'll fight like true Australians,
    Facing danger, wounds or death.

Many Labor supporters and unionists were cautious. The *Australian Worker* wrote: 'We must protect our country. We must keep sacred from the mailed fist this splendid heritage. But we hope no wave of jingo madness will sweep over the land, unbalancing the judgement of its leaders, and inciting its population to wild measures, spurred on by the vile press, to which war is only an increase in circulation, and every corpse a copper. God help Australia! God help England! God help Germany! God help us!'

There were some left-wing unionists, pacifists, and socialists who quickly decided that Australia should not participate in the war. They argued that it was a war started by capitalists, who stood to gain from the manufacture of arms and equipment. It was the poor, exploited worker who would have to fight, and give his life and limb, in their service. Australian men should stay at home with their wives and families. They should not volunteer for a capitalist war in Europe. Let the capitalists fight it! Posters to this effect were displayed, and small meetings condemned the war. At first, however, this small minority was not listened to.

Figure 23.4. World War I AIF enlistment poster.

Figure 23.5. One of the early transports leaving for the Western Front.

The Ranks Form

The Australian government had a small but modern navy. At the start of the war it decided to raise a specially recruited military force of 20 000 men. Both the navy and military force would be placed at the disposal of the British High Command.

The military force, or AIF (Australian Imperial Force), was placed under the command of Brigadier-General W. T. Bridges. He was responsible for its early development. He thought that it should comprise three brigades of infantry and one Light Horse (or cavalry) brigade. It was hoped that many men who had undergone military training in the nation's militia, and who had served in the Boer War, would enlist. Volunteers would make up the balance. High physical standards were set and good pay offered. Privates received six shillings, or 'six bob' a day.

The Commonwealth government had no need to worry about a lack of volunteers. They almost jammed the recruiting offices. City men enlisted first. As news spread to the country, country men enlisted too. Many were swept away on a wave of patriotism. Many thought that the war would be a romantic adventure in their lives, and quickly over. By the end of the first year, 50 000 men had enlisted, and a second division was formed.

The 'six-bob-a-day tourists', once recruited, were given a 'short back and sides' haircut and a coarse uniform consisting of khaki jacket, trousers, shirt, leather boots, leggings, and slouch hat or cap. The slouch hat was a distinctive feature, pinned as it was with a badge which displayed a cluster of radiating rifles with bayonets attached.

Men were trained on sports grounds in cities and camps in the country. Two important training camps were at Liverpool, near Sydney, and Broadmeadows, near Melbourne. Recruits were armed with a heavy Lee and Enfield .303 rifle and long thrusting bayonet.

While they trained, wagons, harnesses, saddles, uniforms, tents, and other supplies were manufactured, food and medical supplies were collected, and ships were refitted as troop transports.

First Action in New Guinea

In September 1914, an Australian Naval and Military Expeditionary Force (ANMEF) seized enemy bases in German New Guinea. News of this action was heavily censored. At the time, Australians were more interested in the German advance on Paris.

The AIF Embarks

When the men of the AIF had completed their training, they marched proudly through city streets to trains, and these trains carried them to ships. All along the way, crowds cheered, waved flags, and wished the men well. A total of 26 Australian transports then made rendezvous with 10 New Zealand transports in the deep waters of King George Sound, on the southern coast of Western Australia.

That was the beginning of the Anzac Corps — Australian and New Zealand Army Corps. The ships left on 1 November for Britain, via the Suez Canal. British and Australian warships formed an escort. On the way, the Australian cruiser HMAS *Sydney* engaged the *Emden*, a German raider, which had been sent to destroy the radio station on the Cocos Islands. The *Emden* was disabled and captured after being beached. Three Australians were killed, and 15 wounded in the action.

Egypt

When the troops reached Egypt they disembarked. News had come through that there was poor weather ahead, there was a lack of accommodation for the men in Britain, and winter was coming on. Canadian troops had been accommodated in Britain only with difficulty. New plans for Dominion troops were also being debated.

Therefore the Anzacs set up camp at Mena, on the outskirts of Cairo, almost in the shade of the Pyramids. There they stood guard duty, drilled, went for route marches and rides across the hot sands, and practised military manoeuvres. For relaxation, they marvelled at the Sphinx and the Pyramids, baited the Egyptians (whom they called 'Wogs'), played two-up, organized horse races, and spent time in the cafés and dives of Cairo and Heliopolis. In Cairo, they met British soldiers, or 'Tommies', for the first time. Many of the Australian troops lacked discipline and respect for regulations, and there were some unpleasant incidents, such as a riot in Cairo. The main trouble-makers were sent home, but by this time the Corps had begun to gain a reputation for lawlessness.

A second contingent, under Colonel John Monash, arrived in February 1915.

Plans

While the Anzacs waited in Egypt, plans were being made in Britain. Turkey had entered the war in October 1914 — only a few days before the Anzac Corps had sailed. The Turks menaced two points — one on the border of the Russian Empire, and the other on the east bank of the Suez Canal. Lord Kitchener, the

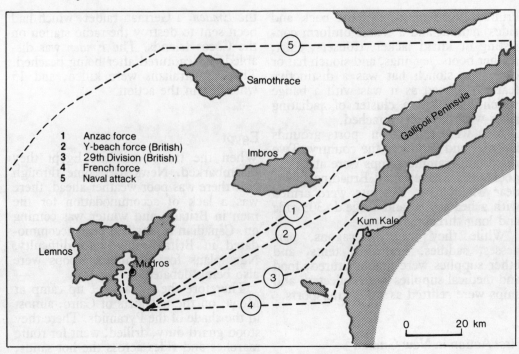

Figure 23.6. The Gallipoli Campaign (a).

Map legend:
1. Anzac force
2. Y-beach force (British)
3. 29th Division (British)
4. French force
5. Naval attack

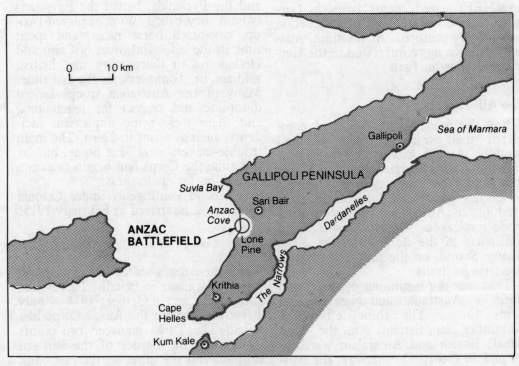

Figure 23.7. The Gallipoli Campaign (b).

Secretary of State for War, hoped to defeat the Turks quickly, and remove this menace. So did Winston S. Churchill, the First Lord of the Admiralty. He believed that an Anglo-French fleet could force an entrance through the Dardanelles, and sail to Constantinople. The fleet could then bombard that ancient city, which hopefully would surrender quickly. With the capital seized, the rest of Turkey would also collapse. This would open a route through to Russia, and allow the allies to attack the enemy in Europe with greater forces.

Churchill's naval action was tried, but failed miserably. Nearly all the ships used were old and, in many cases, needed a refit. The command situation was poor, and the Turks had laid minefields in the narrows and dug in batteries on both shores overlooking the mines. The gunners aboard the ships smashed some of the Turkish batteries, but three ships were lost on a minefield in one day, and the attack had to be called off.

By this time, it became obvious that troops would have to be used in an amphibious assault on the Gallipoli Peninsula. Once landed, these troops could fight their way eastwards, across the peninsula, and take the coastal forts and guns from behind. The ships would then be able to clear the minefields and sail through to Constantinople. General Sir Ian Hamilton was placed in command of a Mediterranean Expeditionary Force, consisting of some 70 000 British, Dominion, Indian, and French troops.

The Anzacs into Action — 25 April 1915

On 1 April (April Fools' Day), the Anzacs were informed that all leave had been cancelled. On 3 April, the men were ordered into trains and taken to the port of Alexandria. There they boarded ships again, and these ships sailed north, towards the Greek island of Lemnos. There they met with other Allied ships,

Figure 23.8. The landing at Anzac Cove.

to form a formidable armada of 200 warships and transports. These ships set sail for Gallipoli on the evening of 24 April.

Before dawn on 25 April, the Anzacs climbed down into small rowing boats, clutching their rifles and equipment. These boats were then towed by steamboats over 4 kilometres to shore. The Anzacs were supposed to land in a small cove one and a half kilometres north of a small promontory called Gaba Tepe, establish a beachhead, and move inland, overcoming the Turks. Unfortunately, there were strong currents, and these currents swept the boats into another cove, later to be named Anzac Cove. Here there was a beach, and behind that a steep hill rising about 100 metres straight up. It was a spot which had been designated impossible for a landing.

As the boats came in, the men tum-

Figure 23.9. Scaling the cliffs at Gaba Tepe.

Figure 23.10. Captain Albert Jacka, VC MC.

bled into the water, and ran up onto the beach. As they came ashore, they were met by rifle and machine-gun fire from the heights above. The Turks were comfortably entrenched, and could pick their marks. For the first time in their history, Australian troops fell wounded and dying together, in the boats, in the water, on the beach, and amongst the scrub on the hill.

A representative of the London *Daily Telegraph* described the initial assault:

The Australians rose to the occasion. Not waiting for orders, or for the boats to reach the beach, they sprang into the sea, and, forming a sort of rough line, rushed at the enemy's trenches.

Their magazines were not charged, so they just went in with cold steel.

It was over in a minute. The Turks in the first trench were either bayoneted or they ran away, and their Maxim was captured.

Then the Australians found themselves facing an almost perpendicular cliff of loose sandstone, covered with thick shrubbery. Somewhere, about halfway up, the enemy had a second trench, strongly held, from which they poured a terrible fire on the troops below and the boats pulling back to the destroyers for the second landing party.

Here was a tough proposition to tackle in the darkness, but those colonials, practical above all else, went about it in a practical way.

They stopped for a few minutes to pull themselves together, got rid of their packs, and charged their magazines.

Then this race of anthletes proceeded to scale the cliffs without responding to the enemy's fire. They lost some men, but did not worry.

In less than a quarter of an hour the Turks were out of their second position, either bayoneted or fleeing.

There has been no finer feat in this war than this sudden landing in the dark and storming the heights, above all holding on whilst the reinforcements were landing ...

The men gained a foothold under

the guns, but were then stopped by the Turks, and could go no further. Meanwhile, more men landed on the beach below. By nightfall, thousands of troops had come ashore. The landing was achieved at tremendous cost, however. Many Australians lay dead and wounded.

Generals Birdwood and Bridges wanted to withdraw the men, but General Hamilton, aboard the *Queen Elizabeth*, refused, and ordered the men to 'dig in' and 'stick it out'. Hence the term 'diggers' was born.

In August, the Anzacs were reinforced by British troops. Attempts were made to move further inland. Some ground was covered, but could not be held. On Sari Bair, there was bitter hand-to-hand fighting, and 4000 men died. By September, the beach and foothills were jammed with some 105 000 men, 20 000 mules, and 3000 horses, plus stores and provisions. By this time, men were huddled in a complex of trenches and dugouts, grumbling endlessly about sniper fire, lack of water, lack of tobacco, lack of mail, and about dysentery which had broken out.

There were heroes amongst the ranks. One was Albert Jacka. Jacka was a country lad who had enlisted at the age of 21. He was a lance-corporal when the Anzacs sailed from Australia. On 19 May 1915, he and four others were attacked by a Turkish platoon. His companions were all killed or wounded, but Jacka was not beaten. He killed all seven Turks single-handed, without being wounded himself. For this, he was awarded the Victoria Cross. He was commissioned in August 1916, and later won the Military Cross.

Another hero was John Simpson. He was 22, an English-born private in the 3rd Field Ambulance. He had difficulty getting ashore. All the men in his boat were killed. Once ashore, he took a donkey and transported wounded troops through bullets and shells for 25 days. Finally he was killed, in mid-May.

Eventually, ugly stories began circu-

lating abroad, spread by pressmen like Keith Murdoch. Leadership was criticized, as well as the immense difficulties of maintaining supplies, and the loss of life. Field Marshal Lord Kitchener visited the Gallipoli beaches and agreed that something had to be done. In early December the British government agreed to withdraw the men. By early January 1916, this had been accomplished.

The Australians lost 7818 men at Gallipoli and sustained 19 441 wounded. The New Zealanders lost some 2500 men, and 5000 were wounded. The French lost as many as the combined Anzac force. The British lost nearly three times as many.

The Western Front

After abandoning Gallipoli, the Anzacs were taken back to Egypt. There they rested, were reinforced, and received new equipment. Early in 1916, the British Command decided to move the men to the front line in France.

Once again, the Anzacs boarded trains, and then ships. This time they sailed to the French port of Marseilles, where they were welcomed enthusiastically by a French crowd. Again they boarded trains, and were taken to 'the Front'. By May, the men were in position near the French village of Armentières.

On the front line, the Anzacs had to face the same fears, frustrations, and discomforts as other troops. There were bombing and strafing raids by aircraft. There were fierce artillery barrages. There was sniping. There was mustard gas — so called because it stained the ground and men's bodies a mustard yellow. Added to this was the fact that the Australians were not used to the biting cold of a European winter. Men sat or stood in trenches, surrounded by mud, with the sound of guns ringing in their ears, and ate or talked or smoked their Woodbines and Navy Cut, and won-

Figure 23.11. *The misery of war at the Western Front — dead and wounded in a railway cutting.*

Figure 23.12. *The First Australian Infantry Battalion at Ypres.*

dered when they would have to fight — again — to survive. At night, the sky was lit up by the flash of guns and the glare of exploding star shells. The dead were buried where they fell, or in cemeteries near by, and the wounded evacuated to London (or 'Blighty'). Men rested on leave in Armentières, and other villages and towns of allied France.

On 19 July, the Australians had their first major engagement with the enemy, at Fromelles. They were supported by British troops, and their objective was to pin down German troops in that area. There was a preliminary bombardment, to 'soften up' the Germans, before the Anzacs went 'over the top'. The Germans had been forewarned, however, and were ready and waiting. They mowed down the advancing Anzacs with machine-gun fire. Men of the 5th Division broke through the German lines, but were forced to retreat again. The attack failed, and cost 5500 casualties.

Four days later, the Anzacs went into action again, at Pozières. Men of the 1st Division closed with enemy in bitter hand-to-hand fighting. Some ground was gained and the men dug in. The Germans struck back again, with massed artillery fire for three solid days. The 1st Division sustained 5300 casualties and was withdrawn, dazed and exhausted, to be replaced by the 2nd Division. The men of this division moved further across 'No Man's Land', and dug in again. Again they were pounded by German artillery. This time there were 6800 casualties. The 2nd Division was then replaced by the 4th Division. Again these men moved forward, losing 4600 men. They were replaced by the 1st Division, which had been rested and reinforced.

And so it went on. The 1st Division lost another 2650 men, and was withdrawn. The 2nd was brought in again and lost another 1300 men. The 4th, brought in again, lost another 2400 men. The 4th managed to reach Mouquet Farm, about one and a half kilometres from the starting point. The men were

Figure 23.13. Regiment of the Australian Light Horse on march near Jerusalem.

then withdrawn, and sent to Ypres, a comparatively quiet sector, to rest. There they dug in for the winter.

The three divisions, 1st, 2nd, and 4th, were soon sent to attack Bapaume, reinforced by the 5th Division. To gain their objective, the Anzacs had to wade through a sea of mud, and many were killed. Twice they tried to get through, and twice they failed. They were withdrawn again. And so this tragic carnage continued... at Bullecourt (1917)... Messines (1917)... Villers Bretonneux (1918)...

War in the Desert

The Anzac Light Horse and Camel Brigades had been left behind in Egypt, as part of a combined force under British command. The function of this combined force was, firstly, to prevent the Turks controlling the Suez Canal, and secondly, to defeat them in the Sinai Peninsula and Palestine.

The Turks attacked at Romani, 37 kilometres from the Canal, but were driven back. The Australians suffered several hundred casualties in this action. General Henry George Chauvel then led the mounted Anzacs against the Turks, and pushed them back into Palestine (1917).

A British commander, General Allenby, then assumed command of operations, and Chauvel took command of the desert column. At Beersheba, in the Judean hills, the Anzacs mounted their first real cavalry charge. Beersheba had to be taken, for its wells. The Anzacs charged through machine-gun and rifle fire, swept through the Turkish lines, and dismounted to fight with rifles and bayonets. Few Anzacs, or their horses, were lost. Allenby then moved 32 kilometres west to take Gaza, then north, to capture Jerusalem. The city had been in Muslim hands for over 600 years, and its fall was celebrated in London as a great victory.

A Reaction at Home

At home, lists of casualties were received. Ministers and priests visited relatives to break the news of soldiers' deaths before their names were pub-

Figure 23.14. Billy Hughes (centre) with a group of Australian soldiers.

AUSTRALIAN LABOR PARTY
Anti-Conscription Campaign Committee.

"VOTE NO MUM

they'll take DAD next"

VOTE ☒ NO

Authorised by
B. Mulvogue,
Trades Hall, Melb.

Fraser & Jenkinson, Print.,
313-5 Queen St.

Figure 23.15. An Australian anti-conscription poster.

lished in newspapers. Australians saw their young men return home limbless, sightless, crippled from mustard gas, and 'shell-shocked'. There was no 'glory' in this. The horrors of Gallipoli, the Western Front, and the desert were brought home to the Australian people, and many began to question the validity of the war. Only a small percentage of the population had opposed the war at the outset. Now the number opposing it grew. Even 'respectable' people began to voice criticism.

In 1916, the Easter Rising occurred in Ireland, and was suppressed brutally by British troops. Irish freedom-fighters were shot, wounded, and imprisoned. The British considered the Irish were traitors, attempting to stab them in the back while they were embroiled in France. However, the Irish wanted to serve neither King nor Kaiser, but only Ireland. They wanted Home Rule. About a quarter of Australia's population was Irish by descent, and many felt sympathy for their relatives in Ireland, and hostility towards Britain, its Empire, and the war effort in general. They joined the growing number of people who opposed the war.

The Conscription Debate

Towards the end of 1915, the Labor prime minister, Billy Hughes, was invited by the British government to visit Europe. There he could study war at close hand. He went, visiting England and France. In England, he attended meetings of the British War Cabinet, and was impressed with Lloyd George, the future prime minister, who was all for ending the war as quickly as possible. In France, he met Georges Clemenceau, the French premier, and visited troops in the trenches.

Hughes returned to Australia determined to involve more Australians in the war. One sure way to do this was to introduce conscription. Late in August, cables were received from the British Army Council and Australian Headquarters in London, asking for reinforcements. The AIF had suffered 28 000 casualties in seven weeks on the Western Front, and there were only 7000 reserves available in Britain. The British authorities were now threatening to break up the Anzac force and place its soldiers in other British units. This was a shrewd move. Hughes would have to do something, or Australians would not have their own military force to represent them; 32 500 men were demanded immediately, plus a further monthly recruitment of 16 500. During June, July, and August, about 6000 men per month had enlisted. This was not nearly

Figure 23.16. Armistice Day in Melbourne, November 1918.

enough. Hughes was thus forced into action.

When Hughes announced his intention to introduce conscription to make up troop numbers, he divided his own party and the people of Australia. He was supported by W. A. Holman, the Labor premier of New South Wales, most newspapers, Protestant churches, the Universal Service League (organized to promote conscription), capitalists, patriots, and conservatives. He was opposed by Dr D. Mannix, the future Roman Catholic Archbishop of Melbourne, T. J. Ryan, the Labor premier of Queensland, unionists, the Industrial Workers of the World (or 'Wobblies'), the Australian Freedom League, Irish nationalists, conscientious objectors, pacifists, socialists, and others. Dr Mannix led the anti-conscription forces in the south, and T. J. Ryan led them in the north. Speeches were made, letters written to newspapers, posters posted, and large meetings voiced protest. Hughes determined he was right, and battled on.

Hughes agreed to two referendums, to let the people of Australia decide the issue. These referendums were held on 28 October 1916, and 20 December 1917. The wording of the first referendum was:

Are you in favour of the Government having, in this grave emergency, the same compulsory powers over citizens in regard to requiring their military service, for the term of this War, outside the Commonwealth, as it now has in regard to military service within the Commonwealth?

The wording of the second referendum was:

Are you in favour of the proposal of the Commonwealth Government for reinforcing the Australian Imperial Force overseas?

Hughes lost both referendums. The first was defeated by a majority of 72 476 'No' votes. (New South Wales, Queensland, and South Australia voted 'No'; Victoria, Western Australia, Tasmania, and the Territories voted 'Yes'.) The second was defeated by a majority of 166 588 'No' votes. (New South Wales, Victoria, Queensland, and South Australia voted 'No'; Western Australia, Tasmania, and the Territories voted 'Yes'.)

The Armistice

The war ended in November 1918, with the surrender of Germany. A Peace Conference was then held in Paris. It was attended by delegates from those nations that had been involved in the war. The guiding spirit at this conference was President Woodrow Wilson of the United States of America. He proposed a 14-point settlement (usually called his 'Fourteen Points'). One of the more important of these points was the setting up of the League of Nations. Hughes, Cook, and others represented Australia.

From the start, Hughes proved an independent delegate at the conference. Lloyd George and others would have preferred him to be a quiet member of a combined Dominion delegation, but he insisted on speaking out, loudly, as a representative of Australia as a nation in its own right. He did not want to treat Germany and her allies kindly, and he fought for, and gained, a number of important, if not highly moral, concessions:

- Japan, who had fought on the side of the Allies, wanted a clause written into the Covenant (agreement) of the new League of Nations guaranteeing racial equality and freedom of migration between members of the League. This would have destroyed Australia's White Australia Policy, and Hughes would have none of it. He managed to have the Japanese proposal defeated.
- For security reasons, Hughes demanded that German New Guinea be annexed to Australia. After much discussion, Australia was given a C-Class mandate over the island. This was almost as effective as full control.
- Hughes insisted that Germany pay heavy reparations (or war damage payments) to compensate for lost Australian lives. He asked for £474 million and was promised £100 million. In the end Australia received only £5 million as Germany was totally unable to repay more.

The Effects of the War

The war had a number of important effects on the course of Australian history:

- Australia had sent almost 302 000 men abroad. Of these, almost 60 000 had been killed or died of wounds and 152 000 wounded or affected by gas. Australia had suffered higher casualties, according to population, than most other countries. This was an incalculable loss. The nation had lost some of her finest young men — who would have become poets, artists, engineers, scientists, craftsmen, and workers. Many who returned home were serious and old before their time.
- A spirit and legend of 'Anzac' was born. Many Australians came to believe that they had proven themselves to be first-rate soldiers. They had been brave, and they had been tough. They had also been on the winning side. Before the war, Australians thought of themselves as a race of bushmen and pioneers. From the time of the Great War onwards, they were to think of themselves, and promote themselves, as both good bushmen and tough soldiers. A whole new national image was born. C. E. W. Bean, an official war historian, wrote:

The arms were handed in. The rifles were locked in the rack. The horses were sold. The guns were sheeted and parked in storage for other gunners. The familiar faded-green uniform disappeared from the streets.

But the Australian Imperial Force is not dead. That famous army of generous men marches still down the long lane of its country's history, with bands playing and rifles slung, with packs on shoulders, white dust on boots, and bayonet scabbards and entrenching tools flapping on countless things — as the fellaheen of Egypt and the French countryfolk knew it.

What these men did nothing can alter now. The good and the bad, the greatness and the smallness of their story will stand. Whatever of glory it contains nothing now can lessen. It rises, as it will always rise, above the mists of ages, a monument to great-hearted men, and for their nation, a possession for ever.

* Some Australian argued that Australia 'came of age' during the Great War. A blood sacrifice was made on the shores of Anzac Cove.
* Australian industry was given a boost during the war (e.g. the establishment of BHP).
* Australians had a new national day to celebrate — Anzac Day, 25 April.

Songs of the First World War

Mademoiselle from Armentières

Oh, Mademoiselle from Armentières,
  Parley Vous?
Oh, Mademoiselle from Armentières,
  Parley Vous?
Oh, Mademoiselle from Armentières,
She hasn't been kissed for forty years,
  Inky, pinky, Parley Vous.

Two Aussie Officers crossed the Rhine,
  Parley Vous,
Two Aussie Officers crossed the Rhine,
  Parley Vous?
Two Aussie Officers crossed the Rhine,
To meet the ladies and taste the wine,
  Inky, pinky, Parley Vous?

Tipperary

It's a long way to Tipperary,
It's a long way to go;
It's a long way to Tipperary,
To the sweetest girl I know.
Goodbye, Piccadilly,
Farewell Leicester Square,
It's a long way to Tipperary,
But my heart's right there.

Pack up your Troubles

Pack up your troubles in your old kit bag,
And smile, boys, smile;
While you've a lucifer to light your fag,
Smile, boys that's the style:
What's the use of worrying?
It never was worth while,
So pack up your troubles in your old kit bag,
And smile, boys, smile.

We are the Ragtime Army

We are the ragtime Army,
The A.N.Z.A.C.;
We cannot shoot, we won't salute,
What blanky use are we?
And when we get to Berlin
The Kaiser he will say,
'Hoch, Hoch, mein Gott,
What an awful rotten lot
Are the A.N.Z.A.C.'

Take Me Back to Dear Old Blighty

Take me back to dear old Blighty,
Put me on the train for London Town,
Take me over there, take me anywhere,
Liverpool or Manchester, well I don't care,
I just want to see my mammy,
With my best girl she'll be waiting there,
Hi tee, iddle, ey ity, Take me back to Blighty,
Blighty is the place for me.

Take me back to bear old Aussie,
Put me on the boat for Melbourne Town,
Take me over there, drop me anywhere,
Sydney, Melbourne, Adelaide, for I don't care,
I just want to see my best girl,
Cuddling up again we soon will be,
Oh, Blighty is a failure,
Take me back t' Australia
Aussie is the place for me.

Questions

(1) What was the reaction of most Australians to the outbreak of war in 1914?

(2) Who commanded the 1st AIF in 1914?

(3) What do the letters ANZAC stand for?

(4) Where were the Anzacs based in Egypt?

(5) Why did the Mediterranean Expeditionary Force land on the beaches of Gallipoli?

(6) Describe some of the difficulties and dangers encountered by troops on the Western Front.

(7) Name three battles on the Western Front in which Australians participated.

(8) How did Australians vote in Hughes's referendums?

(9) What concessions did Hughes win for Australia at the Paris Peace Conference?

(10) Explain what is meant by the term 'Anzac tradition'.

Research

Find out more about the following:
(1) The First World War in general
(2) The 1st AIF
(3) The conscription debate
(4) Prime Minister Hughes
(5) Dr Mannix.

Chapter 24

Between the Wars

The Diggers Return Home

The men who had served their country abroad returned to cheering crowds, waving flags, blaring bands, slaps on the back, and government assistance. Those who suffered from wounds or illness as a result of the war went into repatriation hospitals or remained at home, to be nursed back to health. These thin, pale, shocked young men were said to be 'on susso', that is, they received paid sustenance. Many never recovered. Those who were physically fit turned in their uniforms, purchased 'thirty-bob', 'civvy' suits, and went out to spend their gratuities, before looking for work.

When returned servicemen came to look for work, they found a number of

Figure 24.1. Soldier settlement in Western Australia.

jobs had been taken by women during the war, as part of the war effort. Some patriotic women gave up their jobs for the men. The government also passed legislation that guaranteed preference to returned soldiers. Many were given jobs in the various government services. However, this tended to lower efficiency in those services.

Schemes were also launched to settle returned soldiers on the land. Nearly £50 000 000 was advanced to facilitate

this, and some 37 000 men were settled on small blocks in the country. Many of these men knew little about farming. They were given blocks which were too small to support them and their families, and they could not afford to purchase stock and equipment and repay interest rates. One-third of them quickly left their holdings and, by 1928, half the money invested in the scheme had been written off as lost.

Figure 24.2. During the 1920s, schemes were devised to boost migration to Australia.

Immigration is Boosted

In 1922, the British government passed the *Empire Settlement Act*. This guaranteed loans of up to £3 000 000 a year for 15 years to the Dominions to promote emigration to them and to redistribute the white population of the Empire. In 1925, the British government entered into a £34 000 000 agreement with the Australian Commonwealth government. The two governments promised to lend up to £34 000 000 to the states, over a period of 10 years, for development, on condition that the states guaranteed to settle one assisted immigrant for every £75 received. It was hoped that 450 000 British migrants would settle in Australia. In 1926, the Development and Migration Committee was set up to approve schemes.

Between 1921 and 1929, 323 000 immigrants arrived: 212 000 of them were assisted. This was not as many as theorists had hoped for. Still, Australia's population increased by almost 20 per cent, from 5.4 million to 6.4 million, because of immigration and a rising birth rate.

The Prosperous Twenties

During the 1920s, Australians shared in and enjoyed a generally prosperous economy. There was a great mood of optimism. The war was over. The future promised much.

Imports had been restricted during the war, and this had encouraged the

Figure 24.3. Work began on the Sydney Harbour Bridge in 1923 but was not completed until 1932. The original estimate was £4 million, but by completion well over £9 million had been spent.

growth of small, local industries. After the war, these industries mushroomed. Heavy industries were also established — in iron, steel, and engineering. Steel production doubled. The use of electrical power was expanded (hydro-electricity in Tasmania, and coal-generated electricity in other states). The building industry boomed. Houses, factories, and industrial plants had all to be built.

Millions of hectares were cultivated for the first time. Improved farming methods, including the use of better machinery and superphosphates, meant increased producton.

New towns sprung up across Australia. At Yallourn, in Victoria, for instance, hundreds of homes were built by the State Electricity Commision for the workers who were moved there to mine the area's brown coal.

In all this, returned servicemen and immigrants provided the labour. Industrialists demanded tariff protection, and got it. Unionists continued to press their claims, and achieved them. Farmers demanded bounties of one kind or another, and got them. Therefore prices and wages went up. Things could be made difficult by an occasional drought, or strike, but that was about all. Money for borrowing was always available.

Entertainment in the Twenties

There was a wide variety of entertainment available during the 1920s. Australians went to race meetings (the Melbourne Cup had become the highlight of the racing calendar), cricket matches,

Figure 24.4. Dame Nellie Melba.

Figure 24.5. Gladys Moncrieff.

Figure 24.6. Roy Rene ('Mo').

football matches (Australian Rules was well established in Victoria and Tasmania), aquatic carnivals, regattas, fairs, and agricultural shows. They also went for picnics, walks, boating trips, and to the beach. At the beach, both sexes wore more modern 'bathing costumes'. In the evenings, Australians went to the theatre or cinema, or to dances or balls. Many stayed at home, gathering for a sing-song around the piano, or to listen to radio or play records. Many just sat by the fire, or around the dinner table, and talked.

The Australian Theatre

The Australian theatre was alive and prosperous during the 1920s. Australians could choose from a wide variety of productions, from classical ballet and drama, through musical comedy to vaudeville. Many overseas stars performed in classical productions.

Dame Nellie Melba, a soprano, was regarded as the greatest Australian classical performer. She spent a good deal of her time touring abroad, however. Her last appearance in Australia was at a concert in Geelong, Victoria, in November 1928.

Gladys Moncrieff, 'Our Glad', was popular in musical comedy. She became the equivalent of Britain's Gracie Fields. Her best-remembered role was that of Teresa in J. C. Williamson's production of *The Maid of the Mountains.*

Vaudeville was a mixture of comedy, songs, and chorus line. One of the most popular vaudeville performers was **Roy Rene,** or 'Mo'. He was a comic who indulged in outrageous lampoons and sketches. He was a kindly man, well-loved by Australians. One night he stopped the show to explain to a small girl in the audience that she was meant to laugh when he cried.

The Australian Film Industry

The cinema was strongly established by the 1920s. Films were silent and in black and white. Often a piano player sat beneath or to one side of the small, square screen, and supplied a fitting musical accompaniment to the action. In the cities, films were shown in cinemas. In the country districts they were taken around for exhibition in horse-drawn wagons. Outback, there were no screenings at all.

Australia had helped to pioneer the film industry. *The Kelly Gang*, made in 1905–6, by an Australian unit led by J. and W. Tait, was the first full-length feature film in the world. Unfortunately, no copies of this film still exist.

Popular silent films included *The Enemy Within* and *The Lure of the Bush* (both 1918), *The Sentimental Bloke* (1919), *The Man from Kangaroo*, *On Our Selection*, *Ginger Mick*, *The Jackeroo of Coolabong*, and *The Shadow of Lightning Ridge* (all 1920), *While the Billy Boils* (1921), *Moth of Moonbi* (1926), and a remake of *For the Term of His Natural Life* (1927).

Between 1900 and 1930, the silent period in Australian films, over 150 theatrical films were produced by Australian units. These had to compete with an increasing number of films from overseas, particularly from the USA (Hollywood). Overseas actors and actresses became world-wide idols. These idols included Charlie Chaplin, Buster Keaton, Rudolph Valentino, Greta Garbo, Douglas Fairbanks, Mary Pickford, and many more.

Films with sound ('talkies') appeared first in 1928. The first commercial release of a talkie was *The Jazz Singer*, with Al Jolson. From then on, talkies quickly replaced silent films.

Figure 24.7. An early poster to promote For the Term of His Natural Life, *one of the first 'silent' films to be made in Australia.*

Figure 24.8. A still from the 'talkie' version of the film The Sentimental Bloke, *made in the 1930s.*

Figure 24.9. The phonograph provided a new kind of family entertainment to be enjoyed at home.

Popular Dances and Music

Dances and balls were popular forms of entertainment. Men and women dressed up for these. There were no such things as 'casual' dances. Men wore a suit and tie. Women wore either short 'flapper' dresses or long ball gowns. During this period, jazz came into vogue, played by small groups on piano, drums, double bass, clarinet, and trumpet. To go with the colourful and swinging music, new dances were invented — the Shimmy, the Charleston, and the Black Bottom.

Radio and Phonographs

In the 1920s, radio sets began to appear in homes. At first, radio took the form of a 'crystal set'. The set had no valves, but used a crystal detector of quartz or carborundum on which a fine wire called a 'cat's whisker' rested. The listener had to 'tickle' the cat's whisker to tune in and, because the sounds received were never very loud, she or he had to wear earphones. Several sets of earphones were necessary when guests came to listen in.

Soon it was possible to purchase radio sets with valves and loudspeakers — the loudspeakers taking the form of trumpet-like horns. These early sets had a large, dry battery and 'accumulator', which had to be taken to the shop every week to be recharged.

The early radio stations were all commercial stations. They included 2SB, later 2BL, 2FC, 2KY, and 2UW (Sydney), 2HD (Newcastle), 3AR, 3LO, and 3UZ (Melbourne), 4QG (Brisbane), 4GR (Toowoomba), 5CL and 5DN (Adelaide), 6WF (Perth), and 7ZL (Hobart). By June 1925, 38 000 licences for radio receivers had been issued. This rose to 310 000 in July 1929. The ABC did not commence operations until 1 July 1932.

Australians also played records on phonographs. These records were large, scratchy 78s, which broke easily if dropped. Phonographs had large, horn-shaped speakers like early radios. Popular artists on record were Rudy Vallee, Guy Lombardo, Al Jolson, and — towards the end of the 1920s — a very young Bing Crosby. Music shops did a good trade selling sheet music and records. 'Song pushers' were employed to stand outside shops, singing, to induce passers-by to enter and make a purchase.

Heroes of the Skies

The aeroplane was developed early in the twentieth century by European and American inventors. On 17 December 1903, Orville Wright made the first recorded flight in an aeroplane, at Kitty Hawk in USA. During the First World War, improvements were made in production and design. For instance, ground-to-air radio was developed. By the 1920s, there were an increasing number of aircraft in the skies.

They were exciting days in the history of aviation. Pilots 'flew by the seat of their pants', and were regarded as colourful heroes. They flew dangerous and rickety aircraft, sitting in open cockpits,

Figure 24.10. One of the first airline services to begin operations in the early 1920s was Qantas.

wearing leather helmets and jackets to keep warm, goggles to keep the wind out of their eyes, and scarves to wipe engine oil from their faces. There were no runways in most places, and pilots had to use paddocks, parks, and roadways for take-offs and landings. Fortunately, the aircraft flown were slow, very manoeuvrable biplanes, which could be set down slowly, in a comparatively confined area. Fuel supply was also a problem. Sometimes pilots would land in a bush town and taxi up to the local garage to fill up on petrol from the pumps, or from storage drums.

Some pilots earned their keep by taking passengers for 'joy rides', by putting on air shows called 'flying circuses' and by participating in occasional air races. Pilots also made a living by flying mail. Sometimes there were accidents. On 3 January 1920, Captain A. W. Vigers, MC DFC, crashed in his Sopwith Gnu aircraft while delivering copies of the Melbourne *Herald* to bayside suburbs.

His observer, P. R. Nunn, later died.

Airline services began in the 1920s. Western Australian Airways was the first to become operational, on 3 December 1921. Three flights set out.

Qantas (Queensland and Northern Territory Aerial Services) began on 2 November 1922. Its flight was from Charleville to Cloncurry. This airline was destined to go from strength to strength, and become Australia's overseas airline. Another early, less successful airline was Australia National Airways Ltd. It began in 1929.

Australia produced a number of famous airmen. In 1919, Prime Minister Hughes and his government offered a prize of £10 000 to the first Australian to fly from England to Australia, in a British-made aircraft, within 30 days. This prize were claimed by two young Adelaide pilots, Keith and Ross Smith, and their mechanics, Jim Bennett and Wally Shiers. The brothers were also knighted for their achievement. They

Figure 24.11. Charles Kingsford Smith.

Figure 24.12. 'Bert' Hinkler piloted the first solo flight from England to Australia in 1935.

left England in November 1919, and reached Australia 27 days and 20 hours later. The plane they used was a Vickers Vimy biplane. On their journey out, they spent more time on the ground than in the air, refuelling, repairing their engine, or waiting for bad weather to clear. When they landed at Charleville, they were held up for seven weeks with engine trouble, before flying on to Brisbane. Three other planes attempting to fly the route crashed.

Sir Ross and Lieutenant Bennett were killed in a trial flight in a Vickers Viking in England on 13 April 1922, while preparing for a round-the-world flight. Sir Keith died in 1955.

Another famous pilot, and undoubtedly the most popular, was Charles Kingsford Smith, or 'Smithy'. He was born

at Hamilton, Queensland, in 1897. In 1915, he turned 18 and enlisted in the AIF. He saw action at Gallipoli and in France. In France he joined the Royal Flying Corps and learned to fly. He flew in a fighter squadron, meeting and Germans in 'dog fights', and won the Military Cross. After the war, he made a living by performing acrobatics and stunts in flying circuses and in films in England and the United States. He then returned to Australia and helped to pioneer many new air routes. However, his nagging ambition was to be the first man to fly the Pacific. To do this, he had to purchase a plane. Eventually he obtained financial backing from Sidney Myer of Melbourne and Allan Hancock, an American. He purchased the airframe of a Fokker monoplane that had been used in the Arctic by Sir Hubert Wilkins. He refitted the plane with a new engine and other parts and gave it the name *Southern Cross*.

In 1928, Kingsford Smith realized his dream and made history. He commanded the first flight across the Pacific. Charles Ulm, an Australian, was his co-pilot. Two Americans, Harry Lyon and James Warner, also flew with him. Lyon acted as navigator. The epic flight was made from east to west in three stages: from San Francisco to Honolulu, from Honolulu to Fiji, and from Fiji to Brisbane. The trip took 83 hours and 11 minutes. At the time, the fastest steam ship took 19 days to sail from San Francisco to Sydney.

Smithy disappeared off the coast of Burma in November 1935, during a flight from England to Australia. A companion, J. T. Pethybridge, disappeared with him.

In the same year that Smithy flew the Pacific, another Queensland-born, ex-First World War pilot made history by flying solo from England to Australia. He was Herbert John Louis Hinkler, or 'Bert' Hinkler. His trip took 15½ days, cutting down on the existing record of 28 days. He received a hero's welcome and £2500 in grants from the Queens-

land and Commonwealth governments. He was also awarded the Air Force Cross and was made an honorary squadron leader in the Royal Australian Air Force.

In 1931, Hinkler flew the South Atlantic from west to east in a Canadian-built Puss Moth plane. This remarkable feat of piloting and navigation, in bad weather, earned him world-wide acclaim. He died in 1933. While attempting to fly from England to Australia in a faster time, he crashed in his Puss Moth in the Italian Alps near Arezzo.

The Motor Car

The automobile was developed by European and American inventors towards the end of the nineteenth century and refined early in the twentieth. In 1896, Herbert Thomson, a mechanic from Armadale, Melbourne, built the first car in Australia. It was powered by steam, and between 1898 and 1900 Thomson drove his car all over Victoria. The governor was driven as a passenger in the car and, on one occasion, it was used as a float in a procession. The car was shipped to Sydney for the Royal Easter Show, and was driven back to Melbourne by Thomson. The trip back proved particularly gruelling, and

Figure 24.13. The finish of a car performance test in 1926.

Figure 24.14. The army of the unemployed marching in protest during the Depression.

Thomson was welcomed back by large crowds.

Other cars were built in Australia, but many more were imported from Europe and America. By the 1920s, there were many cars of improved design and performance on the roads, and roads were being developed to meet their needs.

The Depression

In 1929, Wall Street 'crashed' and there was a world-wide slump. Unfortunately, Australia was heavily dependent on the sale of her produce abroad, as well as on imports and borrowed money from abroad. These things had meant a comparatively high standard of living for Australians, even if it had been, to a certain extent, a 'fool's paradise'.

During the course of the Depression, world prices for Australian exports fell dramatically. Fewer goods could be imported, and overseas borrowing became extremely difficult. Overseas loans had been spent on public works. When borrowing ceased, expenditure on public works ceased. This meant that those employed in public works, or in supplying equipment for public works, were thrown out of work. The demand for goods and services declined rapidly, which resulted in smaller and smaller profits and less investment. Production declined. Governments could not raise as much money as before by taxation, and were blamed for the worsening situation. Unemployment increased while productivity fell.

Unemployment figures give a good indication of the course of the Depression. In 1926–27, about 6 per cent of the

Figure 24.15. Queuing to receive food vouchers in Sydney.

work force was unemployed. By 1930, this had risen to 19 per cent. By 1932, the staggering figure of 29 per cent was reached. This meant that about 300 000 workers (mainly men) were unemployed. 1931–32 was the depth of the Depression. However, even by 1935, the national income per head of population was between 10 and 15 per cent lower than before the Depression.

The signs of the Depression soon became obvious. People put up their houses for sale — and could not sell them. Men tramped for kilometres every week, searching for work — and could not find any. When jobs were advertised, long queues formed outside the works, sometimes blocks long. Parks filled with homeless men. Country roads carried men hitching rides and asking for handouts. Shops and businesses closed. Churches did what they could for destitute families. The government offered what assistance (or 'sustenance') it could at local town halls. There, jobs (the few that there were) were advertised, ration books and soup were issued to the starving, and worn-out shoes were mended free of charge. Employment in public works projects such as road building was offered at reduced pay to married men.

Trying to Find a Solution

At first, the Labor government thought it could solve the problem by increasing exports and decreasing imports. A campaign to 'grow more food' was instituted. By 1932, wheat production had increased by 80 per cent, butter production had doubled, mutton production had increased two and a half times, and so on. On the other hand, imports were cut to one-third of what they had been before the Depression.

However, this all failed to have the desired effect, because of the great fall in overseas prices for exports. Politicians in

247

Canberra had to face the fact that Australia's situation would not improve until overseas conditions improved. In the meantime, all Australians could do was share the burden of sacrifice as fairly as possible.

In February 1931, a Premiers' Conference was held, and afterwards the following steps were taken:

• Interest rates were dropped.
• Wages were reduced.
• Government spending was cut back.
• Taxes were increased.
• The Commonwealth Bank issued some credit.

This plan aimed at spreading losses evenly and preventing unemployment rising. However, it probably had little effect. Recovery was tied to overseas recovery, and so was slow and erratic. The Depression of the early 1930s was a painful time in Australia's history, and was not easily forgotten.

The Army of Unemployed

From the Bathurst *Times*, 6 July 1931:

From Goulburn to Pilliga, from the southern parts of Victoria, to the Queensland border, through the Riverina, out west, along the south coast, wherever the road leads, goes the army of unemployed. Many have been so long on the track now that from being an abnormal existence it becomes their normal one.

One remarks casually that he has been out of a job for the past four years, another that he has tramped from Victoria to Bathurst, a third that his last job was when a border railway was being built four years ago. There is developing in Australia a remarkable fraternity, whose numbers now run into tens of thousands — those who form the great army of unemployed which tramps the inland districts of the State, some with the hope of a job in the next town, some content to settle in some established road 'camp', some rather hopeless and others beginning to lose hope through the lack of work for the past six months, twelve months, two years, or whatever it may be.

There are many who do not worry now whether there are any prospects of a job or not

— they merely keep going, 'resting' where a congenial atmosphere is found, or else back on the track, by boot, by 'jumping the rattler', or by obtaining a lift from the friendly lorry driver. The latter, too, has become a well-known figure of the road.

Frequently a driver will pick up a lorry load of campers from under the bridge, Bathurst's 'Hotel Denison', and take them on the next stage to the city or further west. It is noticeable that the drift is always further out — the difficulties of living in the city under the present conditions have been realized by most years ago.

Despite an increasing vigilance, there is still a great deal of the ride-stealing on the railways, mostly a rather precarious ride, but even this is falling off, not because of the campaign conducted against it by railway officials, but rather because many think that one town is as good as the next.

The track certainly gives them a knowledge of their own country — the towns which are the most benevolent, the hard towns, the towns where a big Government job is being carried out and where there is a chance of employment for a time, the names of the cookhouses and their proprietors, the latters' (peculiarities), the places where regular camps are established, and the most profitable stretches of track.

Their conversation reveals an intimate knowledge of these details in a hundred towns, ranging over an area of hundreds of miles, principally in the two south-eastern States. There are hundreds of (stories) told at any of their gatherings, and there is always someone else who can remember yet another story of any particular place which may be mentioned. Generally, however, there is little hint of the prevailing conditions in their conversation. It may touch on any phase of life anywhere in the world, but rarely on the Depression. True, the dole is a general topic here and there, but that is like talking 'shop'. Policemen who handle the dole are another topic — Sergeant So-and-So of one centre, and Constable Somebody of another. Despite what is being said, the police are not looked upon with any enmity by the majority of the unemployed. At least this is not so in the country districts, no matter what influences may be at work among the city members of the fraternity.

It is noticeable that there is a feeling of apathy now — a feeling of months of inactivity, and a sorry phase of the new outlook is the fact that there is less actual search and desire for work than there was in the beginning.

In one group's conversation, the suggestion

was made that the first six months on the track was the worst, to be followed by facetious answers that the worst periods were the first seven years, and the last fourteen. At any rate, after that first spell, the life becomes a normal one.

They are inclined to question some of the facts of unemployment. When one mentioned that there are 125 000 unemployed in the State at present, there was a general chorus of disagreement. Another declared that there was that many in Sydney alone, a second that was probably the number registered at labour exchanges, while a third opined that there were 125 000 men tramping and camping along the Murrumbidgee — a small section of the great army. Then it was suggested that these figures were computed according to the number who obtained the dole. It was strange how the conversation always seemed to drift back to the dole.

The dole had become with most (the same as) a job, the provider of sustenance. But humour was always there, no matter what may have been the experiences of the track. There was always something humorous to tell. And perhaps the grandest example of humour is that which is now being supplied in Bathurst. It has been announced that ration orders will be supplied in an old building in Russell Street, from this week, having been transferred from the police station. And one wag has already coined the suggestion that it be called the 'Millions Club'.

Life during the Thirties

Despite the Depression, the lifestyle of Australians continued to change during the 1930s. Almost every home in the land acquired a radio, or 'wireless'. 'Radiola' was one popular brand. Radio programmes became very popular. Many Australians purchased cars. Cars in the thirties were nearly all heavy sedans, with powerful and reliable engines. The number of commercial air-flights increased and air travel became safer. Buses began running. The railways, too, offered more services.

Entertainment in the 1930s became diverse. The American film industry produced more and more films, promoting and selling a long list of stars to its audience. More and more cinemas, or 'pic-

ture theatres', opened. Many were built in the distinctive 'Odeon' picture-palace style. Vaudeville suffered, and some old vaudeville halls were converted into cinemas. From about 1935 onwards jazz began to give way to 'swing' and the 'big band' sound. Ballroom dancing became more popular, with couples dancing the waltz and foxtrot. More Australians, including women, took to drinking. The cocktail became a popular drink. Bars and lunch counters opened in greater numbers. Skiing became popular, especially in the Snowy Mountains resorts.

Prime Ministers and Politics between the Wars

During the 1920s and 1930s, Australia was governed by the Nationalist Party (1917–23), a Nationalist-Country Party coalition (1923–29), the Australian Labor Party (1929–31), and the United Australia Party (1931–41).

In 1923, Billy Hughes lost the leadership of his Nationalist Party, and was replaced by Stanley Melbourne Bruce. Bruce had been born of a wealthy merchant family in Melbourne. He had been educated at Melbourne Grammar and Cambridge Uiversity, and had served as an officer in the Royal Fusiliers during the Great War. Like many other Australians, he had seen action at Gallipoli. Returning to Australia, he became a member of the federal parliament in 1918. Three years later, he was appointed treasurer by Billy Hughes. In 1923, he became prime minister. It was a meteoric rise — from candidate to prime minister in only five years! He remained prime minister from 1923 to 1929.

Bruce was a shrewd man. He had a sharp mind and was meticulous in his approach. He allied his party with Earle Page and his Country Party. He worked to develop Australia's economy in the 1920s. He created a new basis for Commonwealth-state relations, established the Australian Loan Council, which represented all states in overseas

Figure 24.16. Stanley Melbourne Bruce.

Figure 24.17. Joseph Aloysius Lyons.

borrowing, introduced compulsory voting for all adults over 21 years of age, secured the standing of a Council for Scientific and Industrial Research (later the CSIRO) and, in 1927, moved the federal parliament from Melbourne to Canberra.

Bruce had little time for the unions, and attempted to block their moves for pay rises. He even tried to give the Commonwealth powers to deal with industrial matters. This move was defeated in a referendum. Then, in 1929, Bruce attempted to hand over all industrial relations to the states, and abandon the system of arbitration that had been set up by Hughes and his associates. This proved to be his downfall. His government was brought down in Parliament by one vote in September 1929.

A general election was held and Labor was swept into power. In this election, Bruce also lost his seat in parliament. He was the first prime minister to be thus humiliated. James Henry Scullin was the new prime minister. He was the son of a railwayman at Trawalla, 38 km out of Ballarat, Victoria. An ex-grocer's boy, he had joined the Labor Party at the age of 19, and had risen through the ranks, mainly because of his powers of oratory.

Unfortunately for Scullin, he came to power during the Depression, and the people of Australia were in an angry mood. The people wanted financial experts, not unionists, and they turned their wrath on Scullin and his party. Both were voted out of office in 1931. Bruce, incidentally, was re-elected to parliament in this same election, but there was no prominent position for him. In 1932, he accepted the post of Australian High Commissioner to London, and left the Australian political scene. He remained High Commissioner in London until 1945.

Joseph Lyons, leading the new United Australia Party, became prime minister in 1931, and remained in office until his death in 1939. Lyons came from Tasmania, a state that had never supplied a prime minister before. In Tasmania he had been premier. He had entered federal politics in 1929. He was a quiet, unpretentious man with a country background. He provided just over seven years of stable, though unimaginative government. 'Honest Joe Lyons' the man the street called him, because he placed conscience and responsibility above party politics. Historians have said that his term in office was undistinguished, and that he benefited from the slow recovery from the Depresion which began in 1932. He took part in the Ottawa Conference, where he followed the lead of the United Kingdom faithfully and uncritically. He applied strict censorship to books, plays, films, and broadcasting. He attempted to ban the fledgling Communist Party. He established the States Grants Commission to advise the Commonwealth government on the states' requirements.

Lyons suffered ill health during his last two years in office, and died of a heart attack on 7 April 1939. His body was shipped to his beloved Tasmania, and there laid to rest.

Questions

(1) How were ex-servicemen assisted after the Great War?
(2) What was the mood of the Australian people just after World War I?
(3) What economic development occurred in Australia during the 1920s?
(4) What forms of entertainment were there in the 1920s?
(5) Name three heroes of Australian aviation.
(6) What difficulties did early Australian pilots face?
(7) What were some of the causes of the Depression of 1929–33?
(8) What effect did the Depression have on Australians?
(9) Who was prime minister in 1930?
(10) Who was prime minister in 1933?

Research

Find out more about the following:
(1) Soldier settlement
(2) The Depression
(3) Stanley Melbourne Bruce
(4) James Henry Scullin
(5) Joseph Lyons.

Chapter 25

World War Two: Defending Australia

Figure 25.1. Adolf Hitler, leader of the German Nazi Party, became a ruthless dictator, seeking to create a German empire in Europe.

252

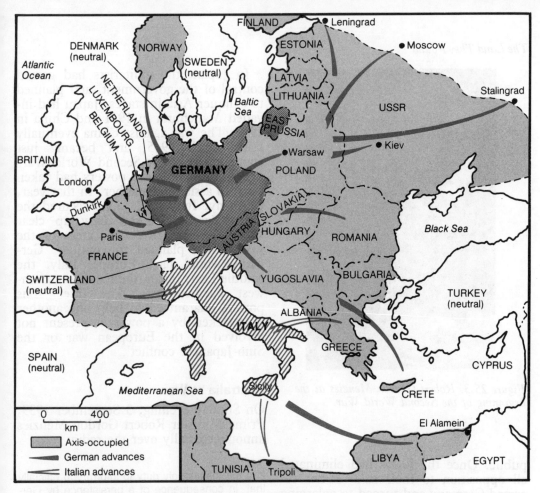

Figure 25.2. Furthest advances of German and Italian troops during the Second World War.

A Worldwide Conflict

The Second World War was two decades in the making and, once begun, it proved to be the most terrible holocaust in the history of mankind. It lasted from 1939 to 1945 and claimed an estimated 35 million lives. Material damage to towns, cities, and industry was also staggering.

Part of the blame for the war must lie with the Treaty of Versailles (1919). The treaty was vengeful. Its terms meant that Germany remained crippled and exhausted. The treaty branded the country as an outcast and left it little chance of entering into friendly, constructive relations with other countries.

Another cause was the Communist Revolution in Russia (1917). It separated Russia from Germany completely, and instilled fear of Russia in the minds of the German middle and upper classes.

There was soaring unemployment, inflation, and poverty in Germany. Would Germany become Communist as well as Russia? That is what many people asked themselves.

Hitler

The time was ripe for a demagogue to appear, and this is what happened. Adolf Hitler, a twisted genius, formed his Nazi (Nationalist Socialist) Party and set about the steady and often ruthless process of taking over the German re-

Figure 25.3. Robert Gordon Menzies at the beginning of the Second World War.

In Japan, the militarists had gained control of the government, and planned to conquer Asia in stages. Japan had invaded Manchuria in 1931 and China in 1932. The war against China eventually lasted until 1945, and became just another part of the Second World War.

By 1940, the three powers had taken steps to assist one another. In that year, Germany, Italy, and Japan secured the Tripartite Pact. They drew up clear spheres of influence over areas of the world they planned to conquer. Germany would have Europe; Italy, the Middle East; Japan, the Far East (southwest Pacific area). The three Axis powers guaranteed to help one another if 'attacked by a power at present not involved in the European war or the Sino-Japanese conflict'.

Australia at War

On Sunday evening, 3 September 1939, Prime Minister Robert Gordon Menzies announced sadly over the radio:

It is my melancholy duty to inform you officially that, in consequence of a persistence by Germany in her invasion of Poland, Great Britain has declared war upon her and that as a result, Australia is also at war.

He added:

Great Britain and France, with the co-operation of the British Dominions, have struggled to avoid this tragedy. They have, as I firmly believe, been patient.

Australia, like Britain and France, was at war with Germany again, for the second time in little more than twenty years.

Australia's Defence Forces

In 1939, Australia's defence forces were run down and in a sorry state. There were about 2800 officers and men in the regular army, and about 80 000 men in the militia. These were organized in four

public. Once the Nazis had eliminated all opposition to their rule, Hitler re-armed Germany and turned to enlarging her 'living space', to make room, and a place in the sun, for all Germans. This meant invading and annexing Austria, Czechoslovakia, and Poland.

When German troops invaded Poland on 1 September 1939, the British and French governments presented an ultimatum. Either Germany should withdraw from Poland, or Britain and France would declare war. Hitler did not reply to the ultimatum, and so war was declared on 3 September 1939.

In the war to come, Hilter had his own allies. In Italy, another dictator held power. He was Benito Mussolini, also known as *Il Duce* (The Leader). At the head of the Fascist Party, he dreamed of restoring the greatness of ancient Rome. In order to create a new Roman Empire, he had invaded Ethiopia in 1935, became involved in the Spanish Civil War in 1936, and invaded Albania in 1939.

Figure 25.4. New recruits arriving at the transit camp at Caulfield, Victoria.

divisions of infantry and two of cavalry. There was also the nucleus of a fifth infantry division. The army was poorly equipped and short of supplies.

The Royal Australian Navy had over 5000 officers and men and only a few light ships. These included the cruisers *Australia, Canberra, Sydney, Hobart, Perth,* and *Adelaide,* the destroyers *Stuart, Vampire, Vendetta, Voyager,* and *Waterhen,* and the sloops *Yarra* and *Swan.* The Navy had no aircraft carriers and no battleships.

The Royal Australian Air Force had just under 3500 officers and men to fly and maintain just over 150 combat aircraft and some other aircraft. Many of these aircraft were obselete.

Australia Mobilizes

The Australian government announced that it would recruit 20000 men. These would form one division and some auxiliary units. The militia woud also be called up in two drafts, and each would be given one month's training. The Air Force would be increased to a force of 32 squadrons. The Australian government offered Number 10 Squadron (composed of Sunderland flying boats) and six other squadrons to flight in Europe. In October 1939, Britain launched the Empire Air Training Scheme, whereby 50000 airmen from the Dominions would be trained each year. Australia's quota was 11000. Once trained, these men would serve with either the Royal Air Force in Britain, or with the Royal Australian Air Force at home.

Lieutenant-General E. K. Squires was appointed Chief of General Staff, Lieutenant-General John Lavarack, 53, was appointed commander of Southern Command, and Lieutenant-General Sir Thomas Blamey, 55, was appointed to command the new 6th Division, then being recruited. Later Blamey would be appointed Commander-in-Chief of Australia's military forces.

The New 6th Division

The men who enlisted went at first into the new 6th Division. Its numbers grew slowly. Some men did not want to fight so did not enlist. Others felt the opposite. They wanted to see action, but feared the division would be held in Australia to defend her shores instead of being sent overseas.

Many of the men who enlisted already had good jobs. Some, however, had been impoverished, especially during the Depression. Critics of the war suggested that the new Division was composed of the dregs of industry and society.

'You'll be sorry!', was the cry from seasoned recruits as newcomers arrived to be given their short-back-and-sides haircut, uniform, physical examinations, injections, and first quarters in makeshift huts.

Accommodation was a problem at first. There was overcrowding, a lack of facilities, and no comfort. The pay was also poor. Unmarried privates received only 5 shillings per day at home, with the promise of an additional 2 shillings per day deferred, after serving overseas.

Figure 25.5. Australian troops and Bren carriers during the attack on the Italian perimeter defences at Bardia.

Married men were to receive 3 shillings per day deferred pay. This was below the basic wage.

Eventually the 6th Division was welded into an effective fighting force with an increasing *esprit de corps*. The men saw themselves as part of a special force, and were proud to belong to it.

Meanwhile, the government was deciding how to handle its defence strategy. Should the 6th, and other units, be held in Australia? Should they be sent overseas? Many people were suspicious of Japan. What moves was it likely to make in the near future? Japan announced that it would remain 'independent', but what did that mean?

Then, on 20 November 1939, the New Zealand government announced that it would send a force to Europe. The spirit of Anzac could not be ignored and, on 29 November, the Australian government announced that it, too, would send a force. It would be the 6th Division. By this time, the Labor Party was putting up only slight opposition to sending Australian troops overseas.

An advance group of the 6th left for Palestine, on orders from Britain. Britain wanted a strong garrison force to protect her bases in the Middle East. On 9 January 1940, men of the 16th Brigade boarded ships in Sydney Harbour, after a rousing farewell. They sailed the following day, to rendezvous with transport ships from New Zealand. The Anzacs were together again. As it was to turn out, however, they were to see little action together. During the course of the war, they were to fight together only in Greece and Crete.

War in the Desert

In Egypt, the Australian 6th Division joined forces with the British 7th Armoured Division (which was equipped with light tanks) under the command of the British General Richard O'Connor. O'Connor was a small, alert man. His orders were to destroy the Italian army, which now occupied eastern

Libya, and had crossed into western Egypt to threaten British bases and the vital Suez Canal. To this end, he had to lead his men into western Egypt and Libya, and attack and destroy Italian bases and fortresses there.

On 3 January 1941, the Australians and British took part in the attack on Bardia. Bardia was a coastal town in Libya which had been heavily fortified by the Italians. Its defences were 17.5 kilometres long and 8 kilometres deep. Two lines of barbed wire had been strung, minefields had been laid, and anti-tank ditches had been dug. The Italian troops were poorly armed, however. They were commanded by General Bergonzoli.

The artillery opened fire first, to 'soften up' the Italian defences. Australian engineers then moved forward and placed bangalore torpedoes under the barbed wire. The wire was blown apart and Australian troops charged through, supported by British tanks. One by one, the Italian posts were stormed. Some Italians fought bravely to the death, while others gave in easily, and began waving white flags. One post — Post 11 — held out stubbornly against all Australian attacks. It was the last to fall. When it did so, Bardia was taken (5 January 1941). Colonel A. Godfrey, commanding officer of the 6th Battalion, shook the hand of the Italian officer commanding Post 11 and congratulated him on his stand.

Some 40 000 prisoners were taken, together with hundreds of artillery pieces, tanks, and equipment. Over 450 Australians were killed or wounded. The 6th division had proved itself. At home in Australia, there were celebrations. Winston Churchill, prime minister of Britain, was jubilant.

General O'Connor moved his combined British–Australian force westwards to attack the port of Tobruk. The force reached the port in three days and dug in, facing another defensive perimeter — this one 48 kilometres long. The siege of Tobruk followed a similar

Figure 25.6. Smoke billows from burning petrol during the shelling of Tobruk.

pattern to that of Bardia. Again, Australian engineers blasted gaps in the Italian wire with bangalore torpedoes, and again Australian infantry and British tanks poured through. In some sections, the fighting was particularly fierce. Some Italian troops fought magnificently. In other sectors, resistance was overcome quickly. The fighting lasted until 22 January. This time, 25 000 Italians were captured, together with guns, tanks, and trucks. Australian casualties were light. At the end of the battle, one soldier hoisted a slouch hat to the top of a flagpole outside the Italian naval headquarters in the town — a jaunty celebration of another Australian victory.

On 30 January, Australian troops captured Derna, a town near Tobruk. Then Giovanni Berta, which was undefended, was occupied. Then Barce, Benghazi, and Giarabub fell to the Allies. The Italian Army was smashed and forced into retreat. Mussolini's empire in North Africa looked like being short-lived.

The 6th Division now handed over to a newly arrived 9th Division, and sailed for Greece. Mussolini's attack on that country had failed, and Hitler was preparing to send in German troops. The 6th joined other Allied troops there, under the command of General Maitland Wilson.

Enter the Desert Fox

Hitler and his generals realized quickly that they were in danger of losing North Africa. Therefore Hitler decided to send a German force to reinforce the Italians. The general he chose was Erwin Rommel, a tank commander who had covered himself with glory during the invasion of France. He would command a new Afrika Korps. Rommel was a fine soldier and was destined to earn the respect of both sides.

Rommel landed with his men and *Panzerkampfwagens* (armoured vehicles) at Tripoli in February 1941, and proceeded to push the Allies back — towards western Egypt again. Defeating the Italians had only put a stronger and more capable enemy in the field. Churchill and the High Command decided to abandon Libya, except for Tobruk. Tobruk was a strategic port.

The task of defending Tobruk fell to Lieutenant-General J. D. Lavarack, commanding the 9th Division, one brigade of the 7th Division, and assorted British troops. Most of the Australian troops were newly arrived in the desert and untried.

To add to the difficulty of the situation, news came through that Hitler had invaded Greece, and that the country would probably fall. Could Tobruk be held against Rommel's Panzers if Greece fell? Many had their doubts. The men at Tobruk waited for the arrival of the Germans. Arrangements were made to supply the garrison by sea, using British and Australian ships.

A combined German and Italian force arrived, and the second battle of Tobruk began on 11 April 1941.

At first, the Germans merely tested the defences around the port, then began attacking in force. The defenders allowed the tanks to break through the perimeter, then rose from their trenches and closed behind them, to fight the advancing German infantry. While they did this, British and Australian artillery stopped the tanks. Lavarack was re-lieved by Lieutenant-General Leslie Morshead, and he ordered raids outside the perimeter against the enemy.

The defenders suffered constant artillery fire and dive-bomb attacks by wailing German Stuka aircraft. Huddled in their dugouts for protection, almost impossible to dislodge, they earned the nickname of 'Desert Rats'. They used every trick possible to hold their position. For instance, to mislead enemy aircraft, they set up dummy gun emplacements.

The Australian government was hardly pleased with their position. It did not want to see the 9th Division destroyed or captured. It might be needed soon to help defend Australia. Therefore Churchill was asked if the men could be withdrawn. He was reluctant to agree, but finally he agreed to replace the Australians with British and Polish troops. The Australians were taken off by sea from August onwards. By the end of October, only one battalion — the 13th — was left. The evacuation of this battalion was delayed because of heavy air strikes on ships. It was evacuated finally on 21 November 1941. Hundreds of Australians were killed and many more wounded defending Tobruk.

By this time the Germans had overrun both Greece and Crete. British, Australian, and New Zealand troops defending Crete were either killed or herded into prisoner-of-war camps after being captured. Some managed to escape. 274 Australians were killed, 507 wounded, and 3109 were taken prisoner.

On 18 November 1941, British forces under General Auchinleck began a counter-offensive against the Germans in Libya, and Tobruk was relieved. However, Rommel came back with reinforcements and captured the town on 21 June 1942. Its fall was a blow to the Allies, but proved only a temporary setback in the desert war.

General (later Viscount) Montgomery, at the head of his 8th Army, heavily outnumbering Rommel's forces, even-

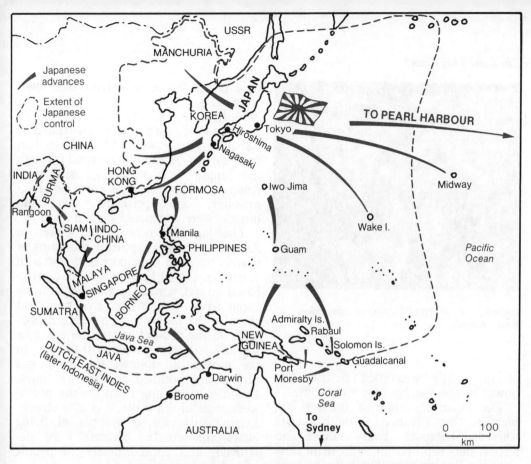

Figure 25.7. The furthest spread of the Japanese Empire, 1942.

tually broke the German commander's power at El Alamein (October–November 1942). The 9th Division was there when this happened, having rested in Syria. The Australians fought with great bravery and determination in support of Montgomery's tanks, and earned high praise from the British commander. Between 23 October and 4 November, the 9th lost 620 men killed, 1944 wounded, and 130 captured.

The Japanese Menace

Japan planned a short, decisive war. It believed that Germany and Italy would win in Europe. Japan would be able to carve out an empire in the Pacific area, which would provide supplies of the raw materials it lacked, such as oil, tin, and rubber. The main threat to Japanese ex-

pansion was the American fleet at Pearl Harbor and a mixed British force at Singapore. Australia was not seen as a great power in the Pacific region.

The Japanese struck quickly, intent on overrunning as much territory as possible and, at the same time, eliminating the American and British counter-forces. An invasion of Malaya was launched on 8 December 1941, with a landing at Kota Bharu. Thailand was invaded at the same time, with landings at Singora and Patani. Just over an hour later, carrier-borne aircraft made a massive air raid on Pearl Harbor, sinking and crippling many American warships. This was the greatest naval defeat since Trafalgar, and brought the USA into the war. On 10 December, Japanese aircraft also sank two British capital ships, the *Repulse* and the *Prince of Wales*, off the coast of Malaya. This

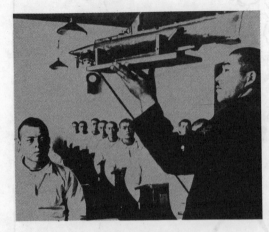

Figure 25.8. Wartime Japanese submariners in naval school.

action greatly weakened British sea-power in the Far East for some time.

The Japanese, some of them riding bicycles, then advanced through Malaya towards Singapore. Every village and airport they captured brought them closer to the British base. These troops were under the command of a British general, A. E. Percival, who had been ordered to hold Singapore at all costs. The Australians at the base were the 8th Division, commanded by Major-General H. Gordon Bennett.

The Japanese outnumbered the Allies and overawed them with the speed of their advance. Bennett and his Australians were not sent into action until most of the Malayan Peninsula had fallen. They could do little but harass and slow down the Japanese troops. Surrender became necessary. Singapore fell on 15 February, after a heavy bombardment. Those troops who had not been killed were rounded up and driven at the point of a bayonet into the notorious Changi prison camp. Later many were sent to work and die on the Burma Railway.

The 7th Division was at sea, returning from the Middle East, when Singapore fell. Churchill asked that these troops be redirected to Burma, but the Australian prime minister, John Curtin, insisted

they return home to defend their own country.

Meanwhile, on the night of 22–23 January 1942, Japanese troops landed in Rabaul. There were 1400 Australian troops there. About 400 escaped through the jungle to New Guinea and then Australia. The rest were killed or taken prisoner. 150 prisoners, including nurses, were butchered on the spot.

The Japanese now moved closer to Australia, quickly capturing the string of islands between Singapore and northern Australia. On 19 February 1942, carrier-based aircraft struck at Darwin, sinking three naval vessels and five merchant ships in the harbour, destroying 23 aircraft on the ground and in the air, killing and wounding about 650 people. In the months to follow, the town was raided and bombed another 55 times. Broome, a pearling town on the north-west coast of Australia, was also struck. During this raid, a number of flying boats and combat aircraft were destroyed, and approximately 70 people were killed or wounded.

On 27 February 1942, the Japanese destroyed an Allied fleet in the Java Sea. They invaded Java the following day. On 8 March, thousands of Allied troops

Figure 25.9. The aftermath of Pearl Harbor following the crippling Japanese air raid in December 1941.

surrendered there. That day, Japanese troops also landed at Lae and Salamaua in New Guinea. The invasion of Australia now seemed imminent.

The American Alliance

Australia had never been threatened with imminent invasion before, and drastic measures had to be taken. John Curtin, the new prime minister, declared war on Japan without consulting Britain. By this time, conscription had been introduced for the militia (they could not be sent overseas to fight), and men were called up in increasing numbers. Women filled many positions in the workforce occupied previously by men. Many went to work in factories, while others drove cars and trucks and worked as couriers on motor cycles. Every effort was made to increase output of war materials. Air-raid precautions, such as the digging of air-raid shelters and blackouts, were introduced. Strict rationing of such items as food and petrol was applied.

Most importantly, Australia now looked to the USA for support. Britain was locked in battle with Germany and Italy in Europe and the Middle East, and could not afford to fight a second war in the Pacific. The loss of the *Repulse* and the *Prince of Wales* and the fall of Singapore had also shattered Australian faith in British sea power. Since Pearl Harbor, however, America had been mobilizing for total war against Japan. She had the population, the industry, and the economy to win a war in the Pacific. At the end of 1941, Curtin had written an article in which he stated:

Without any inhibitions of any kind, I make it quite clear that Australia looks to America, free of any pangs as to our traditional links or kinship with the United Kingdom. We know the problems that the United Kingdom faces. We know the constant threat of invasion. We know the dangers of dispersal of strength, but we know, too, that Australia can go and Britain can still hold on. We are, therefore, determined that Australia shall not go, and we shall exert all our

Figure 25.10. Home wreckage in Darwin after a Japanese bomber raid.

energies towards the shaping of a plan, with the United States as its keystone, which will give to our country some confidence of being able to hold out until the tide of battle swings against the enemy.

Curtin sent a cable to President Franklin D. Roosevelt, recommending that General Douglas MacArthur be appointed Commander-in-Chief of the South-West Pacific Area. Roosevelt was quite happy to oblige. America needed allies in the Pacific, and Australia would be one good base from which to attack Japan. At this time, MacArthur was 62 years of age and blockaded by the Japanese in the Philippines, with his family, at the head of an ill-equipped and hungry Filipino army. He managed to slip out of the Philippines with his family (his wife Jean, and four-year-old son, Arthur) and two officers aboard a PT boat and then an aircraft, and come to Australia, where he assumed command.

MacArthur was unimpressed with Australia's armed forces, and with the plans which had been drawn up by the Australian Chiefs of Staff. The Chiefs of Staff, anticipating a Japanese invasion, argued that it was impossible to defend the entire continent, and that a large

Figure 25.11. Spencer Street Station, Melbourne, 26 March 1942. General Douglas MacArthur (centre) is greeted by service chiefs.

Figure 25.12. US Marines and Australian soldiers have a beer together at the Melbourne Cricket Ground.

part of it would have to be abandoned, temporarily, to the Japanese. They proposed to defend the federal capital, New South Wales, Victoria, and South Australia within a defensive line drawn from Brisbane down to Adelaide.

MacArthur felt that this was too passive a plan. He advocated meeting the Japanese in battle before they reached Australia. This would mean meeting them in the jungle and mountains of New Guinea. To be closer to the action, MacArthur moved his headquarters from Melbourne to Brisbane, then to Port Moresby. Meanwhile, American ships, aircraft, and men began arriving in Australia.

The American Presence

The Americans virtually invaded Australia. For instance, Brisbane became almost an American city. Americans took over whole parks for their camps, in addition to buildings, hotels, and hospitals. Their ships filled harbours, their aircraft, hangars. Their men, on leave, filled the streets, shops, cinemas, and dance halls. 'GI Joe' made quite an impact on Australian society.

In the past, Australians had followed the British way of doing things. In some

ways, they believed in a quiet and reserved way of life. They were frugal and hard-working. The Americans who arrived introduced Australians to an alternative lifestyle. They were well paid and had plenty of money to spend. Their dress uniforms were well tailored and of good material. Indeed, their uniforms made most Australian uniforms look drab. They were awarded medals easily (for instance, a Purple Heart for being wounded) and proudly displayed their medal ribbons, or 'fruit salad', on their uniforms. They brought with them a taste for the latest music, such as 'boogie-woogie', and the latest dances, such as 'juitter-bugging'. They preferred Scotch to beer, played craps not two-up, and gridiron (football) not Australian Rules or rugby. And they bragged endlessly. Private George Huffman boasted: 'I come from God's own country, and I came to this burg (Sydney) expecting to find niggers and kangaroos. I found a bunch of fine people instead.' The newly arrived troops flirted with single and married women, many of whose boyfriends and husbands were interstate or overseas. Several thousand 'war brides' married Americans.

This was all too much for most Australian men, who grumbled that their

Allies were 'over-paid, over-fed, over-sexed, and over here'. There were a number of fights and even brawls. The worst brawl happened in Brisbane, when a number of Australian troops picked a quarrel with some American Military Police. A fight ensued, and some Australians were shot, one fatally. The incident became notorious as 'The Battle of Brisbane'.

The Australian government, incidentally, worried about the arrival of American black troops in Australia, fearing they would want to stay after the war, and thus they would weaken the White Australia policy. As it turned out, this did not happen.

Figure 25.13. One of the three Japanese midget submarines that entered Sydney Harbour.

Victory at Sea

One Japanese target was Port Moresby. In order to capture the town, the Japanese sent a fleet through the Coral Sea, intending to launch an amphibious assault. Between 4–8 May, this fleet was intercepted by an American fleet near the southern end of the Solomon Islands chain. A bitter battle followed, later to be named the Battle of the Coral Sea. The Americans lost one of their two aircraft carriers — the *Lexington* — and 81 aircraft. The Japanese had three aircraft carriers. One, the *Shoho*, was crippled and put out of action, while the third, *Zuikaku*, lost so many aircraft that it was unfit for further action until losses were made up. All told, the Japanese lost 105 aircraft. HMAS *Australia* and *Hobart* took part in the action. After the fighting, both fleets withdrew from the area. There was no outright victory for the Allies, but the assault on Port Moresby had been stopped.

On 31 May, three midget submarines entered Sydney Harbour and torpedoed a ferry that was being used as a depot. All three submarines were destroyed.

Early in June, another Japanese fleet was caught and defeated of Midway Island. During this engagement, the Japanese lost four aircraft carriers. This victory meant that Sydney and other capital cities would not be bombed by carrier-borne aircraft. Pearl Harbor was also saved.

Fighting in New Guinea

After the Battle of the Coral Sea, the Japanese decided to capture Port Moresby by crossing from the north of New Guinea over the rugged Owen Stanley Range, a range of mountains rising to over 4000 metres in some places. The Australian 39th Battalion harassed the advancing enemy, assisted by Papuans (nicknamed the 'Fuzzy Wuzzy Angels'). The Papuans had suffered at the hands of the Japanese and willingly assisted the Australians against them.

By August 1942, the Japanese were much closer to Port Moresby, and were launching an amphibious attack on Milne Bay, on the south-east tip of the island. At Milne Bay, the Australians repulsed the Japanese, thereby inflicting the first defeat on their land forces. The Japanese were also stopped on the Kokoda Trail, on Imita Ridge, just north of Port Moresby. From September 1942 to January 1943, the Australians and Americans forced them back over the Owen Stanley Range. At its height, this bitter campaign absorbed some 54000 Australian and 30000 American troops.

Figure 25.14. The Australian flag is raised as Allied troops enter Kokoda after capturing it from the Japanese.

In March 1943, fighter-bombers of the US Navy destroyed another Japanese fleet in the Battle of the Bismarck Sea. This fleet had been on its way to reinforce Lae. After this battle, MacArthur could make landings at various points along the New Guinea coast, to eliminate Japanese positions. Salamaua fell to the 15th, 17th, and 29th Australian infantry battalions on 11 September 1943, after a particularly fierce battle to take the ridges (e.g. 'Old Vickers') around the town. Meanwhile, the Australian 9th landed on beaches east of Lae and the Australian 7th landed at Nadzab. These two forces then entered Lae on 16 September. They found the town almost deserted. The Japanese, realizing they could not hold their position, had retreated. 500 Australians died in the battle for Salamaua and Lae, 1300 were wounded, 81 Americans died and over 2700 Japanese were killed.

Afterwards, the Australian 7th Division began clearing the heights above the Markham Valley. Finschhafen was captured on 2 October 1943. By the end of 1943 the 5th Division had cleared the Huon Peninsula. By June 1944, all of New Guinea except Wewak had been captured by Allied troops. Wewak was

left until final mopping-up operations in June 1945. Australians then flushed out Japanese troops from the jungle during some bitter clashes.

Beyond New Guinea

MacArthur left New Guinea mainly to the Australians, and they served with great distinction there. They also saw action beyond New Guinea. In September 1944, the 3rd Division began landing on Bougainville Island, and the 5th Division landed in New Britain. On Bougainville, the Japanese fought fanatically, but the Australians drove them to defensive positions by the end of the war. 615 Australians were killed and many more wounded in this campaign. 8500 Japanese were killed; even more died of starvation and disease. Thousands of prisoners were eventually taken. The fighting on New Britain was not as vicious: 100 000 Japanese surrendered there at the end of the war.

On 1 May 1945, the 9th Division landed at Tarakan in Borneo, assisted by American and Austrlian naval and air support. In June, Australian troops captured Brunei and Sarawak. On 1 July, the 7th Division landed with its tanks at Balikpapan.

Meanwhile, the Royal Australian Navy had also been active. Two Australian ships, the *Shropshire* and *Arunta*, took part in another naval battle — the Battle of Leyte Gulf in the Philippines. The cruiser *Australia* should have taken part too, but was struck in the bridge by a Japanese aircraft before the battle. This killed the ship's captain and 28 men, and put the ship out of action. The aircraft was not a *kamikaze* — a plane filled with explosives, flown by a suicide pilot. Soon the Americans would face this new Japanese weapon.

Towards Japan

While the Australian army was fighting the Japanese in New Guinea, Bougainville, New Britain, and Borneo, the

Americans were moving ahead, capturing one Japanese-held island after another, in a determined drive towards Tokyo. The Gilbert Islands, the Marshall Islands, the Marianas, and the Palau Islands all fell to the Americans. The Palau Islands were within striking distance of the Philippines. When MacArthur had left the Philippines to come to Australia, he had promised, 'I shall return.' It gave him great satisfaction to keep that promise. He landed there in October 1944.

Iwo Jima, in the Bonin Islands, was invaded on 19 February 1945. By now, the Japanese were prepared to put up a desperate fight to protect their homeland. It took the Americans 26 days of fierce battle to take that small island, at a cost of 6000 American dead and many more wounded. It was the bloodiest battle in the history of the American Marines. By now, the Americans had resorted to using flame-throwers to defeat their stubbornly entrenched enemy.

On 1 April 1945, another landing was made, this time at Okinawa, in the Ryukyu group, south of Japan. Over 100 000 Japanese sailors, airmen, and soldiers died trying to hold this island. It fell to the Americans in June.

The Americans now made plans to invade Japan itself, and bombing raids were carried out over Japanese cities. B29s dropped incendiary bombs, which caused fires to spread through houses and factories. Many of the houses were constructed from wood and rice paper, and burnt fiercely. In one air raid on Tokyo alone, between 60 000 and 100 000 Japanese were killed. Then, on 6 and 9 August, officially to save American lives and shorten the war, two atmoic bombs were dropped, one on Hiroshima and one on Nagasaki. The Japanese communicated their desire to surrender on 14 August (in the USA). The official surrender took place aboard the USS *Missouri*, in Tokyo Bay, on 2 September 1945. Mamoru Shigemitsu, Japan's foreign minister, signed the surrender on behalf of Japan. MacArthur was there to witness the event, standing at the head of his Allied commanders.

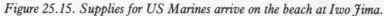

Figure 25.15. Supplies for US Marines arrive on the beach at Iwo Jima.

Figure 25.16. The Japanese foreign minister, Mamoru Shigemitsu, signs the formal documents of surrender on board the USS Missouri *in Tokyo Bay, 2 September 1945.*

By this time, the war in Europe was over, too. Italy had surrendered early in 1945. The combined weight of the USSR, the USA, and Britain and her Commonwealth countries had proved too much for Hitler. Operation Overlord — the Allied landings in Normandy — had proved the beginning of the end. Hitler had committed suicide on 30 April 1945, and on 7 May, General Alfred Jodl had signed an unconditional surrender on behalf of Germany.

VJ Day

The war was over and, in many countries around the world, there were joyous celebrations. Australia celebrated too. In Sydney, people on their way to work stopped to celebrate in the streets. Telephone books, newspapers, and of-

ficial forms were torn up and thrown out of windows, along with streamers. The Union Jack, the Australian flag, and the Stars and Stripes were waved triumphantly. Soldiers, airmen, sailors, nurses, office girls, clerks, and shop attendants formed conga lines, danced the Hokey Pokey, sang songs like *Roll Out the Barrel*, and embraced warmly. Many people became drunk, and many arrests were made. There were celebrations in Melbourne, where the word 'Victory' was scrawled in chalk on the sides of trams. 120 000 people jammed the city centre in Brisbane. Jitterbugging and kissing contests were held in the main street, and soldiers turned their coats inside out and paraded up and down behind a kerosene-tin band. At night, the tall City Hall tower was decorated with lights. In Adelaide, a

Figure 25.17. VJ Day, 15 August 1945. Australians everywhere celebrated the end of the Second World War.

special VJ Day sale was held, together with a Thanksgiving Service and a fireworks display. 30 000 people thronged the City Square in Perth. In Hobart, a beer shortage tended to put a damper on things (a glass of beer cost a shilling). In the country towns and on farms there were quieter, but no less happy, celebrations.

The Effects of the War on Australia

The war had a number of important effects upon the course of Australia's history:

- 21 136 soldiers, 10 562 airmen, and 1854 sailors died, and many more were wounded, physically and emotionally. This, out of a population of barely 7 million.
- Many prisoners of war returned home, having been worked and starved and beaten, almost to the point of death, in Japanese prisoner-of-war camps. Some, in fact, had become walking skeletons. Australians had never been tortured by an enemy before and, for years to come, they were to hate Japan.
- The legend and spirit of Anzac were reinforced. As in the First World War, Australians had proved themselves to be good soldiers.
- The Second World War, unlike the First, brought the nation closer together through a concerted effort and suffering.
- Australia entered into an unofficial defensive alliance with the USA during the war. American forces, particularly the Pacific Fleet, saved Australia from invasion, and govern-

Figure 25.18. John Joseph Curtin.

wealth Employment Service was set up. Federal aid was granted for universities.

• Australian industry was given a boost by the war. Steel production expanded, as did the food-processing and ship-building industries.

• During the war, many women entered the work force. Some rose to positions of responsibility and received good incomes, something that had rarely happened before in Australia. After the war, many of these women remained in the work force. The war partly helped to 'liberate' many women.

• There was great social mobility during the war. Australians were posted interstate and overseas, and mixed with servicemen and civilians of many different nationalities. The war helped to broaden the minds of many Australians.

ment leaders were not to forget this. After the war, they looked more to America, and less to Britain, for security and defence. This was an important turning point in Australia's history.

• During the war, the federal government became more centralized. It took over a good deal of power enjoyed previously by the state governments. These powers included control of finances and taxation, and of import and export licences. After the war, this newly acquired power remained with the federal government. The High Court of Australia gave its approval.

• Government production increased, in such areas as aircraft, weapons, and servicemen's houses.

• Social services were developed, including child endowment, widows' pensions, and unemployment and sickness benefits. The Common-

Prime Ministers and Politics during the War

When Lyons died, leadership of the United Australia Party passed to Robert Gordon Menzies. Menzies was born in Jeparit, in the Victorian wheat belt, on 20 December 1894, and educated at Wesley College, Melbourne, and at Melbourne University, where he read Law. After a successful ten years as a solicitor and barrister, he entered politics and was elected to the Victorian parliament in 1928. He rose quickly to be deputy premier of the state, but then transferred to federal politics. He was elected to represent Kooyong, a fashionable Melbourne suburb. From this, he again rose to become prime minister at the age of 44. An excellent orator, he was conservative, pro-British, and a great admirer of the royal family. His opponents found him arrogant, and hated him.

Menzies was destined not to be prime minister during the war. There was dissatisfaction within the ranks of the

United Australia Party, and the Country Party proved unco-operative. Menzies could not handle the unions, and there was a series of strikes in 1940. Australia could not afford strikes at that time. The press criticized his handling of the war. Menzies then proposed to go to Britain to represent Australia in the United Kingdom War Cabinet. That would have meant he would be away indefinitely.

There was a general election in September 1940, and an equal number of government and opposition members were returned. Therefore Menzies had to rely on the support of two independents. One was A. W. Coles, owner of Coles stores, and the other was A. Wilson, a farmer, who represented a small farming area in Victoria. Menzies was criticized more and more as the war worsened, and finally he was replaced as prime minister in August 1941 by Arthur Fadden, the leader of the Country Party. 'Artie' Fadden hailed from Ingham, Queensland, and had worked as a mill hand, as town clerk of Mackay and as a chartered accountant.

Fadden failed, too, and on 3 October 1941 John Curtin, the Labor leader, moved a motion of 'no confidence' in the government. Coles and Wilson both crossed the floor to vote with Labor. Curtin then became prime minister.

Curtin was born in 1885, in Creswick, Victoria. He became a dedicated socialist and, at 26, secretary of the Victorian Timber Workers Union. In 1916, he went to Western Australia to edit *The Westralian Worker*. He was then elected to parliament to represent Fremantle. He was a quiet, thoughtful man, a reconstructed alcoholic, who welded the

Labor Party together and led the Australian people through the darkest hours of the war. He introduced conscription for service overseas, and moved Australia into a close alliance with the USA.

He died on 5 July 1945, only weeks before the end of the war. He was succeeded by Francis Forde, and then by J. B. Chifley.

Questions

(1) What was the condition of Australia's defence forces in 1939?
(2) Which division was first sent to fight overseas?
(3) Why was Libya invaded by Allied troops?
(4) When did Tobruk fall to the Germans?
(5) Why did the Japanese attack Pearl Harbor?
(6) How did Australian troops suffer after the fall of Singapore?
(7) Why did the Australian government insist that Australian troops be brought home from the Middle East?
(8) What was MacArthur's policy regarding the defence of Australia?
(9) Why was the Battle of the Coral Sea important?
(10) What sacrifices did Australians make during the war?

Research

Find out more about the following men:
(1) Robert Gordon Menzies
(2) Arthur Fadden
(3) John Curtin
(4) Douglas MacArthur
(5) Thomas Blamey.

Chapter 26

Postwar Australia: The Era of Chifley and Menzies

Labor Government, 1941–49

Between the years 1941 and 1949 Australia was governed by the Australian Labor Party (ALP). Three Labor prime ministers held office: John Curtin (1941–45), Francis Forde (one week, 1945), and Joseph Benedict (Ben) Chifley (1945–49).

In the preceding chapter we traced the career of John Curtin. When he died in 1945 Francis Forde became caretaker prime minister for a week, until a new prime minister was appointed. The new prime minister was J. B. Chifley. In this chapter we will look at the life and work of this man.

Figure 26.1. Ben Chifley.

Ben Chifley

Joseph Benedict Chifley was born in Bathurst, NSW, in 1885. His family was of the working class. He left school at the age of 15 and eventually joined the railways. He became active in union politics. In 1917 he took part in an extensive locomotive strike. After that he helped to establish the Australian Federated Union of Locomotive Enginemen. He entered parliament in 1928. In 1931 he lost his seat in the House of Representatives, and was not returned until 1940.

Chifley was dedicated to social reform, and to the creation of a welfare state. His dream is well expressed in his vision of 'the light on the hill':

I try to think of the Labor movement not as putting an extra sixpence into somebody's pocket or making somebody Prime Minister or Premier, but as a movement bringing something better to the people, better standards of living, greater happiness to the mass of the people. We have a great objective — the light on the hill — which we aim to reach by working for the betterment of mankind not only here but anywhere we may give a helping hand. If it were not for that, the Labor movement would not be worth fighting for.

Labor's Foreign Policy

In foreign affairs, Chifley's Labor government was a firm supporter of the United Nations. Dr H. V. Evatt, the deputy leader of the ALP, played an important part in the debates at the San Francisco Conference in 1945, which set up the new world body. Evatt had great faith in the United Nations. He believed it could succeed, unlike the old League of Nations, in bringing peace and justice to the world.

Chifley's government supported independence movements in Asia. For instance, it sided with the Indonesians against their former colonial Dutch masters. Chifley put pressure on the Netherlands to grant Indonesia its independence. The ALP was opposed to all forms of colonialism.

Social Services Strengthened at Home

At home, Chifley and his government were dedicated to maintaining full employment. This had been achieved during the war years. Chifley did not want to see a percentage of the working population unemployed, which had happened in the past. Many people had bitter memories of the Depression years.

Besides maintaining full employment, Chifley also wanted to continue expanding social services. In 1946 a referendum was held. Chifley asked Australians to vote to amend the Constitution so as to give the federal government wider powers in the payment of social services. The majority of voters voted in favour of the amendment. The new section of the Constitution empowered the federal government to make provision for maternity allowances, widows' pensions, child endowment, unemployment benefit, pharmaceutical, sickness and hospital benefits, medical and dental services, benefits to students, etc.

Attempts to Nationalize Industry

Chifley and his government hoped to nationalize Australia's main industries. They did not believe that such industries should be controlled by the wealthy, or by overseas interests. In 1945 the Chifley

government passed an Act that created the Australian National Airlines Commission. The plan was that this commission would monopolize interstate air services. Immediately, however, private airline companies such as Australian National Airways (ANA) complained. The matter was heard in the High Court, which ruled that the federal government could not interfere with private enterprise. Chifley responded by setting up Trans Australia Airlines (TAA), a government airline.

Having failed to nationalize the air-transport industry, Chifley next tried to nationalize banking. He argued that bank nationalization was necessary to preserve full employment and prevent booms and slumps. He also feared that the private banks would ultimately weaken the powers of the Commonwealth Bank.

Chifley was supported by many unions, and by members of the Communist Party. The opposition in parliament complained that Labor was trying to turn Australia into a socialist country. In the future, the opposition warned, Australians would be denied freedom of choice. Private bank employees also feared for their jobs. A campaign was launched to defeat Chifley on the banks issue. Public meetings were held and petitions were drawn up.

On 15 October 1947, Chifley introduced legislation to nationalize the banks. After debate, the Banking Bill was passed. However, 11 trading banks and three state governments (Victoria, South Australia, and Western Australia) challenged the law in the High Court. On 11 August 1948, the High Court ruled that the main provisions of the Act were unconstitutional and therefore invalid. Labor's plans for nationalizing industry foundered.

The Holden

Until 1948, every car on Australian roads was either fully imported or made

Figure 26.2. Chifley with the first Holden, 1948.

up of a locally manufactured body on an imported chassis. Lawrence J. Hartnett, the managing director of General Motors–Holden's Ltd, saw no reason why Australians could not produce a car of their own — using the new integral-construction method, which built the body and chassis as one unit. Chifley believed this was a splendid idea. He believed that the building of such a car would be good for Australia, and good for employment. Many workers who had previously been employed in munitions factories could be employed building the new car.

In order to pave the way for the construction of Australia's first car, Chifley repealed a law passed in 1940 whereby only Australian Consolidated Industries Ltd could legally make cars in Australia. Hartnett took his plans to the United States, and presented them to Alfred P. Sloan, the chairman of General Motors. Sloan was not sure, at first, about the proposal. Did not Australia have a Labor government? Was it not true that many Australians were dedicated socialists? Chifley arranged for the Commonwealth Bank and the Bank of Adelaide to put up £3 000 000 to launch the project. Sloan then agreed to go ahead.

The first Holdens (the 48/215 model) began rolling off the assembly line at the rate of ten a day on 29 November 1948. The car had an integrally constructed body and chassis, and a six-cylinder overhead-valve engine. The car was based on an American prototype. It proved very popular, and was the first of many models.

The Snowy Mountains Scheme Begun

Early in July 1949, Chifley set up the Snowy Mountains Hydro-Electric Authority. Funds were provided for an ambitious 20-year construction project: to trap the waters of the Snowy River, and its tributary the Eucumbene, and direct them through a series of tunnels under the Great Dividing Range into the Murrumbidgee River and Murray River, so as to provide energy for hydro-electric power stations and water for irrigation. William Hudson, an eminent New Zealand engineer, was appointed to head the Authority. He was later knighted for his work.

The opposition was not interested in Chifley's ambitious project. When the project was inaugurated on 17 October 1949 by the governor-general, William McKell, nearly all the members of the opposition boycotted the ceremony.

Figure 26.3. Construction of the Eucumbene-Tumut tunnel, Snowy Mountains Scheme.

Industrial Unrest

Industrial unrest created serious problems for Chifley and his government. By the end of the war, unions such as the Miners' Federation, the Waterside Workers' Federation, the Seamen's Union, and the Metal Trades Union had been infiltrated by members of the Communist Party. Communist members were bent on a course of confrontation. In 1949 the Great Coal Strike occurred, in all states except Western Australia. When the miners did not go back to work, Chifley fined strikers and froze the funds of the Miners' Federation. When these measures failed, Chifley sent in the army to break the strike. This angered many workers: they felt that the ALP was beginning to lose touch with the feelings of ordinary Australians.

Labor Loses Office

A general election was held in 1949. During the election campaigns, Robert Gordon Menzies, leader of the new Liberal Party, attacked Chifley and his government. He said the government was too dedicated to socialist priciples. Chifley had also kept up petrol rationing, which was unnecessary. Menzies promised a freer, more prosperous country if re-elected. He promised to ban the Communist Party, and to put value back in the pound. His slogan was, 'Tip out the socialists and fill up the bowsers'.

Leslie Haylen, a veteran Labor politician, wrote in his memoirs:

In my middle class—worker type of electorate of Parkes, for every criticism levelled at Labor on the banking issue I got a hundred protests about rationing and shortages, the persistence of controls long after the war was over and the shortage of petrol. Petrol rationing was the big issue. True enough the Banking crisis had shaken Labor to its foundations, but the pragmatic electors I watched going to the polls in 1949 left no doubt in my mind that they were going to flatten us on petrol, butter, rationing, housing, boredom with controls and the desire

to get something out of life now the war had been over for four years.

The ALP was defeated in the election. The Liberal–Country Party coalition won 74 seats in the new parliament. No one realized at this point that the coalition would hold office for the next 23 years!

Menzies is Prime Minister Again

Menzies's early career was sketched at the end of the preceding chapter. You will remember that Menzies was forced to resign as prime minister in 1941. In October 1944, he formed a new party, the Liberal Party of Australia. Principles and policies were quickly worked out. The new party was defeated in the election of 1946, but, as we have just seen, it won office in the election of 1949.

Menzies Tries to Ban the Communist Party

In April 1950, Menzies introduced the Communist Party Dissolution Bill into the House of Representatives. If the Bill were passed, the Communist Party would be declared an illegal association. Any organization affiliated with the party would be dissolved. Any person declared to be a Communist would be disqualified from working in a government department, or from holding office in a trade union.

Menzies's introduction of the Bill was well timed. Within 24 hours, Sir Charles Lowe, a Royal Commissioner appointed by the Victorian government to look into Communist activities, reported that the Communist Party was aiming to seize complete power in Australia. One of its aims was:

(f) Armed insurrection . . . (if necessary) the seizure of power by the proletariat and the smashing of the State as we know it.

The Bill was passed later in 1950. When it became law, Commonwealth police questioned many people, most of

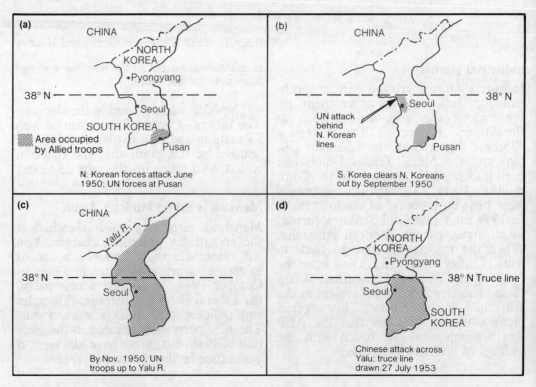

(a)
CHINA
NORTH KOREA
•Pyongyang
38° N — — — — — —
•Seoul
SOUTH KOREA
Area occupied by Allied troops
Pusan
N. Korean forces attack June 1950; UN forces at Pusan

(b)
CHINA
38° N
•Seoul
UN attack behind N. Korean lines
Pusan
S. Korea clears N. Koreans out by September 1950

(c)
CHINA
Yalu R.
38° N
Seoul •
By Nov. 1950, UN troops up to Yalu R.

(d)
CHINA
NORTH KOREA
•Pyongyang
38° N Truce line
Seoul •
SOUTH KOREA
Chinese attack across Yalu; truce line drawn 27 July 1953

Figure 26.4. The Korean War, 1950–53: the changing situation. Shading shows Allied-occupied areas.

them not Communists. The trade unions and the Communist Party challenged the Act in the High Court. The Court found that the Act was invalid, because it interfered with civil liberties. But Menzies did not give up easily. He declared: 'This is not the end of the fight against Communism. It is merely the beginning.'

A double dissolution of both houses of parliament followed: Menzies won control of both houses in the election. He then called a referendum. He asked the voters of Australia to vote in favour of changing the Constitution so as to allow his government to pass laws to deal with Communism. By now Chifley was dead, and the leader of the Labor Party was Dr Herbert Vere Evatt. Evatt campaigned for a 'No' vote in the poll. He accused Menzies of using the Communism issue to conceal the country's inflation problem. He also accused Menzies of trying to turn Australia into a right-wing dictatorship.

The referendum was conducted on 22 September 1951. The outcome was that the 'No' votes outnumbered the 'Yes' votes. There were 'No' majorities in New South Wales, Victoria, and South

Australia. Most Australians felt that Australian Communists should be allowed free speech and organization. Many thought the Communist union leaders had done well in winning better award conditions for workers.

The Korean War

The Korean War began on 25 June 1950, when Communist troops from North Korea (the Democratic People's Republic of Korea) crossed the 38th parallel of north latitude and invaded South Korea (the Republic of Korea). The aim of the Communist forces was to unite all of Korea under one Communist government, guided and supported by Russia. The Communists probably hoped that the United States would not move against them. President Truman had said in January 1950 that he would not fight a war in China or Korea, since they lay outside the American defence perimeter. Also, the US Eighth Army in Japan was run down and not ready for combat.

The North Korean gamble did not pay off. Truman and his advisers were angered by the North's aggression, and decided to assist the Republic of Korea. This was done through the United Nations. A special UN force was enlisted, consisting of US troops supported by troops from a number of other countries. Britain, Canada, India, Australia, and New Zealand were all represented. General Douglas MacArthur, hero of the recent Pacific war against Japan, was made allied commander.

The North Koreans pushed back the South Koreans and conquered most of South Korea. But UN forces commanded by MacArthur drove the Communists back, almost to the Chinese border (the Yalu River). China then intervened. Thousands of Chinese troops crossed the border, and with North Korean forces drove the UN forces south, across the 38th parallel, back into South Korea. The UN forces then recovered, and advanced to a line approximating the former border between North and South Korea. This became the cease-fire line.

Peace talks were held at Panmunjon. The war ended on 27 July 1953. The result: the North Koreans failed to unite all of Korea under a Communist government. South Korea ended up with a few extra square kilometres of territory.

Australia's Involvement

Four days after the North Koreans crossed the 38th parallel, Menzies announced that Australian warships on duty in Japanese waters would be placed at the disposal of the United Nations. The next day Menzies announced that No. 77 Squadron would also be made available, and that Australian troops in Japan would not be brought back home, as had been decided in May. Not long afterwards, Menzies announced that Australia would raise a special land force for service in Korea.

The special force was made up of a brigade of volunteers from the permanent army, the British Commonwealth Occupation Force (BCOF) in Japan, and World War Two veterans. There were many volunteers. Privates was paid 13/9 (thirteen shillings and ninepence) a day — two shillings a day more than ordin-

Figure 26.5. Korean War. Australian soldiers passing through a Korean village on their way to defensive positions.

ary regular privates. Married men got an extra 4/9 a day.

In Korea, Australian servicemen joined other UN forces fighting the Communists. Australian Mustangs and Meteors escorted American Superfortresses and B26s on bombing missions, and bombed, rocketed and strafed enemy ground positions and troop movements. Occasionally, Meteors encountered Russian-built MiGs. During its three years in Korea, 77 Squadron flew a total of 4836 missions — made up of 18 872 individual sorties. It lost 35 pilots; it shot down three MiGs and three other enemy fighters, and destroyed abut 3700 buildings, 1500 vehicles, and 16 bridges.

Australian warships saw action throughout the Korean War. In December 1950, *Warramunga* and *Bataan* joined three Canadian ships and one American ship in evacuating between 7000 and 8000 wounded troops and refugees from Chinnampo, about 50 kilometres up the Taedong River. Late in 1951 the frigate *Murchison* spent 44 days on the Imjin River shelling enemy positions. In October 1951, the Australian aircraft carrier *Sydney* sailed into action, replacing the British carrier *Glory*. Her pilots flew Sea Fury and Firefly aircraft against the enemy. On one occasion, *Sydney*'s pilots flew 401 sorties in eight days. Other Australian ships that saw action were the destroyers *Anzac* and *Tobruk*, and the frigates *Condamine* and *Culgoa*.

On the ground, Australian troops met the enemy in a number of engagements. At Yongyu, north of the North Korean capital of Pyongyang, troops of C Company advanced on the enemy under cover of a Sherman tank, and then charged with fixed bayonets. The North Koreans suffered heavy casualties and fled; seven Australians were wounded. Later, Brigadier B. A. Coad said: 'All the fighting had to be done with infantry weapons and nothing else — the Bren gun, the rifle, the bayonet and the grenade. This was down the Australians'

street'. Further fighting followed, during which the Australians lost 17 dead and more than 50 wounded.

Australians were involved in the Battle of Broken Bridge. It was fought on the Taenyong River, two kilometres south of Pakchon, on 25 October 1950. The Australians crossed the river at the expense of eight dead and 22 wounded. Another important battle for the Australians was Chongju. Chongju lies north-west of Pakchon, only 64 km south of the Chinese border. It was the furthest north the Australians reached. They lost eight men killed and 30 wounded in the battle and its aftermath.

At Kapyong, on 23 and 24 April (Anzac eve) 1951, the Australians made a stand against advancing Chinese. They blunted the Chinese advance, losing 31 killed and 58 wounded. For its valour at Kapyong, the 3rd Battalion RAR was presented with the US Presidential Citation. During Operation Commando, Australian troops helped establish the Jamestown Line, just north of the 38th parallel.

All told, 281 Australian servicemen died, or were not accounted for, and some 1257 were wounded, during the Korean War. The war did not make a big impact on Australians as a whole. When Australian servicemen returned home, the *Bulletin* published a cartoon showing a civilian saying to a soldier: 'Been to Korea, you say, Dig. Where's Korea?'

Menzies's Foreign Policy

Menzies was emotionally attached to Britain, and to the British Commonwealth. At the same time, he believed that Australia's friendship with the United States should be continued, for purposes of security and development. He believed that Australia needed great and powerful friends. The United States was the most powerful friend available. It could help defend Australia against the spread of Communism in Asia.

In 1951 Australia formalized its alliance with the United States and New Zealand. The three countries all signed the ANZUS Treaty. The key article in this treaty reads:

Each Party recognizes that an armed attack in the Pacific Area on any of the Parties would be dangerous to its own peace and safety and declares that it would act to meet the common danger in accordance with its constitutional processes.

The signing of ANZUS was an important event. The United States expected Australia to be an active military ally in the future.

Figure 26.6. Vladimir and Evdokia Petrov.

The Petrov Affair

On 13 April 1954, Menzies announced in parliament that Vladimir Petrov, a Soviet diplomat, had defected from the USSR, had renounced Communism, and had asked the Australian government for political asylum. That asylum had been granted. Petrov had also given the government 'a great number of documents', which named some Australians involved in spy activities. Menzies said the government would set up a Royal Commission into espionage in Australia.

His announcement was made only weeks before an election. He intended to make full use of the Petrov affair to attack the opposition and trade union leaders. Evatt issued a statement saying that the Labor Party would support the fullest inquiry into the matter. It would also see to it that anyone found guilty of spying was prosecuted.

There followed an incident that well illustrates the strong emotions generated by the Cold War. The Soviet ambassador in Australia, Generalov, said Petrov's allegations were 'nonsense from beginning to end'. Mrs Evdokia Petrov said she was not seeking political asylum, and that she wished to return to Russia. On 19 April, three Soviet agents, Kislytsin, Jarkov, and Karpinsky, bustled her aboard an airliner at Mascot Airport, Sydney. W. W. Wentworth, a government member, claimed that Mrs Petrov had committed a crime in the eyes of the Soviet state, and would probably be executed.

The aircraft took off. One of the stewardesses, Joyce Bull, acting on government instructions, asked Mrs Petrov

Figure 26.7. Sir Robert Menzies (1963).

whether she was really leaving Australia of her own free will. Mrs Petrov told her that she doubted that her husband really wanted to defect. Miss Bull gained the impression that Evdokia Petrov would like to stay in Australia. The news was radioed ahead to Darwin. When the plane landed, the Soviet escorts were overpowered and Mrs Petrov 'rescued'. When she was offered political asylum she hesitated, not knowing whether to accept or not. Finally, after speaking with her husband on the telephone, she decided to stay in Australia. The Petrovs changed their name and went into hiding.

Menzies picked the judges he wanted for his Royal Commission. The hearing dragged on for many months. During that time, Menzies won his election by 64 seats to 57. The Commissioners published their report in August 1955: they did not identify one individual who could be prosecuted for an illegal act. The Petrov affair ended diplomatic representation between the USSR and Australia until 1959.

The Opposition Divides

After World War Two, anti-Communist eeling developed steadily within the ranks of the ALP. Anti-Communist groups were organized, to work within unions. These groups were directed by two men who were not members of the Labor Party: one was B. A. Santamaria, a Melbourne lawyer and leading member of the Catholic Social Movement; the other was Dr Daniel Mannix, Roman Catholic Archbishop of Melbourne.

The most agitation occurred within the Victorian branch of the ALP. The fedeal executive of the ALP met in Canberra on 27 and 28 October 1954 to consider charges against the branch. In November a number of members were interviewed. The federal executive then dismissed the Victorian executive, and called for the election of a new executive by the Labor Party in Victoria. The ALP State Conference went ahead and elected a new executive.

The members of the old executive did not give up, however. Victorian members, and some members from other states, formed a new political party. At first it was called the Australian Labor Party (Anti-Communist). Later the name was changed to Democratic Labor Party (DLP). The new party claimed at first to be the real Labor Party, and even spent two years trying, unsuccessfully, to obtain the Labor Party headquarters in Melbourne.

The DLP was unable to attract the political support that the ALP did. Still, it settled upon a policy of helping to keep the ALP out of government. At election time it attacked the ALP and union leaders, saying that they were too soft on Communism. It also recommended that its supporters give second preference on the ballot paper to the Liberal Party. For a time, Catholics were encouraged by their church leaders to vote for the DLP.

Menzies was, of course, glad of the split in the labour movement. It made it that much easier for him to stay in government.

The Suez Crisis

The Suez Crisis of 1956 gave Menzies the chance to perform on the international political stage.

On 26 July 1956, Egypt's president Nasser announced that he had nationalized the Suez Canal. This threatened all shipping that passed through it. An international conference was held in London to discuss the matter. Menzies attended, with his minister for external affairs, R. G. Casey. The seizure of the canal threatened Australia. Menzies appeared on British television and argued that Nasser's seizure was an illegal act, because in 1888 the Egyptian government had granted a concession to the canal's international company until 1968. As recently as June 1956, Nasser had ratified the concession.

Menzies was chosen by the London conference as chairman of a committee to visit Cairo. In Egypt, he warned Nasser that Britain and France would be obliged to use force if the canal were not re-opened. But Nasser was not easily intimidated. In the USA, President Eisenhower was opposed to the use of force to re-open the canal.

Menzies's mission to Egypt failed. He returned to Britain suffering from dysentery. After his return to Australia, war broke out between Egypt and Israel. Two days later Britain and France launched a military operation to 'protect' the canal. They occupied Port Said, Ismailia, and Suez. Menzies said of the operations that it was 'practical and courageous'. Shortly afterwards, the European powers were ordered to leave by the General Assembly of the United Nations. UN troops were sent to supervise a cease-fire.

The Olympic Games, 1956

In 1949 the International Olympic Committee met in Rome and decided that Melbourne would host the 1956 Olympic Games. Melbourne had time to prepare and build for the Games. However, preparations were marred by squabbles and bickering, and by changes of sites. Progress was slow. Avery Brundage, president of the IOC, visited Melbourne and warned the city that if preparations did not speed up and improve, the Games would be shifted elsewhere. The result was that a new man, Lewis Luxton, was appointed deputy chairman of the Olym-

Figure 26.8. Opening day at the 1956 Olympic Games, Melbourne Cricket Ground. Ron Clarke (Australia) bears the Olympic flame around the track.

Figure 26.9. Graham Kennedy in 1958.

pic Organizing Committee. He made things happen.

Those responsible for the Games also had to contend with political problems. The Hungarians hated the Russians because the Soviet Union had invaded their country. Athletes from both countries intended to compete. Would there be trouble? The Dutch and Spanish decided not to come as a protest against the Soviet invasion of Hungary. The People's Republic of China decided not to attend because Taiwan was being allowed to compete; the Communist Chinese were angry that Taiwan should be recognized. Egypt and Lebanon decided not at attend because of events in the Middle East.

The Games, the sixteenth of the modern era, were opened on Thursday, 22 November 1956, by the Duke of Edinburgh, in the Melbourne Cricket Ground. More than 100 000 people attended the opening ceremony. Ron Clarke, the Australian runner, lit the Olympic flame with a torch flown from Greece to Cairns and carried south by runners.

In the Olympic events that followed, Australian athletes did very well. The USSR won the most medals: 98 all told, 37 of them gold. The United States came second, winning 74 medals, 32 of them gold. Australia came third, winning 35 medals, 13 of them gold. Australia won must of its gold medals for swimming. Murray Rose, Jon Henricks, David Thiele, Dawn Fraser, Lorraine Crapp, Faith Leech, and Sandra Morgan became national heroes and heroines. Betty Cuthbert and Shirley Strickland earned their glory on the running track.

Popular Forms of Entertainment

During the Menzies era, Australians watched television, listened to the radio, played records, went to 'the pictures' (cinema) or the theatre, attended dances, parties or barbecues, played sport or watched it, and enjoyed visits to the beach and the countryside.

Television

Television came comparatively late to Australia. Frank Packer's TCN9 Sydney began to transmit geometric test patterns and demonstration programmes on 16 July 1956. The station went to air officially on 16 September 1956. Bruce Gyngell opened the station broadcast by saying simply: 'Good evening, ladies and gentlemen, welcome to television'. TCN9's first programmes were broadcast from a tiny church hall in Surry Hills, Sydney, because the TCN9 studios were not yet completed.

Shortly afterwards, GTV9 Melbourne opened, broadcasting programmes from a converted jam factory in Richmond. By the end of 1956 Australia had two commercial stations and one ABC national station. There was on co-axial cable or microwave link connecting Sydney and Melborne. Melbourne viewers were able to watch the Olympic Games live on their sets; Sydney could offer only a film coverage of the Games. In the years that followed, television stations were established in the other states.

During the 1950s, 1960s, and early 1970s, television programmes were broadcast in black and white. Most programmes were produced in the United States and Britain; a few were produced in Australia. Successful early Australian programmes included *In Melbourne Tonight* with Graham Kennedy and Bert Newton; *Theatre Royal* with George Wallace Junior and Eddie Edwards; *Bandstand* with Brian Henderson (featuring regulars such as Col Joye, Patsy Ann Noble, and Judy Stone); *The Hit Parade*; *Pick-a-Box*, with Bob and Dolly Dyer; *Consider Your Verdict*, a courtroom melodrama; and *Homicide*, a police drama.

Radio

Radio programmes were varied and popular during the early years of the Menzies era. Listeners were treated to quiz shows, dramas, comedies, news, interviews, sports reports, hit parades, etc. Undoubtedly the two biggest names in radio were Bob Dyer and Jack Davey. Neither was Australian — Bob Dyer came from Nashville, Tennessee; Jack Davery from New Zealand. Both were based in Sydney, and were friendly rivals. Both became notorious for their pranks and antics on radio. Tragically, Jack Davey died from cancer at the age of 49. Bob Dyer made a successful transfer to television.

Going to the Pictures

During the early 1950s, before television became established, one of the most popular outings was to the cinema. Australians drove their Holdens, Morris Minors, Ford Zephyrs, or Customlines to town, to visit a city cinema, or to the local suburban one. Those without cars rode on buses, trolley buses, trams, or trains, or simply walked. Cinemas screened very full programmes, which included one or two news bulletins, cartoons, a serial (e.g. *Batman*), previews of coming attractions, and two films. Some films were screened in black and white, some in colour. For a short time, three-dimensional films were popular. Members of the audience donned cardboard-framed coloured spectacles and viewed gimmicky films such as *House of Wax*. In 1954 *The Robe* appeared, in colour and Cinemascope. It established a trend towards large, colourful presentations in Cinemascope, Vistavison or Todd-AO, and stereophonic sound.

During the 1950s the Australian film industry slumped sadly. There was enormous competition from Hollywood. Films shot in Australia included *Bitter Springs, The Glenrowan Affair, Kangaroo Kid, Kangaroo, Wherever She Goes, Night Club, The Phantom Stockman, King of the Coral Sea, Long John Silver, Captain Thunderbolt, Jedda*, and *Robbery Under Arms*. Undoubtedly the most popular Australian film star was Chips Rafferty. Tall, lean, and resourceful, he was everyone's idea of the Australian bushman. Two other popular male stars were Peter Finch and Errol Flynn. Both of these men became very successful actors overseas. Two players who captured the interest of Australians were the Aboriginal stars of *Jedda*, Ngarla Kunoth and Robert Tudawali.

The Theatre

Those who went to the theatre enjoyed lavish musical productions such as *Oklahoma!*, *Brigadoon*, *Kiss Me Kate*, *South Pacific*, *Call Me Madam*, *Paint Your Wagon*, *The Pajama Game*, and *My Fair Lady*. All of these were imported shows; none was set in Australia. Australian performers were usually employed to appear on stage. Some overseas stars who came to Australia to perform became very popular with audiences. One of these stars was Evie Hayes. She starred in *Call Me Madam* in 1954.

There was also drama, ballet, and opera. In 1954 the Australian Elizabethan Theatre Trust was formed. It produced a number of classical plays. Two popular and controversial Australian plays that were produced during the Menzies era were Ray Lawler's *Summer of the Seventeenth Doll* and Alan Seymour's *The One Day of the Year*.

Australian ballet was led at this time by Czech-born Edouard Borovansky. Dancers who established themselves with audiences included Kathleen Gorham, Peggy Sager, Vassilie Trunoff, Elaine Fifield, Marilyn Jones, and Garth Welch. Robert Helpmann, already world famous, danced in Australia occasionally.

Opera had a battle to survive during the 1950s and 1960s. The Elizabethan Trust Opera Company, an arm of the Australian Elizabethan Theatre Trust, presented a number of operas (e.g. Mozart's *The Marriage of Figaro*, *Don Giovanni*, *The Magic Flute*, and *Cosi fan tutte*). Successful Australian performers included Joan Sutherland, Joan Ham-

Figure 26.10. Johnny O'Keefe in action.

mond, Elsie Morison, Ronald Dowd, and Max Worthley. Joan Sutherland was very successful overseas.

Rock 'n' Roll

In 1955 the Western world was swamped by a new form of popular music called rock 'n' roll. This music began in the United States. The leaders were American singers such as Bill Haley and the Comets, Little Richard, Jerry Lee Lewis, and Elvis Presley. Australian teenagers listened to them on the radio, bought their records and flocked to see them on the screen. Popular early rock 'n' roll films were *Rock Around the Clock*, *Don't Knock the Rock*, *Love Me Tender*, and *Loving You* (the two last-named were Presley's first films). Cinema managers groaned as audiences clapped, stamped and screamed when their favourite artists appeared on the screen. Rock 'n' roll dances and concerts also became popular. Young Australians found a new form of dress. Boys wore blue jeans, shirts, duffle coats, leather jackets, and blue-suede shoes, and greased their hair with Brylcreem or Californian Poppy and swept it up to overlap behind their ears. Girls favoured jeans, blouses and jumpers, skirts and blouses, and full dresses. Dresses were sometimes worn over a layer of rope-circled petticoats, which took flight during dancing. The ponytail was a popular hairstyle. Many parents took one look at Elvis's gyrations, or his clothes and hairstyle, and thought rock 'n' roll was evil. Many hoped it would not last.

Australia soon produced its own young singing stars. They included Johnny O'Keefe ('The Wild One'), Col Joye, Lucky Starr, Dig Richards, The Deltones, Rob E. G., Johnny Devlin, Judy Stone, Lana Cantrell, Patsy Ann Noble (now Tricia Noble), and Little Pattie. Two popular television shows were Johnny O'Keefe's *Six O'Clock Rock* and Brian Henderson's *Bandstand*. Australian performers slavishly copied their American counterparts.

Beatlemania

Towards the end of the Menzies era, fashions in dress, hair, and music began to change. In 1963–64, Australian teenagers found a new overseas singing group to rave about. This group was The Bealtes. George, Paul, John, and Ringo visited Australia in mid-1964 and were given a tumultuous reception. In Melbourne, a large crowd gathered outside the Southern Cross Hotel, where the young singers from Liverpool were staying: 250 of the crowd, mostly young girls, had to be treated for minor injuries, hysteria, and fainting.

Vietnam: A Fateful Decision is Made

We have seen how Menzies feared the spread of Communism in Asia, and also how he favoured close ties with the United States. In the mid-1960s the USA became increasingly involved in South Vietnam. US policy was to support the South Vietnamese government against Communist aggression, both from within and from outside the country. Menzies was an enthusiastic supporter of a large American and allied commitment in South Vietnam. He believed this would enhance Australia's security.

On 29 April 1965, Menzies announced in the House of Representatives that his government would send a battalion of troops to South Vietnam. The announcement took many by surprise. The House was half empty. Arthur Calwell, who had succeeded Evatt as leader of the ALP, and his deputy Gough Whitlam, had left Canberra few hours earlier to help campaign for a forthcoming election in New South Wales.

Menzies's announcement was an important one, historically speaking. The Vietnam War was destined to become one of the most controversial wars in history. It was to divide Australian society, as well as American society, and contribute to the eventual fall of the Liberal-Country Party government. We will see how this happened in Chapter 27.

Introduction of Decimal Currency

The notion of introducing decimal currency to replace the complex imperial system of pounds, shillings, and pence was not a new one. In 1902, a select committee of the first Commonwealth parliament reported in favour of decimalization. However, Australia did not switch to decimal currency at that time because the rest of the British Empire would not change. In 1937 a Royal Commission on banking recommended a change to decimal currency; nothing came of its recommendation.

In 1957, business-interest groups formed the Decimal Currency Council and campaigned for the introduction of decimal currency. The Council won widespread support. Many business people realized that decimal currency was more suited to mechanized office procedures and computers. The federal government set up the Decimal Currency Committee. It worked out the details of Australia's future currency.

For a while there was some debate over what the new notes and coins should be called. In June 1963, Menzies announced that the main unit of the currency would be the Royal. Immediately there was widespread opposition to the name. In October, Harold Holt, the federal treasurer, announced that the new unit would be the Dollar.

The Decimal Currency Board organized a conversion programme. For two years Australians were educated and prepared. The change-over occurred on 14 February 1966. During the two years that followed the change-over, the old and new currencies were used together. Only new decimal notes and coins were introduced, while the old currency was slowly withdrawn.

Menzies Retires

Lord Casey, the governor-general, accepted Menzies's resignation on 21 January 1966, and appointed Harold Holt, Menzies's political heir, as the new prime minister.

Menzies had proved himself to be no ordinary Australian politician. He had founded his own party. He had led that party from 1944 to 1966. He had re-mained prime minister from December 1949 to January 1966. To date, no other Australian federal political leader has held power for so long a period.

Questions

(1) In what year did Chifley become prime minister?
(2) What were Chifley's aims as prime minister?
(3) When did the first Holden appear?
(4) Who was appointed to head the Snowy Mountains Hydro-Electric Authority?
(5) Why did the ALP lose office in 1949?
(6) Why did Menzies try to ban the Communist Party?
(7) What part did Australia play in the Korean War?
(8) How did Menzies use Vladimir Petrov?
(9) Who was Robert Tudawali?
(10) Why did Menzies commit Australian troops to South Vietnam?

Research

Find out more about the following:
(1) The Holden car
(2) The Snowy Mountains Scheme
(3) The Korean War
(4) Early television
(5) Life in Australia during the 1950s and 1960s.

Chapter 27

Federal Politics, 1966–89

Harold Holt: Menzies's Successor

Harold Edward Holt was born in Sydney on 5 August 1908, but spent a good deal of his life in Melbourne. Like Menzies, he attended Wesley College, and went on to Melbourne University to study law. He entered the federal parliament in 1935, representing the electorate of Fawkner. In 1939 (the year the Second World War began) Holt became minister without portfolio in the Menzies government. In 1940, Menzies made him minister for labour and national service. When Menzies was voted back as prime minister, Holt was given the portfolios of labour and national service, and immigration. He became the deputy leader of the Liberal Party in 1956. Two years later he became treasurer, remaining in this portfolio during the disastrous credit squeeze of 1960–61. It nearly cost the Liberal–Country Party the 1961 general election. In 1966, Holt became prime minister, at the age of 57. Holt's rise was helped by the fact that he never challenged or threatened Menzies, and that he attracted enough friends and supporters in the Liberal–Country Party coalition.

Holt brought a fresh, modern image to the office of prime minister. In Cabinet, he regarded himself as a first among equals. He was not a strict authoritarian, as Menzies had tended to be. In public, he was relaxed and natural. He enjoyed scuba-diving and swimming, and was photographed with his bikini-clad daughters-in-law. Menzies would never have dreamed of posing for photographers half-naked, or in a wetsuit. Holt enjoyed company, and preferred dining out at restaurants and hotels to eating at home. His wife Zara bubbled over with the joy of life, and was as popular on television as her husband.

Figure 27.1. Harold Holt.

Figure 27.2. The Vietnam War.

The Vietnam Issue

When Holt became prime mininster, he continued Menzies's policy of supporting the United States in South Vietnam. He visited President Lyndon Baines Johnson (LBJ) in America in 1966, and promised him increased support in the war effort. Australians were told they should be prepared to go 'all the way with LBJ' in South Vietnam.

Some Australians were opposed to this idea. Among them were pacifists; they objected to war of any kind. Some objected to conscription, which had been re-introduced by Menzies in November 1964. Under the new scheme, young men had to register for two years of National Service when they reached their twentieth birthday. Service was calculated according to birth dates, which were selected at random. Some believed the war in Vietnam was an unjust war. They did not think Australia should be involved in such a war.

Before going any further, it will be necessary to sketch the troubled history of Vietnam.

A War-torn Country

Vietnam is a small country in South-east Asia. It has suffered a number of invasions in the past. The ancient Chinese conquered and ruled the northern part

Figure 27.3. Australian troops escorting villagers from Duc Hoa after a military operation during the Vietnam War.

of the country, calling it Annam, or 'Pacified South' — a name that angered the Vietnamese. In the nineteenth century the French occupied all of the country, along with Laos and Cambodia. The French drove the Chinese out of the north of Vietnam during the Franco-Chinese War (1883–85). In 1941 the Japanese invaded Vietnam. The Japanese army ruled the country, while French officials administered it. When the Japanese surrendered to the Allies in 1945, the Chinese Nationalists, under Chiang Kaishek, moved into the north of Vietnam, while French forces moved back into the south. Chiang Kaishek allowed Ho Chi Minh, a Communist guerrilla leader, to set up a Communist state in the north, with Hanoi its capital. Chiang Kaishek then withdrew.

When Chiang Kaishek left Vietnam, the French moved back into the north, seizing Hanoi and its port of Haiphong. Driven into the jungle, Ho and his guerrillas fought the French. Despite American assistance, the French lost the war. They were surrounded and overwhelmed at the battle of Dienbienphu, in 1954.

After the French surrender, a decision was made in Geneva to divide Vietnam along the 17th parallel of north latitude. Ho and his Communists were granted power in the north, while in the south a new 'democratic' government was set up under Ngo Dinh Diem, a right-wing Nationalist. US authorities moved many anti-Communist Vietnamese south, because they feared for their safety. This divided and separated families and friends. The division of Vietnam also cut off the industrial north from the rice bowl of the fertile Mekong River delta in the south.

From the beginning, Ho was determined to unite all of Vietnam under his Communist government. He guided and assisted a resistance movement in the south. Many Vietnamese in the south organized themselves, or were organized, into small groups of Viet Cong (VC). They attacked government posts and Diem's ARVN troops (Army of the Republic of Vietnam). Ho also sent troops south, to assist the Viet Cong.

Ho's task was made easier when Diem proved to be a petty tyrant. Diem would not allow elections, and he placed those who opposed him in concentration camps. He did not carry out essential reforms. Eventually, he was assassinated, in November 1963. Diem's successors, Nguyen Cao Ky and Nguyen Van Thieu, were not strong leaders.

At first the US government sent military advisers and aid to South Vietnam. Then, when it became clear that the ARVN forces were no match for the Viet Cong and northern regiments, it sent US troops. Allied troops (Australian, New Zealand, South Korean, Filipino) followed. Communist supply routes, such as the Ho Chi Minh Trail, and staging areas were bombed from the air. (By the end of the war, the tonnage in bombs dropped was to exceed that of the Second World War!) Villages were searched for weapons. Many suspects were interrogated and tortured. ARVN and allied forces engaged the Communists in the jungle.

President Johnson and his military advisers, and leaders such as Holt, believed that they had to stop the spread of Communism in South Vietnam. They believed that if they did not stop it there, it would spread to other countries in South-east Asia. They saw Communist aggression in South Vietnam as part of an international conspiracy, inspired and led by the USSR and Red China.

Labor parliamentarians and other people opposed to involvement in South Vietnam argued that the Vietnamese people should be allowed to sort out their own problems, that the Vietnamese Communists posed no threat to other countries, and that Ho and his Communists were probably better than the regime of Diem and his successors.

The Protests Escalate

From 1966 onwards, protests against

Australia's involvement in the Vietnam War grew louder and more insistent. Calwell, leader of the ALP, condemned the war as 'unwinnable', and led mass demonstrations against the South Vietnamese prime minister, Nguyen Cao Ky, when he visited Australia in 1967. Young men refused to register for National Service, and were supported by Labor politicans and others. At the time, the law provided for two years' imprisonment for those refusing to register. A few young men were imprisoned for their conscientious beliefs.

In October 1966, President Johnson visited Australia, complete with armed guards and hovering helicopter — security measures new to Australians. Large crowds turned out to welcome him. Others turned out to demonstrate their opposition to the war. Almost everywhere the president went, he was confronted by bands of protestors waving placards denouncing US policy in Vietnam. In St Kilda Road, Melbourne, university students splashed the president's car with red paint. In Sydney, young demonstrators lay down on the road in front of the president's motorcade.

The 1966 Elections

In 1966 there was a general election, fought mainly on the Vietnam issue. Holt argued that Australia should be involved in the war. Arthur Calwell argued that Australia should not be involved. Holt projected a more modern and positive image than Calwell. Calwell was an old-style politician; he lacked the glamour and presence of Holt. Although the Vietnam War was beginning to divide Australian society, it had not at that stage divided it enough to topple the Liberal–Country Party coalition. In 1966 the voting age was 21. Many young opponents of the war could not yet vote. Holt won the election by 82 seats to 41. It was the best win for any party since federation.

Problems for Holt

After the election, Holt had to worry about continuing and increasing criticism of Australia's involvement in South Vietnam. He was also accused of wasting taxpayers' money on VIP aircraft, and of not handling well the matter of the *Melbourne–Voyager* collision. In 1964, the aircraft carrier *Melbourne* rammed the destroyer *Voyager*, an accident that caused the death of 82 men. A Royal Commission in 1964 found that the *Voyager* had been responsible. However, many politicians and others were not satisfied, and they wanted Holt to order a second Royal Commission.

Death of Holt

Holt did not see out his three-year term as prime minister. On Sunday, 17 December 1967, he went swimming at Cheviot Beach, near Portsea, Victoria. Tragically he disappeared in the surf, and was never seen again. The artist Clifton Pugh, a diving companion of the prime mininster, described Holt's last day on Cheviot Beach:

I think he probably wanted to show off a little bit. I believe there was a young bloke and his young girl there and I think it was the story of the old bull and the young bull. You know, out he goes without his wetsuit. He'd had a few drinks and you get puffed very quickly. The young bloke had much more sense. He went a little way and came back. Apparently, right at that time, the tide changed and the water became an absolute millrace. And then, in that water is a lot of debris and kelp up to thirty feet long whipping about. He might have just got a bit exhausted. He could have been hit on the head by a bit of debris, or caught by a bit of kelp. It's all holes there and rock caverns. I think he probably just got pulled under.

A number of dignitaries attended a special memorial service for Holt in Melbourne. They included Lyndon Johnson, British Labour prime minister Harold Wilson, and Prince Charles. President Johnson appeared deeply moved by the service.

John Gorton

Holt's disappearance led to a bitter struggle within the Liberal–Country Party coalition. John McEwen, 67, the leader of the Country Party, was sworn in by Lord Casey, the governor-general, as caretaker prime minister. Some Liberals wanted William McMahon, the treasurer and deputy leader of the Liberal Party, to be the next prime minister. McEwen announced that the Country Party would not remain a partner of the Liberal Party if McMahon were made the next prime minister. Leslie Bury, Paul Hasluck, Billy Snedden, and Senator John Gorton each wanted to be the next prime minister. A group of behind-the-scenes Liberals, including Malcolm Fraser, supported Gorton. He was finally accepted as Holt's successor. Gorton became prime minister, and moved from the Senate to the House of Representatives (winning Holt's seat of Higgins).

John Grey Gorton was born on 9 September 1911. During World War II he served as a fighter pilot, and was severely wounded in action — he had to have plastic surgery. His face had a crag-

Figure 27.4. John Grey Gorton.

gy appearance because of this operation. In parliament, Gorton clashed with Menzies. He remained on the backbench for nine years because of his differences with the Liberal leader. Eventually he was made navy minister.

As prime mininster, Gorton projected

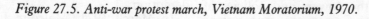

Figure 27.5. Anti-war protest march, Vietnam Moratorium, 1970.

a rugged, independent, all-round Australian image. In public he appeared even more relaxed and informal than Holt. In government, he liked to make decisions on his own. He expected to lead, and others to follow. He did not like delegating authority to committees. He promoted his supporters, and demoted those who did not agree with him. He was accused of keeping his backbenchers in the dark. As time passed, his political enemies increased in number.

Gorton in Trouble

Gorton continued Menzies's policy of supporting the United States in South Vietnam. By 1968 there were some 8000 Australian soldiers in the war zone, 40 per cent of them National Servicemen. More Australians joined the ranks of those opposing conscription and involvement. Gorton had to face criticism from the opposition in parliament, and from people opposed to the war across Australia. Suddenly, moral issues were fashionable and important. People questioned such things as capital punishment (after the hanging of Ronald Ryan in Melbourne) and the powers and policies of the RSL. Was Gorton too conserative? Many thought so.

A general election was held in October 1969. This time Labor was led by Edward Gough Whitlam. Whitlam had won leadership of the ALP when Arthur Calwell retired from politics after the 1966 election. Once again, Vietnam was an issue. Gorton argued that Australia should be involved in the war; Whitlam argued that Australia should not be involved. The government won the election, but lost many seats. The Liberal Party won 46 seats, the Country Party 20 seats and the ALP 59 seats. The Liberal-Country Party coalition was left with a majority of only seven seats.

Withdrawal from Vietnam

By 1970 it had become obvious to the

Americans that they were not going to win the war in South Vietnam. The United States had also become deeply divided and angry over the war. President Johnson's successor (after 1968) was Richard Nixon. He began a slow withdrawal of US forces from South Vietnam. Gorton was obliged to do the same. The move was as necessary for Australia as it was for the US. Late in 1971, the first Australian troops were withdrawn from South Vietnam. By the end of 1972, all Australian troops had been withdrawn.

Fall of Gorton

Many Liberals blamed Gorton for the loss of seats to the Labor Party in the 1969 election. Many feared that the Liberal-Country Party government would lose the next election if he remained prime mininster. Some were angry because of the way they had been treated by Gorton. Some said the prime minister had fallen under the spell of his attractive secretary, Ainslie Gotto, and that she had a part to play in cabinet reshuffles. Dudley Erwin, a deposed minister, openly blamed Gotto for his demotion.

In March 1971, Malcolm Fraser and Gorton fell out over a statement on defence. Fraser announced he could no longer work with Gorton, and resigned as minister for defence. Shortly afterwards, Fraser attacked Gorton in the House of Representatives:

Since his election to office, the Prime Minister has seriously damaged the Liberal Party and cast aside the stability and sense of direction of earlier times. He has a dangerous reluctance to consult Canbinet, and an obstinate determination to get his own way ... because of his unreasoned drive to get his own way, his obstinacy, impetuous and emotional reactions, has imposed strains upon the Liberal Party, the government and the Public Service. I do not believe he is fit to hold the great office of Prime Minister.

Journalists joined in the attack on

Figure 27.6. William McMahon.

Gorton. On 10 March 1971, the Liberal Party met to settle the problem of leadership. A vote was taken on Gorton's suitability as leader, and the result was a tie. Strangely, Gorton then cast his own vote against himself and stepped down. McMahon was then elected leader.

William McMahon

Like Menzies, Holt, and Gorton, William McMahon (born on 23 February 1908) was educated at a private school. Like Menzies and Holt, he studied law at university (in this case, Sydney University). He was elected to federal parliament in 1949, to represent the seat of Lowe. He became the minister for navy and air (1951–54), mininster for social services (1954–56), minister for primary industry (1956–58), minister for labour and national service (1958–66), treasurer (1966–68), and minister for foreign affairs (1969–71). McMahon was 63 when he became prime minister.

McMahon looked old, and was pedantic. He did not have the total support of his party, and he was unable to give it inspired leadership. Many Australians found it difficult to accept him as a leader.

At first Gorton was McMahon's deputy, and minister for defence. In August 1971, McMahon dismissed him for a series of articles he wrote for a newspaper to defend himself against criticism of his leadership while prime minister.

By 1972 McMahon had the lowest popular standing of a prime minister in 22 years. A general election was held in December 1972. The Australian Labor Party, led by Whitlam, won that election. After 23 years in government, the Liberal and Country Party members took their seats on the opposition benches.

Reasons for the ALP's Success

Gough Whitlam and the ALP won the 1972 election for a number of reasons:

- The coalition had probably been in government for too long. It had grown tired. In had become disunited.
- The ALP had been 23 years in opposition. Many Australian voters believed in giving the ALP 'a fair go'. Whitlam's compaign slogan for the 1972 election was 'It's Time'. It was a good slogan, and many voters were moved by it.
- The ALP's campaign was very slick and commercial. It made maximum use of television, and television personalities. Australians everywhere were depicted as wanting change.
- The Liberal–Country Party government's election campaign was poorly handled. McMahon's policy speech was wooden and inept.
- The coalition's commitment to South Vietnam was still fresh in Australians' minds. Young men of conscience were still in jail. Many Australians thought this was wrong.

Figure 27.7. Gough Whitlam.

• There was a new mood of change in Australia. New topics were being debated: land rights for Aborigines, women's liberation, abortion, homosexuals' rights, etc. The ALP was seen as a party that would make changes where needed in a responsible way. The coalition was seen as being opposed to change, too conservative.

Gough Whitlam

Edward Gough Whitlam was born on 11 July 1916, in Melbourne. He attended Knox Grammar School (Sydney), Telopea Park High School (Canberra), and Canberra Grammar School, and finished his education at Sydney University, where he studied arts and law. During the Second World War he served as a member of air crew in the RAAF. After the war he became a lawyer, and then a politician. He represented Werriwa, New South Wales, in the House of Representatives between 1952 and 1978. He rose to become deputy leader of the Labor Party (1960–67), and leader (1967–77). He was 56 years old when he became prime minister in 1972.

As prime minister, Whitlam was filled with reforming zeal. His government ended Australia's military support for the government of South Vietnam, which was soon to fall to Ho and his Communists. It abolished conscription and ordered the release of young conscientious objectors who had been imprisoned. It recognized the People's Republic of China. For too long, Whitlam argued, the Chinese people had been ignored. Chinese administrators, and others, were invited to visit Australia. Whitlam was not anti-American: he maintained the ANZUS treaty.

At home, Whitlam spent large sums of money on social services. He was committed to building up the public sector. One of the most important things he did was to introduce compulsory medical insurance, known as Medibank. All workers were obliged to contribute to Medibank, and in return received, when necessary, free medical treatment and hospitalization. Money was given to schools, colleges, universities, hospitals, clinics, and old people's homes. University fees were abolished. A new Family Court was established.

Whitlam's government soon ran into difficulties. It tried to do too much, too quickly, and many Australians became concerned for the future. Overseas there were growing economic problems. Whitlam's economic measures made these worse at home. Inflation and unemployment grew steadily. Whitlam's critics argued that he was spending far too much, in an irresponsible manner. For instance, they said that many young people no longer wished to work. Many 'hippies' and others preferred to live off unemployment benefits as 'dole bludgers'. The dole was far too easy to obtain. The government was also criticized for spending money on such things as the controversial modern painting *Blue Poles*. Many also criticized Whitlam's centralist policy. Some were concerned that money was not being spent on such things as the armed forces.

Amid growing criticism of the government, Billy Mackie Snedden, the new leader of the Liberal Party, threatened to block Labor's proposed legislation in the Senate. This would have made Labor's government unworkable. Whitlam responded by calling a double dissolution of both houses of parliament (May 1974). Whitlam's government was returned to office, but with a reduced majority, and still lacking control of the Senate. The election of 1974, incidentally, saw the end of the Democratic Labor Party as a force in federal politics.

Scandal weakened the Labor government. Some of Whitlam's ministers were criticized for their lack of ability. Dr James F. Cairns, the deputy prime minister, was attacked for his relationship with Juni Morosi, an office co-

ordinator and assistant. Some said that Whitlam and his wife, Margaret, were going to divorce. These ugly rumours harmed the national image of the Labor government. Then it was discovered that Cairns and another mininster, Rex Connor, intended to borrow large sums of money from untraditional sources in the Middle East. There was an outcry from the opposition over this.

The Dismissal

In October 1975, the opposition in the Senate blocked Labor's budget bills. This cut off the supply of money to all government departments and authorities, and made the Labor government unworkable. But Whitlam refused to agree to a double dissolution of parliament and fresh elections. The deadlock continued for weeks, and grew into a consitutional crisis. It seemed that neither the government nor the opposition-controlled Senate would give way. On 11 November (Remembrance Day) 1975,

Figure 27.8. The steps of Parliament House, Canberra, 11 November 1975. The governor-general's official secretary reads out the proclamation dissolving parliament as Gough Whitlam, his government dismissed by Sir John Kerr, looks on.

Figure 27.9. Malcolm Fraser.

Malcolm Fraser

John Malcolm Fraser was born on 21 May 1930. He was educated at Melbourne Church of England Grammar School, and at Oxford University. He obtained an MA degree from Oxford. After completing his education, Fraser became a grazier and a politican. He entered parliament representing the seat of Wannon, Victoria, in 1955. He served under Menzies, Holt, McEwen, Gorton, and McMahon: mininster for the army (1966–68), minister for education and science (1968–69 and 1971–72), and minister for defence (1969–71). In 1975 he became leader of the Liberal Party. We have been how he withdrew his support from Gorton in 1971, and how he was later installed as caretaker prime minister by Sir John Kerr, in 1975. Fraser was 45 when he became prime minister.

After being made caretaker prime minister, Fraser won three successive general elections (December, 1975; 1977; and 1980). Fraser proved himself a strict and serious leader. He developed a number of cabinet committees to assist in the governing of Australia. He insisted on loyalty from this ministers and backbenchers. He did, however, clash with
Don Chipp and Andrew Peacock.

On the international front, Fraser kept close ties with Britain and the USA. He maintained the recognition of the People's Republic of China, but very vigorously attacked the expansionism of the USSR (especially in Afghanistan). He was an opponent of South Africa's apartheid policies. He also tried to interest foreign heads of state in finding ways to help underdeveloped countries. To ensure the defence of Australia, his government maintained and defended the presence of American bases on Australian soil (e.g. Pine Gap), and gave American bombers the right to refuel in and fly over northern Australia on navigational exercises.

At home, Fraser slowly and systematically reversed most of Labor's policies.

Sir John Kerr, the governor-general, called Whitlam to Government House, Canberra, and withdrew his commission as prime minister. Minutes later, Malcolm Fraser was sworn in as caretaker prime minister.

Whitlam and his colleagues, and Labor supporters everywhere, were stunned by Kerr's action. Whitlam made a bitter statement to members of the media on the steps of Parliament House, Canberra:

Well may we say 'God save the Queen', because nothing will save the Governor-General. The proclamation which you have just heard read by the Governor-General's official secretary was countersigned 'Malcolm Fraser' who will undoubtedly go down in Australian history from Remembrance Day 1975 as Kerr's cur.

Demonstrations against the governor-general followed. Many staunch Labor supporters vowed never to forget the date on which Whitlam was dismissed.

Figure 27.10. Robert Hawke.

Medibank was dismantled. Funds to educational institutions, hospitals, and old people's homes were cut back. Unemployment benefits were made more difficult to obtain. The private sector was strengthened, the public sector weakened.

One serious problem confronting Fraser in the early 1980s was a worsening world recession. This affected Australia's economy. As a result of the recession, and of strikes and wage demands at home, Australia's inflation and unemployment rates soared. A damaging drought also harmed the economy.

The 1983 Election: Bob Hawke

On 5 March 1983, Australia went to the polls once again. Fraser had decided to call an early election. But a sudden change of Labor leadership, with Bob Hawke taking over from Bill Hayden (who had led the opposition since Whitlam's resignation, and who now stepped

aside for Hawke), contributed significantly to the sweeping Labor victory. Malcolm Fraser, the second-longest-serving prime minister, announced his resignation as Liberal leader; Andrew Peacock was elected by the party as its new leader a few days later.

Robert James Lee Hawke was born in Bordertown, SA, on 9 December 1929. He was educated at the Perth Modern School and the University of Western Australia, graduating BA and LLB. He also studied at Oxford after winning a Rhodes Scholarship in 1952. Hawke was president of the Australian Council of Trade Unions (ACTU) from 1970 to 1980, and president of the ALP from 1973 to 1978. He entered parliament in 1980, for the seat of Wills (Victoria).

In the 1983 campaign Hawke pledged to strive, if elected, towards 'national reconciliation' and to introduce a 'consensus' style of government, and promised that a national economic summit conference would be held at which all the important community groups would be represented. The problems of the nation, he believed, could be solved only by discussion — by the constructive exchange of opinion among the competing sectors of society, such as the employers and the unions.

The economic summit was held in April 1983 in an atmosphere, for the most part, of co-operation and cautious optimism.

An important factor in Labor's 1983 election victory was Hawke's promise to stop the damming of the Franklin River in south-west Tasmania. In July 1983 the High Court ruled that the new federal government could stop the Tasmanian government from building the dam.

Hawke's Second and Third Terms

In December 1984 the Hawke Labor Government was returned to office. Many people believed that a third victory in a row would be impossible. However, in July 1987 Hawke led Labor to such a victory.

The continued electoral success of the Labor government has been based on:

- A steady decline in the unemployment rate — from nearly 10 per cent in the early 1980s to about 7 per cent in 1987.
- A steady decline in the inflation rate — from more than 10 per cent in 1982 to about 5 per cent in 1987.
- The continued agreement of unions to keep wage demands within limits decided by arbitration. This 'accord' was the permanent result of the 1983 economic sumit.
- High rates of profitability for major businesses.
- The ability of the treasurer, Paul Keating, to cut the deficit in each year's annual budget.
- Severe divisions among Labor's opponents. Among the Liberals, John Howard defeated Andrew Peacock and became party leader. This did little to restore confidence in the party because many voters and Liberal Party members still supported Peacock. The Nationals divided badly. Sinclair remained leader of the party, but in early 1987 Sir Joh Bjelke-Petersen demanded that the National Party break its long-standing coalition with the Liberal Party. Sir Joh appeared to believe that breakaway group of Nationals under his leadership could win enough seats to become the major conservative party, and therefore the next government. Few National Party members followed Sir Joh's instructions, but his actions confused many undecided voters. The coalition partners seemed to disagree so severely with each other that voters rejected them as a government.

By the end of 1988, Labor was facing an election some time in 1989 or 1990 and the possibility of a fourth victory. However, the Liberal and National parties had patched up many of their differences, Sir Joh Bjelke-Petersen had lost office in Queensland, and some commentators believed that Bob Hawke would retire before or soon after the next election. Would Australian voters re-elect a Labor government led by anybody else but Hawke?

Questions

(1) When did Harold Holt become prime minister?
(2) What do you know about Holt's foreign policy?
(3) Who succeeded Holt as caretaker prime minister?
(4) Who hoped to succeed Holt as prime minister?
(5) Why did Gorton make enemies within is own party?
(6) How many seats did the ALP win in the 1969 election?
(7) Why did Gorton begin to withdraw Australian servicemen from South Vietnam?
(8) Why did Whitlam win the 1972 election?
(9) How did the ALP lose office in 1975?
(10) What were some of the policies of the Fraser government?

Research

Find out more about the following people:
(1) Harold Holt
(2) John Gorton
(3) William McMahon
(4) Gough Whitlam
(5) Malcolm Fraser.

Chapter 28

Social and Economic Change

A Developing Economy

During the twentieth century, Australia's economy has greatly expanded as new sources of prosperity have been tapped.

In 1949 a lone prospector called John Michael White stumbled across uranium deposits at Rum Jungle, in the Northern Territory. The deposits were proved in 1951, and White was paid a reward of £25 000 by the federal government. Over the years that followed, Australia began mining uranium for export to countries with nuclear industries. But some Australians feared that the uranium could be used in the manufacture of nuclear weapons, and the issue became very controversial. For a time, unions banned the handling of uranium. In the early 1980s, the federal government allowed some export of uranium on condition it would be used only for peaceful purposes.

In 1953, the first major oil discovery was made near Exmouth Gulf in Western Australia, by Ampol Exploration Limited. In 1961 a more important oil discovery was made at the Moonie field in southern Queensland. In 1964 oil and gas were discovered at Barrow Island, north-west of Exmouth Gulf. Finally,

Figure 28.1. Iron ore. Aerial view of Mount Tom Price open-cut operations, Hamersley Ranges, Western Australia.

The Land They Found

offshore oil and gas were discovered in Bass Strait. Today Australia produces about 70 per cent of its oil needs. It imports the rest. Large sums of money are being invested in the continuing search for oil.

In 1955 reserves of high-grade bauxite were discovered at Weipa, north Queensland, on the Gulf of Carpentaria. The field proved to be the largest in the world. The area was extensively developed. Today, bauxite is carried from the Weipa port to Gladstone in Queensland or Bell Bay in Tasmania, to be used in the manufacture of aluminium.

In 1952 a grazier and prospector called Lang Hancock discovered iron ore near his Hamersley station in the Pilbara region of Western Australia — the first of many finds by him. The Rio Tinto Mining Company of Australia Ltd investigated the area. In September 1962 two of the company's geologists discovered ore at Mount Tom Price. An international consortium of companies set up Hamersley Iron Pty Ltd to mine the ore, rail it to the coast, and ship it from Dampier to countries overseas, such as Japan. Large-scale export commenced in 1966.

In 1966 large deposits of nickel were discovered at Kambalda in Western Australia. In 1969 a small mining company, Poseidon NL, announced that it had discovered nickel at Mt Windarra in Western Australia. Poseidon shares skyrocketed from 80 cents a share, in September 1969, to $290 a share in February 1970. Many investors hoped to cash in one the fluctuations of the shares. The boom ended when one company, Mineral Securities Australia Ltd, collapsed.

By the 1980s Australia was becoming a great manufacturing nation. More and more factories were built, to produce new consumer products such as cars, refrigerators, washing machines, dryers, television sets, audio equipment, motormowers, etc. The new factories offered employment to tens of thousands. Many factories were owned by foreign companies.

Increase in Population

During the 1960s, 1970s, and early 1980s, Australia's population continued to increase. Many migrants came to Australia from European countries such as Britain, Italy, and Greece, and from Asian countries such as Malaysia and Vietnam. Those who arrived came seeking a new life in Australia.

Increase in population created a demand for more homes, shops, schools, clinics, hospitals, etc. Cities and towns grew in size, spreading out into what was formerly waste land, farm land, and forest. Trees were bulldozed to make way for housing estates. Freeways were constructed to accommodate an increasing number of vehicles.

A New, Cosmopolitan Culture

Migrants introduced Australians of British descent to new languages, attitudes, religions, foods, and music. New arrivals and their children filled whole suburbs. Second-language newspapers, films, radio, and television appeared. Australians were obliged to reassess their outlooked on culture and race. Unfortunately, some were racially prejudiced against the newcomers.

Women's Liberation

Until the early 1970s, women did not enjoy the same rights and privileges in Australian society as men. They were discriminated against in the workforce and in public amenities such as hotels and clubs. Early in the 1970s many women began to fight for equal status with men. One of the leaders of the movement was an expatriate Australian, Germaine Greer.

Germaine Greer was born in 1939, into a conservative middle-class Mel-

Figure 28.2. Germaine Greer in the 1970s.

minated against and punished in Australian society. Those who admitted tio having committed a homosexual act were summonsed to appear in court, and were either imprisoned or ordered to undergo psychiatric counselling.

Campaigns for 'gay rights' began in the 1970s. Many homosexuals spoke out in public against public bias, and against laws prohibiting private acts between adults of the same sex. Their arguments moved some politicans and judges. By the early 1980s, homosexuality was no longer illegal in the ACT, South Australia, and Victoria. In the other states it was tolerated, between consenting adults in private, providing no complaint was made.

The Abortion Debate

Abortion was long considered a serious offence in all states. Doctors were not allowed to perform abortions, and 'backyard abortionists' made a living from breaking the law. Today the feelings of many (but by no means all) politicans, judges, police officers, and doctors are different. In the early 1980s abortion was legal in South Australia and the Northern Territory. There, women could obtain abortions performed by trained doctors and surgeons, in clinics and hospitals. In the ACT, New South Wales, Victoria, Tasmania, and Western Australia, women who required abortions were usually able to obtain them. Queensland did not allow abortion. Abortion was vigorously opposed throughout Australia by the Roman Catholic Church and the Right to Life Association.

bourne family. As a girl she was sent to convent schools. She then attended university, where she studied arts. She obtained her BA from Melbourne University, her MA from Sydney University, and her PhD from Cambridge. Living in Britain, Greer wrote a book on women's liberation called *The Female Eunuch*. This book became a best-seller, and inspired many women around the world to fight for their rights. She came to Australia, in 1972 appeared on television, and led a march of thousands of women through the streets of Sydney.

During the 1970s some women activists advised women to 'burn their bras' (i.e. not to dress to please men) and to fight for their rights. The Whitlam government did what it could to help women. Elizabeth Reid was appointed special adviser to the prime minister. Whitlam sponsored a Women and Politics Conference in Canberra, and women representatives were sent to a conference in Mexico in 1975 held to mark International Women's Year. In 1978 Malcolm Fraser set up a National Women's Advisory Council to give women a voice at federal government level.

Gay Liberation

Until recently, homosexuals were discri-

Test-tube Babies

Earlier this century many people laughed at the idea of 'test-tube babies', protesting that such a thing would be scientifically impossible. In 1968 the staff of Monash University's department of obstetrics and gynaecology began working towards a method of *in vitro* fertilization and embryo transfer. The first attempt to fertilize a human egg outside the womb was made at the Queen victoria Hospital, Melbourne, in 1973, but the embryo survived only for several days. The first two babies conceived outside the womb were born in Britain; but in June 1980 the world's third 'test-tube baby', Candice Reed, was born at the Royal Women's Hospital, Melbourne. Subsequently the Melbourne doctors had increasing success with their method.

The term *in vitro* is Latin for 'in glass'. Doctors take the egg from the woman's womb through a narrow incision in her abdomen, using a *laparoscope* (an instrument like a little telescope) and an *aspirating needle* (a delicate suction intrument), and place the egg in a glass dish with the man's sperm. The dish is then warmed in an incubator until the egg becomes fertilized and the embryo

begins to grow. When this happens, the embryo is transferred to the woman's uterus (womb) using a thin tube. Once back in the womb, the embryo develops normally; the woman gives birth in the normal manner.

This work, by people such as Professor Carl Wood, Professor John Leeton, and Dr Alan Trounson, has created all kinds of new moral and legal questions — questions that will require much time and a good deal of informed discussion and debate before they can be resolved.

Land Rights for Aborigines

In 1970, Australia celebrated the two hundredth anniversary of Cook's discovery of the east coast. Queen Elizabeth II visited Australia, to share in the celebrations. This made no impression on the Aborigines. They went down to Captain Cook's landing place at Kurnell, and threw wreaths into the water. As far as the Aborigines were concerned, the

Figure 28.3. An Aboriginal land rights march in Melbourne.

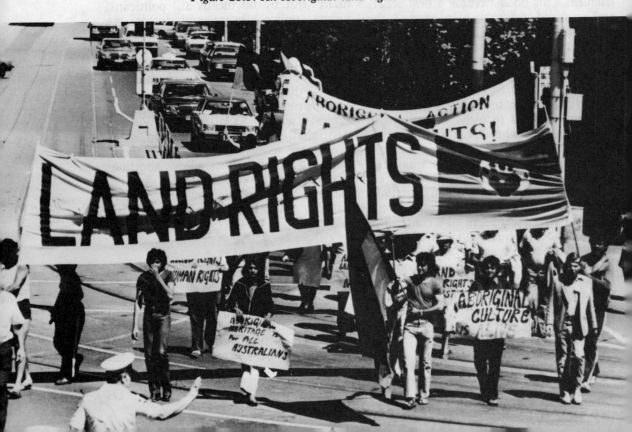

arrival of the European was not an event to celebrate.

The first white settlers condemned the Aborigines as primitive and uncivilized. According to the white settlers, the Aborigines were only slightly more advanced than apes. Aborigines were driven off their land. Their tribal culture was destroyed. Many were murdered. In time, the authorities stopped most of the atrocities, and Christian missionaries worked to convert the Aborigines to European ways. For a time, some white Australians wanted separate development for the Aborigines.

In the 1960s, a small number of Aborigines began to fight for land rights. They wanted the return of tribal land, and the right to live on that land or to do whatever they wished with it.

One of the earliest and most important struggles for land rights occurred at Wattie Creek, about 600 km south of Darwin, in the late 1960s and early 1970s. There, a number of Gurindji people worked on Wave Hill station, owned by the British company Vestey Ltd, which paid the Gurindjis less than a quarter of the minimum wage paid to white workers. Sometimes they paid the Aborigines no money at all: instead they gave them salt beef, bread, flour, sugar, tea, and tobacco.

One day in 1966, Vincent Lingiari, a tribal elder, and his people took some wire and fenced off part of the Vestey land. A long legal battle ensued. Vestey left the matter up to the federal government. The federal government left it up to Vestey. Communists and waterside workers supported the Gurindjis. Both the Liberal and Labor governments were moved to assist the Gurindjis. Whitlam's government purchased some 3250 square kilometres of Wave Hill station for them.

The remarkable stand made by the Gurindjis was celebrated in a song by Ted Egan:

Poor Bugger Blackfella, Gurindji,
Long time work, no wages we,
Work for Good Old Lord Vestey,
Little bit flour, sugar and tea.
From Lord Vestey to the Gurindji.

Poor Bugger Blackfella, this country,
Government law, him talk along we,
Can't givit land long blackfella, see,
Only spoilim Gurindji,
Poor Bugger Me, Gurindji.

Poor Bugger Blackfella, Guindji,
Suppose we buy im back country,
What you reckon proper fee?
Might be flour, sugar and tea,
From the Gurindji to the Lord Vestey,
Oh Poor Bugger Me.

Since the victory of the Gurindjis, many applications have been made by the Aborigines to the courts for the return of tribal land. The Fraser government was reluctant to oppose the Aboriginal land-rights movement.

Some Aborigines have sought acceptance in white Australian society. These include Pastor Sir Doug Nicholls, Lionel Rose, and Evonne Goolagong (later Cawley). Doug Nicholls became governor of South Australia (1976–77); Neville Bonner, the first Aboriginal member of parliament; Lionel Rose, world bantamweight boxing champion (1968–69); and Evonne Goolagong became a winner at Wimbledon in 1971 and 1980.

The Computer Revolution

Australia in the 1980s is experiencing a revolution of immense consequences — the computer revolution.

Do you know what a computer is? A computer is a machine that can count, calculate, store and sort data, and then present the results in a convenient form. It does this much faster than a human being. Computers can also be programmed to operate other machines, such as 'robots' in factories.

Soon you will be living in the twenty-first century. In that century, much of the boring, repetitive or dangerious work that people have to do will be done by computers. This will mean that you will have more time for creative and leisure activities.

Questions

(1) How has Australia's economy changed during this century?
(2) What was found at Mount Tom Price?
(3) Why do migrants come to Australia?
(4) How have migrants contributed to Australian society and culture?
(5) Why is Germaine Greer important?
(6) When was International Women's Year?
(7) When did 'gay rights' campaigns commence?
(8) What happened at Wattie Creek in the 1960s?
(9) Why do many Aborigines want land rights?
(10) How are computers beginning to change Australian society?

Research

Find out more about the following:
(1) Australian immigration
(2) The Women's Liberation movement
(3) The Aboriginal land rights movement
(4) Australian mineral industries
(5) Computers.

Index